GLOBETROTTER™

Travel Atlas

SOUTH AFRICA

New Holland Publishers (UK) Ltd
London • Cape Town • Sydney • Auckland

First edition 1994
Second impression 1995
Third impression 1996
Fourth impression 1997
Second edition 1997
Second impression 1998
Third impression 2000

10 9 8 7 6 5 4

24 Nutford Place
London W1H 6DQ
United Kingdom

80 McKenzie Street
Cape Town 8001
South Africa

14 Aquatic Drive
Frenchs Forest, NSW 2086
Australia

218 Lake Road
Northcote, Auckland
New Zealand

ISBN 1 85974 582 2

Manager Globetrotter Maps: John Loubser
Text: Peter Joyce, Claudia Dos Santos
Editor: Claudia Dos Santos
Design and DTP: Lyndall du Toit, Claudia Dos Santos
Compiler/Verifier: Elaine Fick

Reproduction by Hirt & Carter, Cape Town
Printed and bound by Trident Press (Pty) Ltd

Cover: *Chapman's Peak Drive is one of the Western Cape's most spectacular mountain passes.*
Title Page: *The picturesque Wilderness coastline, part of the well-known Garden Route, is a popular destination for visitors.*

Photographic Credits

Photo Access/Walter Knirr, page 10; **Herman Potgieter**, page 33; **SIL/Shaen Adey**, front cover, pages 49, 59; **SIL/CLB**, page 24;**SIL/Roger de la Harpe**, pages 30, 67; **SIL/Gerhard Dreyer**, title page, page 40; **SIL/Walter Knirr**, pages 16, 18, 54, 70 (bottom), 72, 80; **SIL/Peter Pickford**, page 74; **SIL/Erhardt Thiel**, pages 46, 48, 53; **SIL/Hein von Hörsten**, pages 35, 39, 62; **SIL/ Lanz von Hörsten**, pages 20, 42, 45, 78; **SIL/ Keith Young**, pages 26, 28, 57, 61, 70 (top); *[SIL: Struik Image Library; CLB: Colour Library]*

Emergency Telephone Numbers
Notrufnummern
Appels d'Urgence

Police Polizeirevier Poste de police	**10111**
Telephone enquiries Telefon Auskunft Information téléphonique	**1023**
Ambulance Krankenwagen Ambulances	**10177**

This brightly coloured South African flag was first raised at midnight on 26 April 1994. For most South Africans it is a symbol of hope, uniting the nation in their effort to reconciliate and become a truly democratic society.

CONTENTS

KEY TOURIST AREAS

GAUTENG 10
- Greater Johannesburg 12
- Pretoria 16
- Pilanesberg and Sun City 18
- Kruger National Park 20

MPUMALANGA 22
- Nelspruit 23

KWAZULU-NATAL
- North Coast 24
- South Coast 26
- Durban 28
- Drakensberg Mountain Resorts 30
- Historic Battlefields 32

WILD COAST 33

EASTERN CAPE 34
- Port Elizabeth 36
- East London 37

GARDEN ROUTE 38
- George 40
- Knysna 41

CAPE WINELANDS 42
- Stellenbosch and Paarl 44

WEST COAST 45

CAPE PENINSULA 46
- Kirstenbosch 48
- Cape Town 49
- V & A Waterfront 52

FREE STATE 54
- Bloemfontein 56
- Kimberley 57

MAIN MAP SECTION

Key and Legend 58

EASTERN AND WESTERN CAPE 59

GREAT KAROO 64

NORTHERN CAPE 68

KIMBERLEY AND BLOEMFONTEIN 70

NORTHEASTERN FREE STATE 72

NORTHERN KWAZULU-NATAL 74

NORTH WEST AND NORTHERN PROVINCE 78

MPUMALANGA AND NORTHERN PROVINCE 80

INDEX

For ease of use, the INDEX has been divided into two sections:

- the first focuses on the KEY TOURIST AREA MAPS and related text and photographs.
- the second deals with the MAIN MAP SECTION only, facilitating the easy location of cities, towns and villages.

NATIONAL ROUTE PLANNER

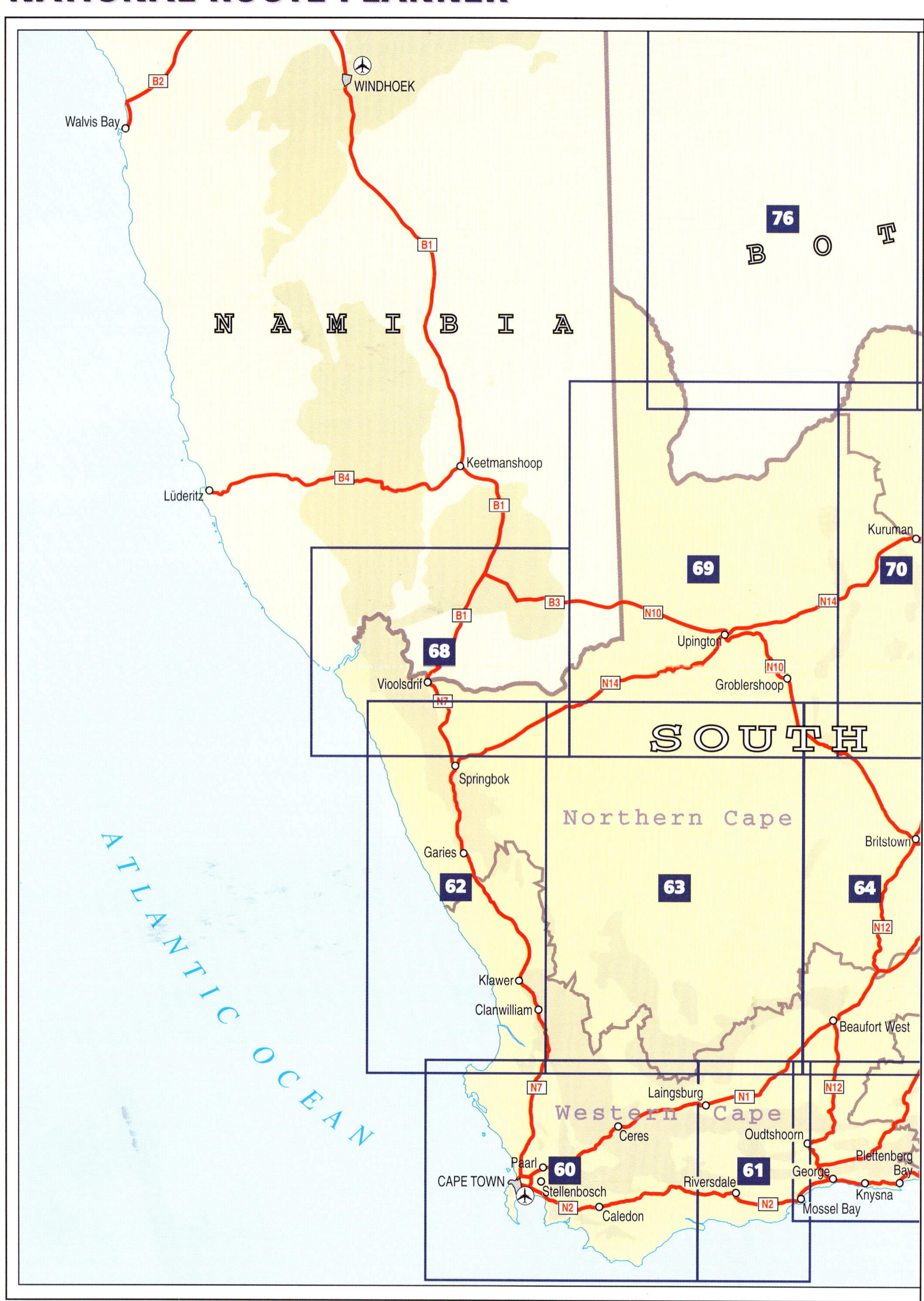

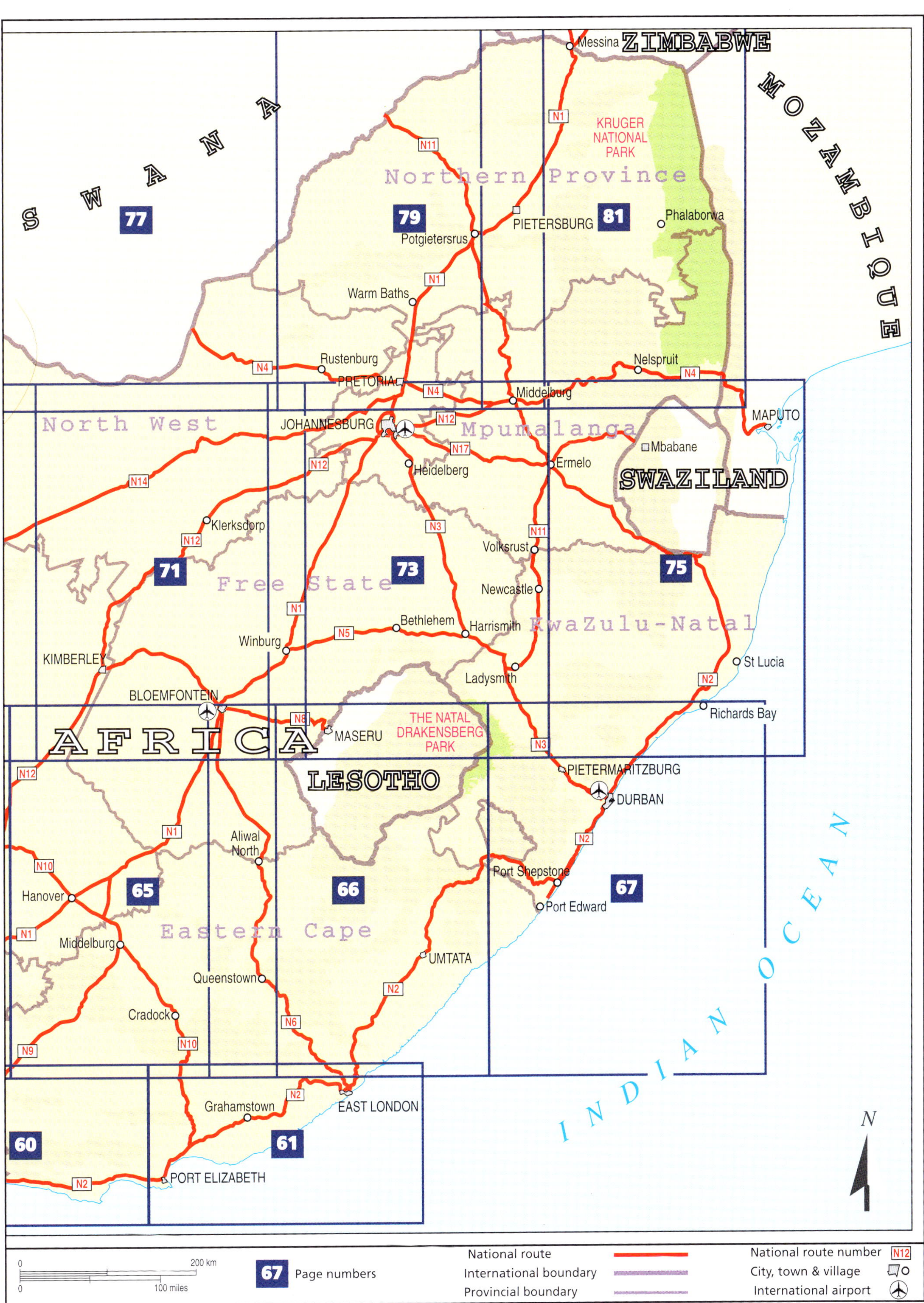
ZIMBABWE
MOZAMBIQUE
BOTSWANA
SWAZILAND
LESOTHO
AFRICA
INDIAN OCEAN
Northern Province
North West
Mpumalanga
Free State
KwaZulu-Natal
Eastern Cape
KRUGER NATIONAL PARK
THE NATAL DRAKENSBERG PARK
Messina
Phalaborwa
PIETERSBURG
Potgietersrus
Warm Baths
Rustenburg
PRETORIA
Nelspruit
Middelburg
MAPUTO
Mbabane
JOHANNESBURG
Heidelberg
Ermelo
Klerksdorp
Volksrust
Newcastle
Bethlehem
Harrismith
Winburg
KIMBERLEY
Ladysmith
St Lucia
BLOEMFONTEIN
Richards Bay
MASERU
PIETERMARITZBURG
DURBAN
Aliwal North
Hanover
Port Shepstone
Port Edward
Middelburg
UMTATA
Queenstown
Cradock
Grahamstown
EAST LONDON
PORT ELIZABETH
N1
N2
N3
N4
N5
N6
N8
N9
N10
N11
N12
N14
N17
77
79
81
71
73
75
65
66
67
60
61
N
0
200 km
0
100 miles
67 Page numbers
National route
International boundary
Provincial boundary
National route number
City, town & village
International airport

KEY TOURIST AREAS

Gauteng
Gauteng Area Map.. 11
Greater Johannesburg Area Map.................. 13
Johannesburg City Plan............................... 14-15
Pretoria City Plan.. 17
North West
Pilanesberg National Park............................ 19
Sun City Complex... 19
Northern Province & Mpumalanga
Kruger National Park.................................... 21
Mpumalanga
Mpumalanga Area Map................................ 22
Nelspruit Town Plan..................................... 23
KwaZulu-Natal
KwaZulu-Natal North Coast.......................... 25
KwaZulu-Natal South Coast.......................... 27
Durban City Plan... 29
Pietermaritzburg City Plan............................ 29
Drakensberg Mountain Resorts.................... 31
Historic Battlefields....................................... 32
Eastern Cape
Wild Coast Area Map.................................... 33
Eastern Cape Area Map................................ 34-35
Port Elizabeth City Plan................................ 36
East London City Plan.................................. 37
Western Cape
Garden Route Area Map............................... 38-39
George Town Plan... 40
Knysna Town Plan... 41
Cape Winelands.. 42-43
Stellenbosch Town Plan............................... 44
Paarl Town Plan.. 44
West Coast Tourist Area Map....................... 45
Cape Peninsula Area Map............................ 47
Kirstenbosch National Botanical Gardens...... 48
Cape Town City Plan.................................... 50-51
Waterfront 3D Map & Waterfront Plan............ 52-53
Free State
Free State Area Map..................................... 55
Bloemfontein City Plan................................. 56
Northern Cape
Kimberley City Plan....................................... 57

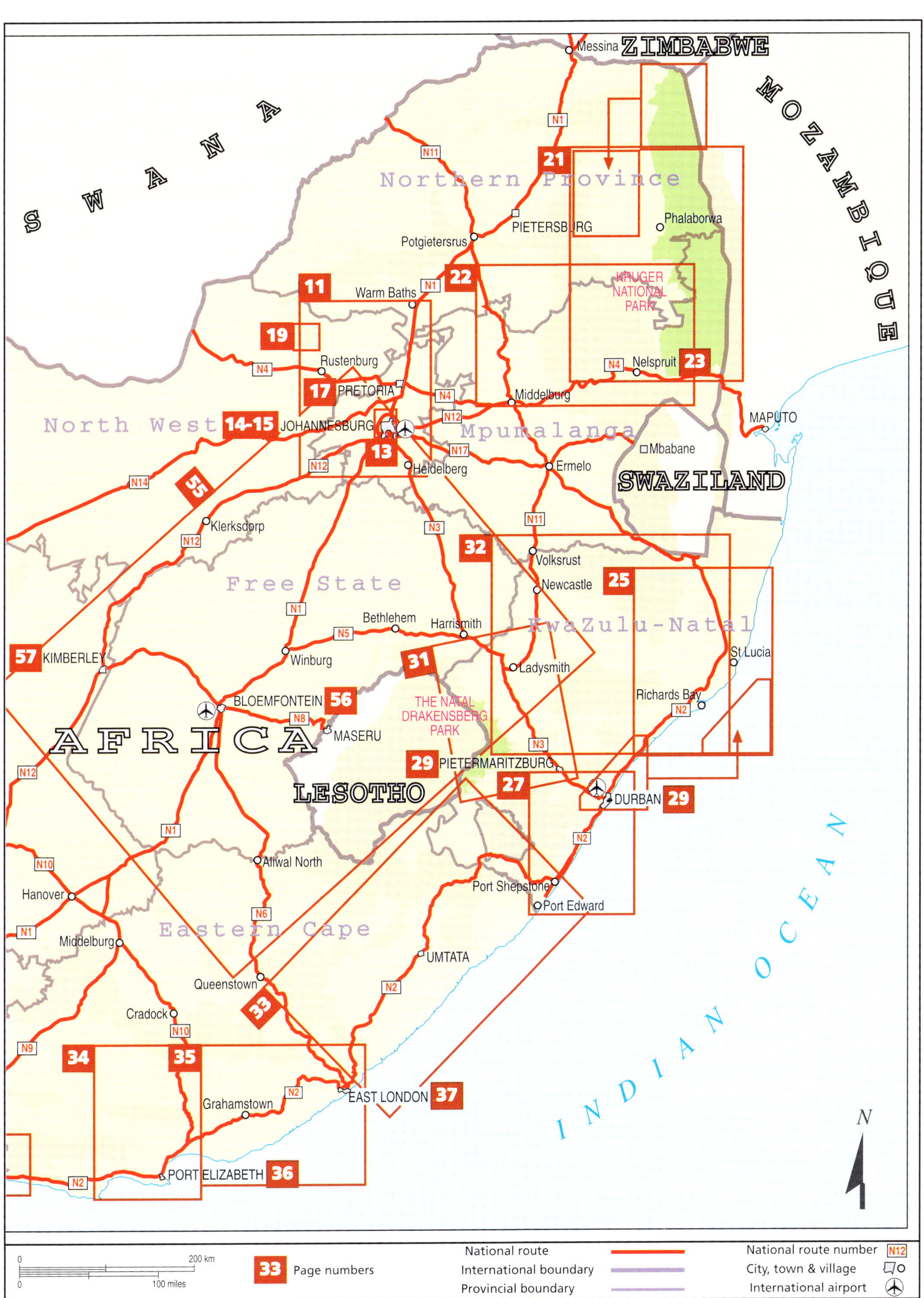
ZIMBABWE
MOZAMBIQUE
SWANA
Messina
N1
N11
21
Northern Province
PIETERSBURG
Phalaborwa
Potgietersrus
22
KRUGER NATIONAL PARK
11
Warm Baths
19
Rustenburg
N4
Nelspruit
23
17
PRETORIA
Middelburg
North West
14-15
JOHANNESBURG
N12
Mpumalanga
MAPUTO
Mbabane
13
N17
Heidelberg
Ermelo
SWAZILAND
55
N14
N3
Klerksdorp
32
Volksrust
Free State
Newcastle
25
Bethlehem
N5
Harrismith
KwaZulu-Natal
57
KIMBERLEY
Winburg
31
Ladysmith
St Lucia
BLOEMFONTEIN
56
THE NATAL DRAKENSBERG PARK
Richards Bay
N8
N2
AFRICA
MASERU
29
PIETERMARITZBURG
27
LESOTHO
DURBAN
N10
Aliwal North
Hanover
Port Shepstone
Port Edward
N6
Eastern Cape
Middelburg
UMTATA
Queenstown
33
Cradock
N9
34
35
Grahamstown
EAST LONDON
37
PORT ELIZABETH
36
INDIAN OCEAN
N
0
200 km
100 miles
33
Page numbers
National route
International boundary
Provincial boundary
National route number
City, town & village
International airport

DISTANCE CHART

APPROXIMATE DISTANCES IN KILOMETRES	BLOEMFONTEIN	CAPE TOWN	DURBAN	EAST LONDON	GABORONE	GRAHAMSTOWN	JOHANNESBURG	KIMBERLEY	MAPUTO	MASERU	MBABANE	PORT ELIZABETH	PRETORIA	WELKOM	WINDHOEK
BEAUFORT WEST	547	457	1178	605	1042	492	942	504	1349	609	1129	501	1000	697	1629
BLOEMFONTEIN		1004	634	584	622	601	398	177	897	157	677	677	456	153	1593
BRITSTOWN	398	710	1032	609	791	496	725	253	1289	555	1075	572	783	551	1378
CAPE TOWN	1004		1753	1099	1501	899	1402	962	1900	1160	1680	769	1460	1156	1500
COLESBERG	228	778	860	488	848	375	624	292	1123	383	903	451	682	379	1573
DE AAR	346	762	980	557	843	444	744	305	1243	503	1023	520	802	499	1430
DURBAN	634	1753		674	979	854	578	811	625	590	562	984	636	564	2227
EAST LONDON	584	1079	674		1206	180	982	780	1301	630	1238	310	1040	737	1987
GABORONE	622	1501	979	1206		1223	358	538	957	702	719	1299	350	479	1735
GEORGE	773	438	1319	645	1361	465	1171	762	1670	913	1450	335	1229	926	1887
GRAAFF-REINET	424	787	942	395	1012	282	822	490	1321	599	1101	291	880	577	1697
GRAHAMSTOWN	601	899	854	172	1223		999	667	1478	692	1418	138	1057	754	1856
HARRISMITH	328	1331	306	822	673	929	274	505	649	284	468	1068	332	258	1921
JOHANNESBURG	398	1402	578	982	358	999		472	599	438	361	1075	58	258	1801
KEETMANSHOOP	1088	995	1722	1482	1230	1351	1296	911	1895	1245	1657	1445	1354	1205	505
KIMBERLEY	177	962	811	780	538	667	472		1071	334	833	743	530	294	1416
KLERKSDORP	288	1271	645	872	334	889	164	308	763	368	525	1009	222	145	1693
KROONSTAD	211	1214	537	795	442	812	187	339	742	247	522	888	245	71	1724
LADYSMITH	410	1413	236	752	755	932	356	587	567	366	386	1062	414	340	2008
MAFIKENG	464	1343	821	1048	158	1065	287	380	886	544	648	1141	294	321	1577
MAPUTO	897	1900	625	1301	957	1478	599	1071		853	223	1609	583	813	2400
MASERU	157	1160	590	630	702	692	438	334	853		633	822	488	249	1750
MBABANE	677	1680	562	1238	719	1418	361	833	223	633		1548	372	451	2162
MESSINA	928	1932	1118	1512	696	1529	530	1002	725	960	808	1605	476	788	2331
NELSPRUIT	757	1762	707	1226	672	1358	355	827	244	713	173	1434	322	639	2156
OUDTSHOORN	743	506	1294	704	1241	532	1141	703	1705	959	1417	394	1199	896	1828
PIETERMARITZBURG	555	1674	79	595	900	775	499	732	706	511	640	905	557	485	2148
PIETERSBURG	717	1721	897	1301	485	1318	319	791	605	749	515	1394	267	577	2120
PORT ELIZABETH	677	769	984	310	1299	130	1075	743	1609	822	1548		1133	830	1950
PRETORIA	456	1460	636	1040	350	1057	58	530	583	488	372	1133		316	1859
QUEENSTOWN	377	1069	676	207	999	260	775	334	1302	473	1240	399	833	525	1829
UMTATA	570	1314	439	235	1192	415	869	747	1064	616	1003	545	928	718	2066
UPINGTON	588	894	1222	982	730	851	796	411	1395	745	1157	945	854	669	1005
WELKOM	153	1156	564	737	479	754	258	294	813	249	451	830	316		1679
WINDHOEK	1593	1500	2227	1987	1735	1856	1801	1416	2400	1750	2162	1950	1859	1679	

DISTANCE IN KM FROM CAPE TOWN	
Bloemfontein	1004
Durban	1753
Johannesburg	1402
Kimberley	962
Port Elizabeth	769

Distance Charts

In order to calculate the distance between two of the country's major centres, locate the name of the first town or city on the vertical or horizontal column on the chart (see left), then locate the name of the other on the second column and read off the number where the vertical and horizontal lines intersect.

CAPE TOWN	J	F	M	A	M	J	J	A	S	O	N	D
AV. TEMP. °C	21	21	20	17	15	13	12	13	14	16	18	20
AV. TEMP. °F	70	70	68	63	59	55	54	55	57	61	64	68
DAILY SUN hrs	11	10	9	7	6	6	6	7	8	9	10	11
RAINFALL mm	14	17	19	39	74	92	70	75	39	37	15	17
RAINFALL in	0.6	0.7	0.7	2	3	4	3	3	2	1.5	0.6	0.7
SEA TEMP. °C	15	14	13	13	12	12	12	13	13	14	14	14
SEA TEMP. °F	59	57	55	55	54	54	54	55	55	57	57	57

Climate Charts

Above is an example of a Climate Chart. These occur throughout the atlas, and give the average temperatures and rainfall for the relevant region or city.

Toll Road Chart

Various South African provinces are served by time-saving toll roads. The chart below identifies the names of these toll roads, the locations of the toll plazas, points between which the toll roads stretch and grid references for locating these roads on the maps in this book.

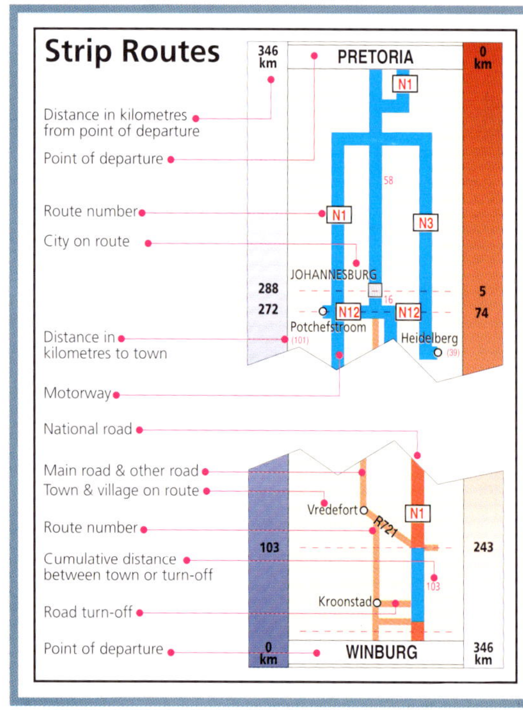

TOLL ROADS

ROUTE	PROVINCE	NAME	TOLL PLAZA	LOCATION
N1	Western Cape	HUGUENOT TUNNEL	HUGUENOT	DU TOITS KLOOF
N1	Free State	KROONVAAL	VAAL	UNCLE CHARLIES–KROONSTAD
N1	Gauteng		GRASMERE	JHB–VANDERBIJLPARK
N1	Northern Province	KRANSKOP	KRANSKOP	WARMBATHS–MIDDELFONTEIN
N2	Western Cape	TSITSIKAMMA	TSITSIKAMMA	THE CRAGS & STORMS RIVER
N2	KwaZulu-Natal	SOUTH COAST	ORIBI	SOUTHBROOM–MARBURG
N2	KwaZulu-Natal		IZOTSHA	SOUTHBROOM–MARBURG
N2	KwaZulu-Natal	NORTH COAST	TONGAAT	UMDLOTI–BALLITO
N2	KwaZulu-Natal		UMVOTI	SHAKASKRAAL / STANGER
N2	KwaZulu-Natal		MTUNZINI	MTUNZINI / FELIXTON
N3	Free State	HIGHVELD	WILGE	VILLIERS–WARDEN
N3	KwaZulu-Natal	MIDLANDS	TUGELA	KEEVERSFONTEIN–FRERE
N3	KwaZulu-Natal		MOOI RIVER	FRERE–CEDARA
N3	KwaZulu-Natal	MARIANNHILL	MARIANNHILL	ASSAGAY–PINETOWN
N4	Gauteng	MAGALIES	QUAGGA	PRETORIA–ATTERIDGEVILLE
N4	Gauteng		PELINDABA	ATTERIDGEVILLE–PELINDABA
N17	Gauteng	WITWATERSRAND	DALPARK	SPRINGS–DALPARK
N17	Gauteng		DENNE ROAD	SPRINGS–DALPARK
N17	Gauteng		GOSFORTH	DALPARK–RAND AIRPORT

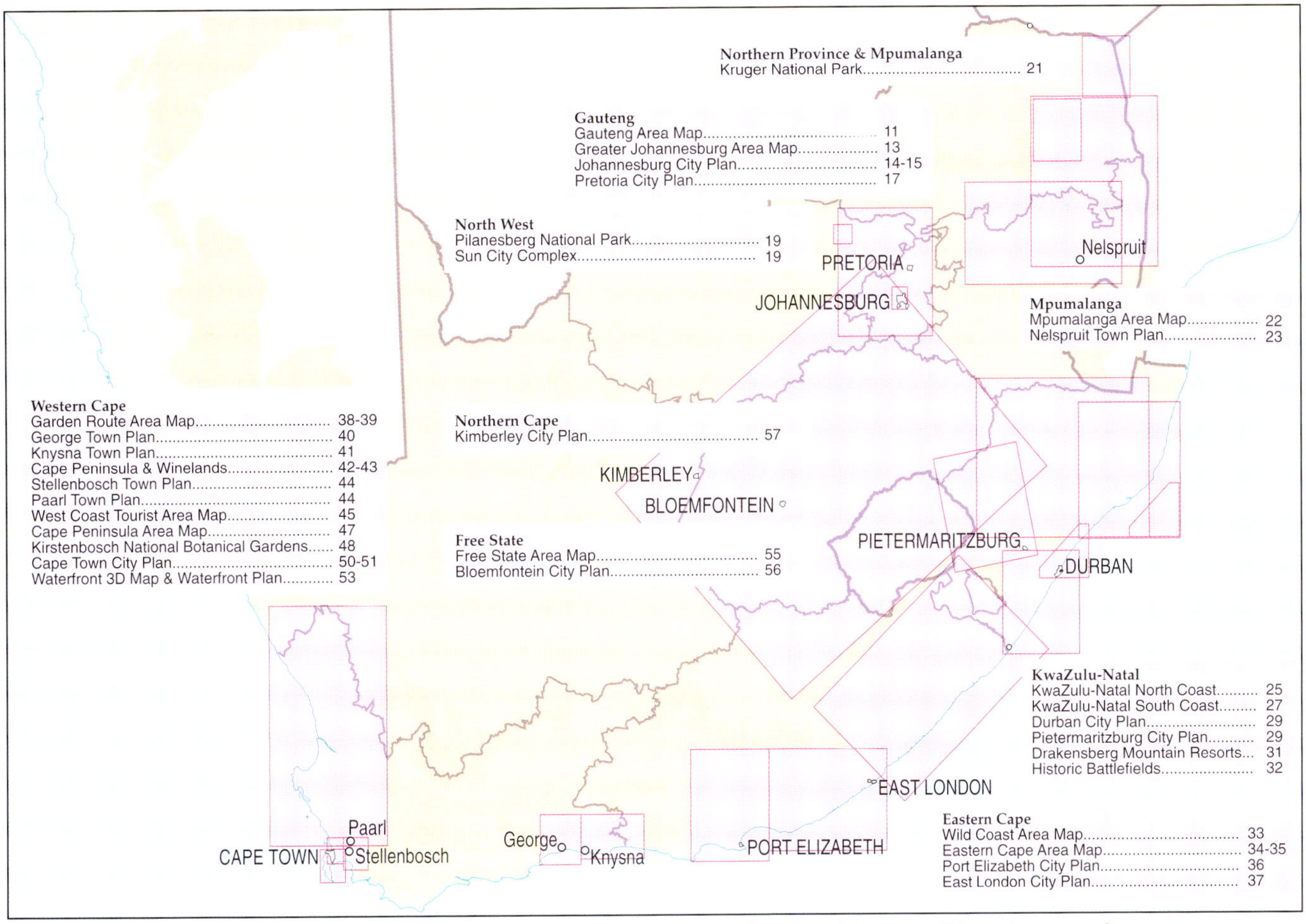

Northern Province & Mpumalanga
Kruger National Park ... 21

Gauteng
Gauteng Area Map ... 11
Greater Johannesburg Area Map ... 13
Johannesburg City Plan ... 14-15
Pretoria City Plan ... 17

North West
Pilanesberg National Park ... 19
Sun City Complex ... 19

Mpumalanga
Mpumalanga Area Map ... 22
Nelspruit Town Plan ... 23

Western Cape
Garden Route Area Map ... 38-39
George Town Plan ... 40
Knysna Town Plan ... 41
Cape Peninsula & Winelands ... 42-43
Stellenbosch Town Plan ... 44
Paarl Town Plan ... 44
West Coast Tourist Area Map ... 45
Cape Peninsula Area Map ... 47
Kirstenbosch National Botanical Gardens ... 48
Cape Town City Plan ... 50-51
Waterfront 3D Map & Waterfront Plan ... 53

Northern Cape
Kimberley City Plan ... 57

Free State
Free State Area Map ... 55
Bloemfontein City Plan ... 56

KwaZulu-Natal
KwaZulu-Natal North Coast ... 25
KwaZulu-Natal South Coast ... 27
Durban City Plan ... 29
Pietermaritzburg City Plan ... 29
Drakensberg Mountain Resorts ... 31
Historic Battlefields ... 32

Eastern Cape
Wild Coast Area Map ... 33
Eastern Cape Area Map ... 34-35
Port Elizabeth City Plan ... 36
East London City Plan ... 37

PRETORIA
JOHANNESBURG
Nelspruit
KIMBERLEY
BLOEMFONTEIN
PIETERMARITZBURG
DURBAN
EAST LONDON
PORT ELIZABETH
George
Knysna
Paarl
Stellenbosch
CAPE TOWN

Area Map Legend

National road / Nationalstraße / Route nationale
Motorway / Autobahn / Autoroute
Principal road / Regionalstraße / Route de liaison régionale
Main road / Hauptstraße / Route principale — Tarred, Untarred
Minor road / Nebenstraße / Route secondaire — Tarred, Untarred
Route numbers / Routenummern / Numéros de routes — N4, R28, R518
Distances in kilometres / Entfernungen in Kilometern / Distance en kilomètres — 19, 15
Scenic route / Malerische Landschaft / Route panoramique
Mountain pass / Bergpass / Col — Du Toits
Motorway & interchange / Autobahn mit Kreuzungen / Autoroute avec échangeur
Railway / Eisenbahn / Chemin de fer
International boundary / Internationale Grenze / Frontière internationale
Provincial boundary / Provinz Grenze / Frontière provinciale
Game & nature reserve / Wild- und Naturschutzgebiet / Réserve naturelle — Inyati N.R.
Battle site / Ehemaliges Schlachtfeld / Lieu de bataille historique — Ulundi
Mountain range / Gebirge / Chaîne de montagnes — LEBOMBO
Border post / Grenzübergang / Poste de contrôle — Lebombo
Provincial name / Provinz / Nom du département — Western Cape
Airport / Flughafen / Aéroport — INT., Other
Place of interest / Sehenswürdigkeit / Endroit à voir — Baobab Tree
Railway station (selected) / Bahnhöfe (Auswahl) / Gare
Area name / Gebiet / Nom de la région — Ciskei
Toll road / Gebührenpfl. Straße / Route à péage
Peak in metres / Höhe in Metern / Sommet (en mètres) — Table Mtn. 1140m
Water feature / Gewässer / Hydrographie — River, Dam, Swamp
Safe bathing beach / Geschützter Badestrand / Baignade autorisée
Major petrol stop / Große Tankstelle / Station-service
Hotel (selected) / Hotel (Auswahl) / Hôtel
Camp / Ferienlager / Camp

City and Town Plan Legend

Motorway and slip road / Autobahn mit Ausfahrt / Autoroute et jonction
Main road and mall / Haupt- und Einkaufsstraßen / Route principale et Mall — MALL
Road / Straße / Route
Railway / Eisenbahn / Chemin de fer
Park and sports field / Park und Sportplatz / Parc et terrain de sports
Route numbers / Routenummern / Numéros de routes — 24, 4, 27
Hospital / Krankenhaus / Hôpital
Caravan park / Wohnwagenpark / Camping pour caravanes
Hotel / Hotel / Hôtel — MANOR
Bus terminus / Endstation / Terminus d'autobus
Building of interest / Wichtiges Bauwerk / Monument à voir
Place of interest / Sehenswürdigkeit / Endroit à voir — Castle
City / Großstadt / Grande ville
Major town / Bedeutende Stadt / Ville
Town / Stadt / Ville secondaire
Place of worship / Gotteshaus / Lieu du culte
Police station / Polizeirevier / Poste de police
Parking area / Parkplatz / Parking
Post office / Postamt / Bureau de poste
Information centre / Auskunftsbüro / Centre d'information
Library / Bibliothek / Bibliothèque
Built-up area / Wohngebiet / Agglomération
One-way street / Einbahnstraße / Rue à sens-unique
Golf course / Golfplatz / Terrain de golf
Major petrol stop / Große Tankstelle / Station-service
Small town / Kleinstadt / Grand village
Large village / Größere Ortschaft / Village
Village / Dorf / Petit village

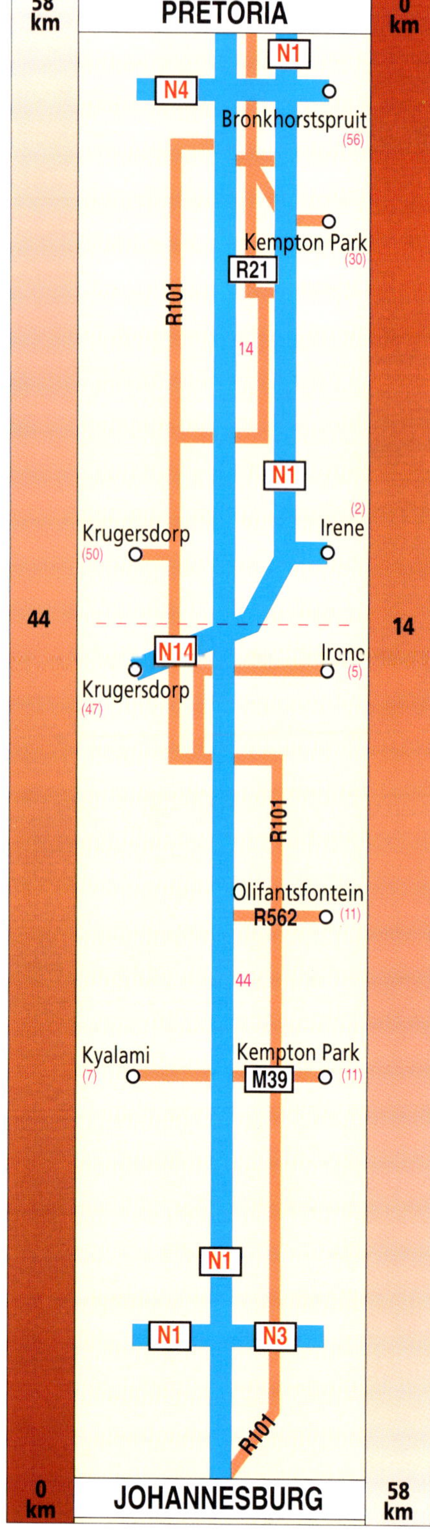

GAUTENG

Johannesburg, bustling financial capital of Gauteng and South Africa's largest metropolis, and stately Pretoria, the country's administrative capital, are located 56km (35 miles) apart on the highest part of the interior plateau known as the Highveld. South of Johannesburg sprawls the urban conglomerate of Soweto, as well as a concentration of important industrial towns like Germiston, Vereeniging and Vanderbijlpark, while to the north lie Johannesburg's affluent garden suburbs. All these come together to form what is known as Gauteng – South Africa's pulsating economic heartland.

MAIN ATTRACTIONS

Johannesburg: South Africa's commercial and financial capital, a modern city dominated by concrete-and-glass giants.
Pretoria: the lovely 'Jacaranda City' offering a wealth of historic buildings; in October its avenues are strewn with lilac blossoms.
Sterkfontein Caves: northwest of Krugersdorp; source of artefacts from the dawn of humankind.
Hartbeespoort Dam: large body of water, picturesquely situated at the foothills of the Magaliesberg mountain range; popular with many anglers, campers and watersports enthusiasts.
Carousel Entertainment World and **Morula Sun:** dine in style, watch an entertaining show, or gamble the night away at one of these chic casino resorts.

DISTANCE IN KM FROM JOHANNESBURG	
Bloemfontein	398
Cape Town	1402
Durban	578
Nelspruit	355
Port Elizabeth	1075

USEFUL CONTACTS

Police, tel: 1-0111 (national number).
Ambulance, tel: 1-0177 (national number).
Johannesburg General Hospital, tel: (011) 488-4911, fax: 643-1612.
Johannesburg Metropolitan Tourism Association, tel: (011) 336-4961, fax: 336-4965; tourist information.
Computicket, tel: (011) 445-8445; for booking of theatre and cinema shows.
First National Bank, tel: (011) 371-1212; lost or stolen credit cards.
AA of South Africa, tel: (011) 799-1000.
SATOUR, Pretoria, tel: (012) 347-0600.

TRAVEL TIPS

A network of well-signposted roads and highways links the centres in this region. Speed limits apply to usual urban zones like schools and hospitals. As in crowded city areas worldwide, crime presents a growing problem. Common sense, however, goes a long way towards preventing potentially unpleasant situations. Below follow some safety guidelines:

- Plan your itinerary before setting out.
- Don't leave your vehicle if it is bumped from behind, but rather proceed to a populated and well-lit area.
- Never park in poorly lit areas.
- Don't walk around alone after dusk.
- Leave your personal belongings and valuables safely stored in the hotel when you venture out.

Below: *The Randburg Waterfront, capturing the spirited ambience of a Mediterranean marina, has become a popular haunt for young and old alike.*

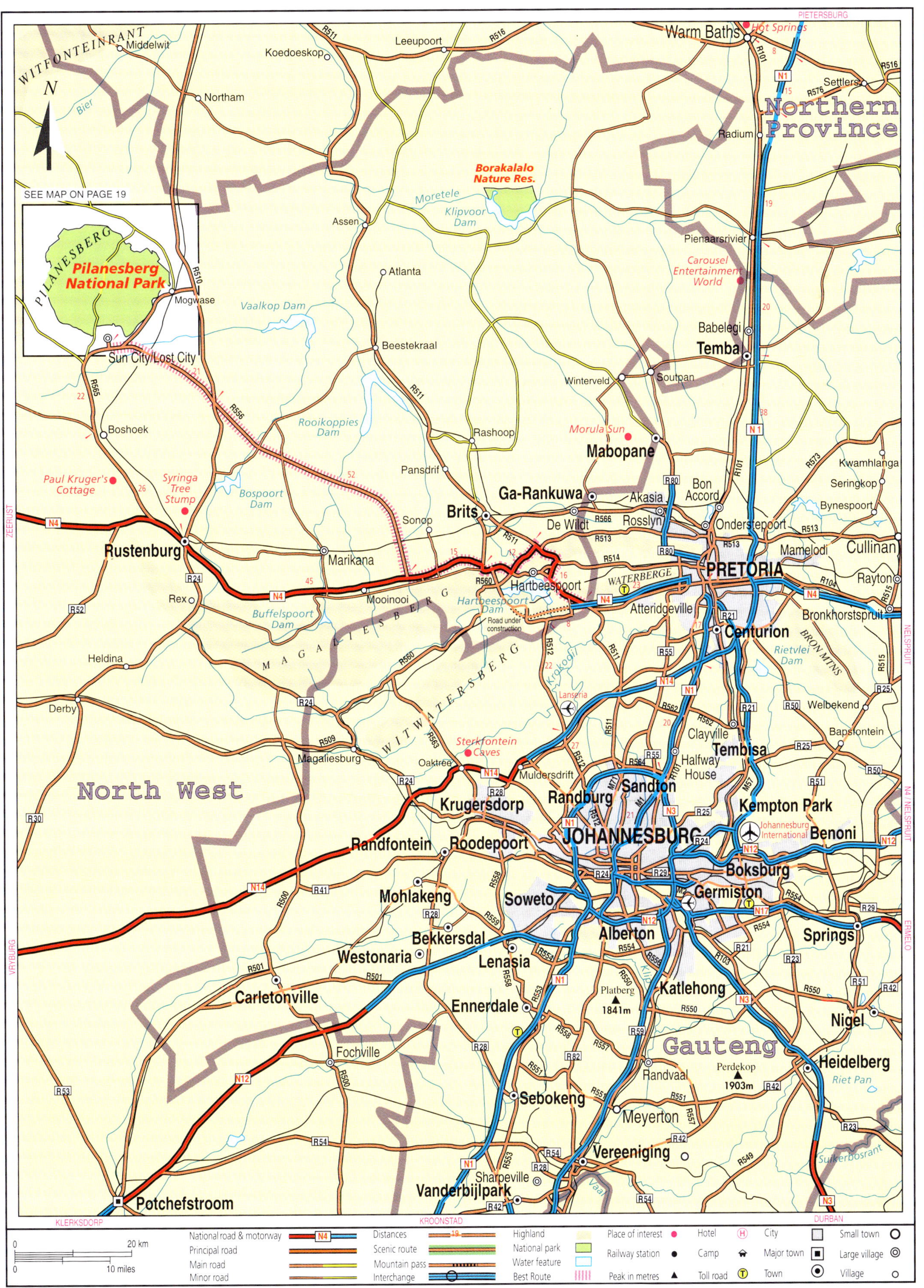
PIETERSBURG
Warm Baths
Hot Springs
Leeupoort
Koedoeskop
Middelwit
WITFONTEINRANT
Northam
Bier
N
Settlers
Northern Province
Radium
Borakalalo Nature Res.
Moretele
Klipvoor Dam
SEE MAP ON PAGE 19
Assen
Pienaarsrivier
PILANESBERG
Pilanesberg National Park
Mogwase
Carousel Entertainment World
Atlanta
Vaalkop Dam
Babelegi
Beestekraal
Temba
Sun City/Lost City
Winterveld
Soutpan
Boshoek
Rooikoppies Dam
Rashoop
Morula Sun
Mabopane
Paul Kruger's Cottage
Syringa Tree Stump
Pansdrif
Ga-Rankuwa
Akasia
Bon Accord
Kwamhlanga
Seringkop
Bospoort Dam
Brits
De Wildt
Rosslyn
Onderstepoort
Bynespoort
Sonop
Rustenburg
Marikana
Mamelodi
Cullinan
PRETORIA
Rayton
Hartbeespoort
WATERBERGE
Rex
Mooinooi
Hartbeespoort Dam
Atteridgeville
Bronkhorstspruit
Buffelspoort Dam
Road under construction
Centurion
MAGALIESBERG
BRONKHORSTSPRUIT
Rietvlei Dam
Heldina
Lanseria
Krokodil
WITWATERSBERG
Welbekend
Derby
Clayville
Tembisa
Bapsfontein
Sterkfontein Caves
Magaliesburg
Halfway House
Oaktree
Muldersdrift
Sandton
North West
Randburg
Krugersdorp
Kempton Park
Johannesburg International
Benoni
JOHANNESBURG
Randfontein
Roodepoort
Boksburg
Mohlakeng
Soweto
Germiston
Alberton
Springs
Bekkersdal
Westonaria
Lenasia
Katlehong
Carletonville
Platberg 1841m
Ennerdale
Nigel
Gauteng
Fochville
Randvaal
Perdekop 1903m
Heidelberg
Riet Pan
Sebokeng
Meyerton
Vereeniging
Suikerbosrant
Sharpeville
Vanderbijlpark
Vaal
Potchefstroom
ZEERUST
VRYBURG
KLERKSDORP
KROONSTAD
DURBAN
NELSPRUIT
N4 / NELSPRUIT
ERMELO
0 20 km
0 10 miles
National road & motorway
Principal road
Main road
Minor road
Distances
Scenic route
Mountain pass
Interchange
Highland
National park
Water feature
Best Route
Place of interest
Railway station
Peak in metres
Hotel
Camp
Toll road
City
Major town
Town
Small town
Large village
Village

GREATER JOHANNESBURG

The huge, yellow mine dumps and rusting headgear of the abandoned gold mines to the south of modern Johannesburg are evocative reminders of the days when the city was essentially a diggers' camp – a visit to Gold Reef City lets you relive the exciting gold-rush past. To the north, wealthy garden suburbs like Sandton and Randburg offer upmarket shopping centres, fashionable boutiques, souvenir shops, an impressive range of cosmopolitan and ethnic restaurants, and numerous entertainment venues. Informal art and craft markets are regularly held in the many parks, and there are no less than 11 challenging golf courses.

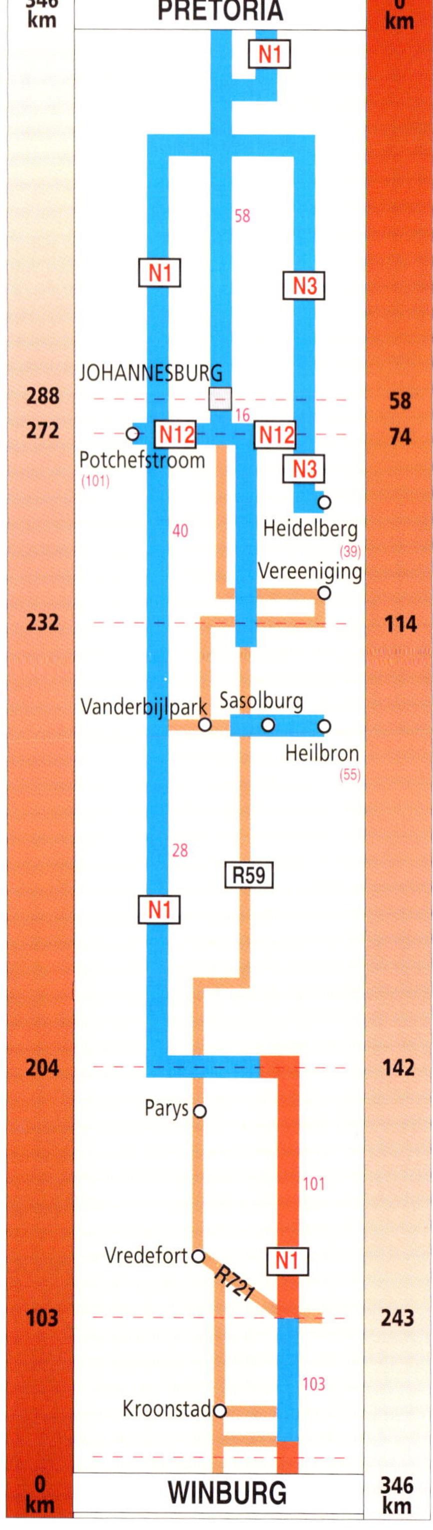

MAIN ATTRACTIONS

Gold Reef City: experience Johannesburg during the gold rush days. Descend deep into a mine, see traditional and 'gum-boot' dances, visit the interesting museums and the fairground.
Randburg Waterfront: attractive complex with live entertainment, restaurants, shops and pubs.
MuseumAfrica: next to the Market Theatre; fascinating displays and artefacts illustrate South Africa's turbulent history from prehistory to the present.
Flea markets: the Johannesburg (at the Market Theatre) and Bruma Lake flea markets offer most anything, every Saturday.
Soweto: interesting tours with reputable operators give an insight into the birthplace of the country's freedom movement.
Traditional Herbalist Shop: at 14 Diagonal Street; marvel at the skins, bones, roots and herbs used by tribal doctors.

Events and Festivals

Lexington PGA Golf Tournament: International and Southern African golfing greats meet in **January** to fight it out for this prestigious title.
Rand Show: in **April** the National Exhibition Centre (southwest of Johannesburg) hosts the biggest consumer show in Africa, featuring local and international products.
Johannesburg Pops Festival: in **April** traditional and contemporary musicians, choirs and soloists get together for the most vibrant 3-day outdoor concert in southern Africa.
International Eisteddfod of South Africa: during **September/October** the city of Roodepoort hums with acitivity as musicians and dancers from around the world compete for honours in this cultural event.
Guinness Jazz Festival: in **September/October**; jazz extravaganza featuring exciting local and international talent.

JHB	J	F	M	A	M	J	J	A	S	O	N	D
AV. TEMP. °C	20	20	18	16	13	10	10	13	16	18	18	19
AV. TEMP. °F	68	68	64	61	55	50	50	55	61	64	64	66
DAILY SUN hrs	8	8	8	8	9	9	9	10	9	9	8	8
RAINFALL mm	131	95	81	55	19	7	6	6	26	72	114	106
RAINFALL in	5.5	4	3.5	2.5	0.7	0.3	0.2	0.2	1	3	4.5	4.5

ACCOMMODATION

Carlton Hotel *****, corner of Main and Kruis streets, tel: (011) 331-8911, fax: 331-3555; convenient, central location.
Holiday Inn Garden Court *****, tel: (011) 336-7011, fax: 336-0515; in the city centre.
Sandton Sun and Towers Intercontinental *****, Sandton City, tel: (011) 780-5000, fax: 780-5002; luxurious accommodation.
Gold Reef Protea Hotel ****, tel: (011) 496-1626, fax: 496-1636; Victorian charm, located right in the theme park.
City Lodge Morningside ***, tel: (011) 884-9500, fax: 884-9440; 30 minutes from the airport in lovely Sandton.
Holiday Inn Garden Court Milpark ***, Auckland Park, tel: (011) 726-5100, fax: 726-8615; some 6km (4½ miles) from the city centre.
Karos Johannesburger ***, tel: (011) 725-3753, fax: 725-6309; located in the heart of town.
Airport Formula One, tel: (011) 392-1453, fax: 974-3845; budget accommodation close to the International Airport.
City Lodge Airport, tel: 392-1750, fax: 392-2644; only 5 minutes from the airport.
Bed and Breakfast (central booking office), tel: (011) 482-2206, fax: 726-6915; assists travellers with finding accommodation.

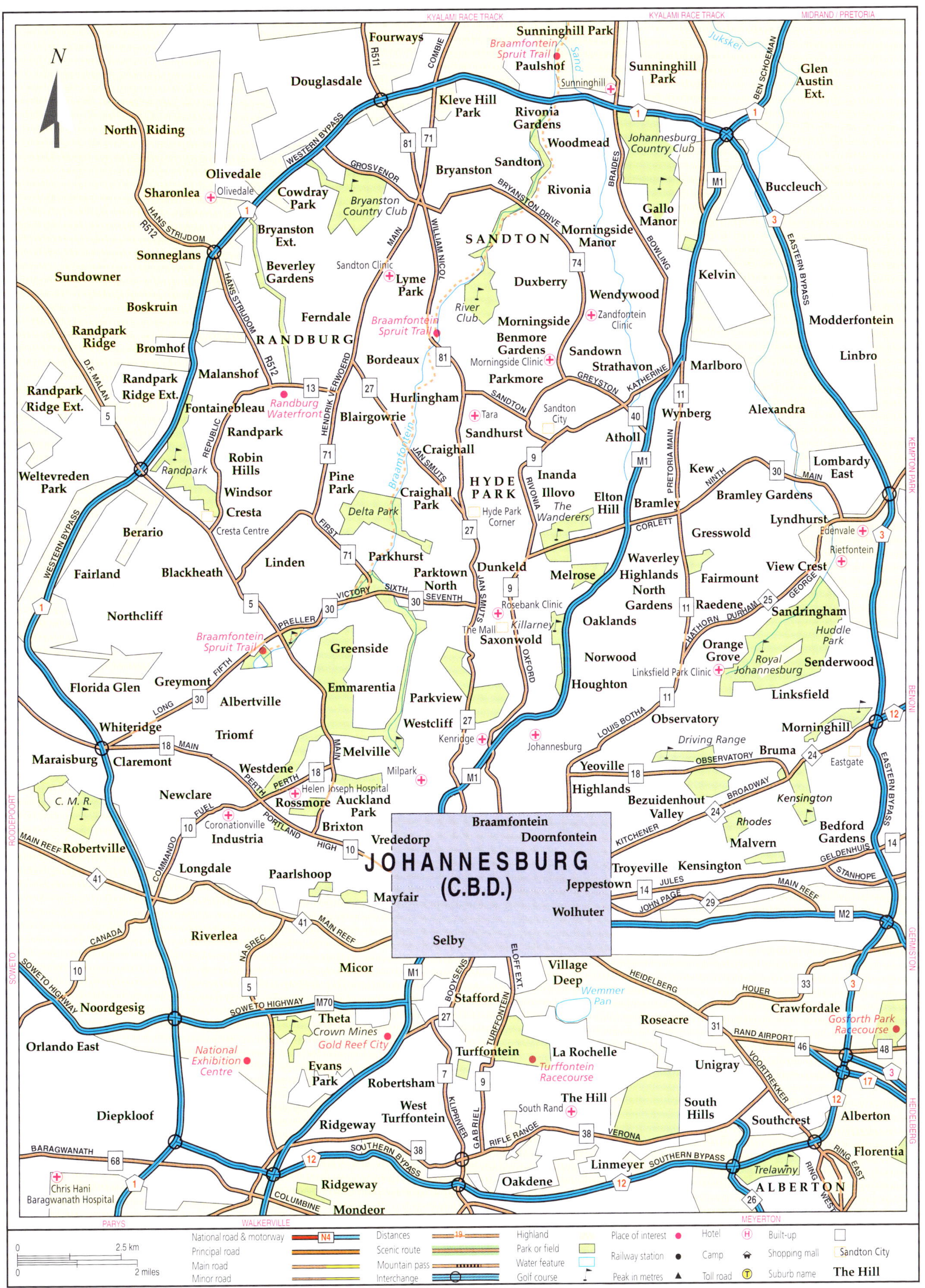

KEY TOURIST AREAS

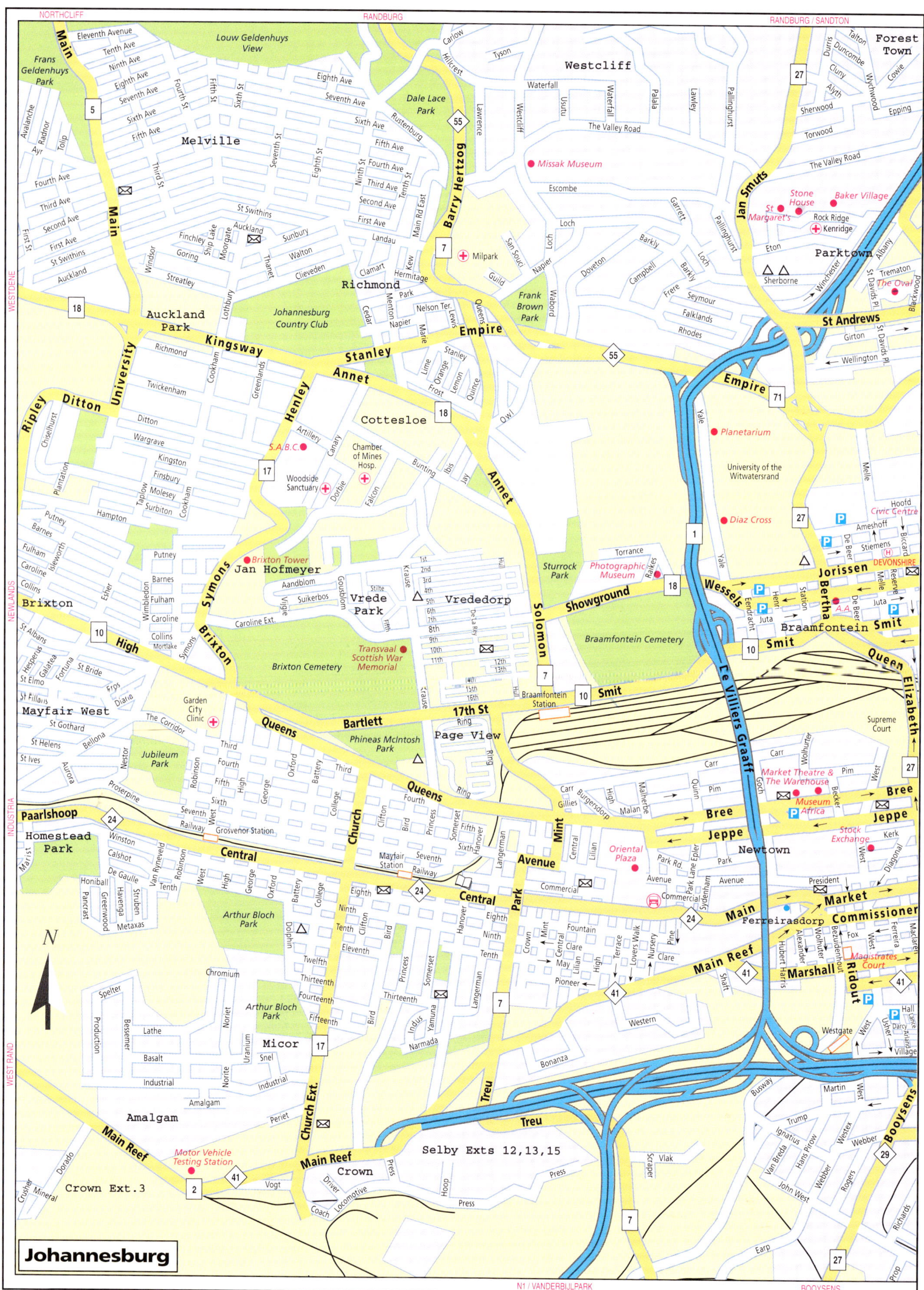
Johannesburg
NORTHCLIFF
RANDBURG
RANDBURG / SANDTON
WESTDENE
NEWLANDS
INDUSTRIA
WEST RAND
N1 / VANDERBIJLPARK
BOOYSENS
Frans Geldenhuys Park
Louw Geldenhuys View
Melville
Westcliff
Forest Town
Dale Lace Park
Missak Museum
Stone House
Baker Village
St Margaret's
Kenridge
Parktown
Sherborne
The Oval
Milpark
Richmond
Frank Brown Park
Auckland Park
Johannesburg Country Club
St Andrews
Empire
Kingsway
Stanley
Annet
University
Ditton
Ripley
Cottesloe
Planetarium
University of the Witwatersrand
S.A.B.C.
Chamber of Mines Hosp.
Woodside Sanctuary
Diaz Cross
Civic Centre
DEVONSHIRE
Brixton Tower
Jan Hofmeyer
Vrede Park
Vrededorp
Sturrock Park
Photographic Museum
Showground
Jorissen
Wessels
Bertha
Braamfontein
Braamfontein Cemetery
Brixton
High
Transvaal Scottish War Memorial
Brixton Cemetery
Braamfontein Station
Smit
Queens
Elizabeth
Mayfair West
Garden City Clinic
Bartlett
17th St
Page View
Phineas McIntosh Park
Jubilee Park
Supreme Court
Market Theatre & The Warehouse
Museum Africa
Bree
Jeppe
Stock Exchange
Newtown
Paarlshoop
Homestead Park
Grosvenor Station
Central
Church
Mayfair Station
Avenue
Mint
Oriental Plaza
Market
Commissioner
Ferreirasdorp
Main
Arthur Bloch Park
Park
Main Reef
Marshall
Magistrates Court
Ridout
Micor
Amalgam
Church Ext.
Treu
Selby Exts 12,13,15
Motor Vehicle Testing Station
Crown
Crown Ext.3
Boysens
Village
N

KEY TOURIST AREAS

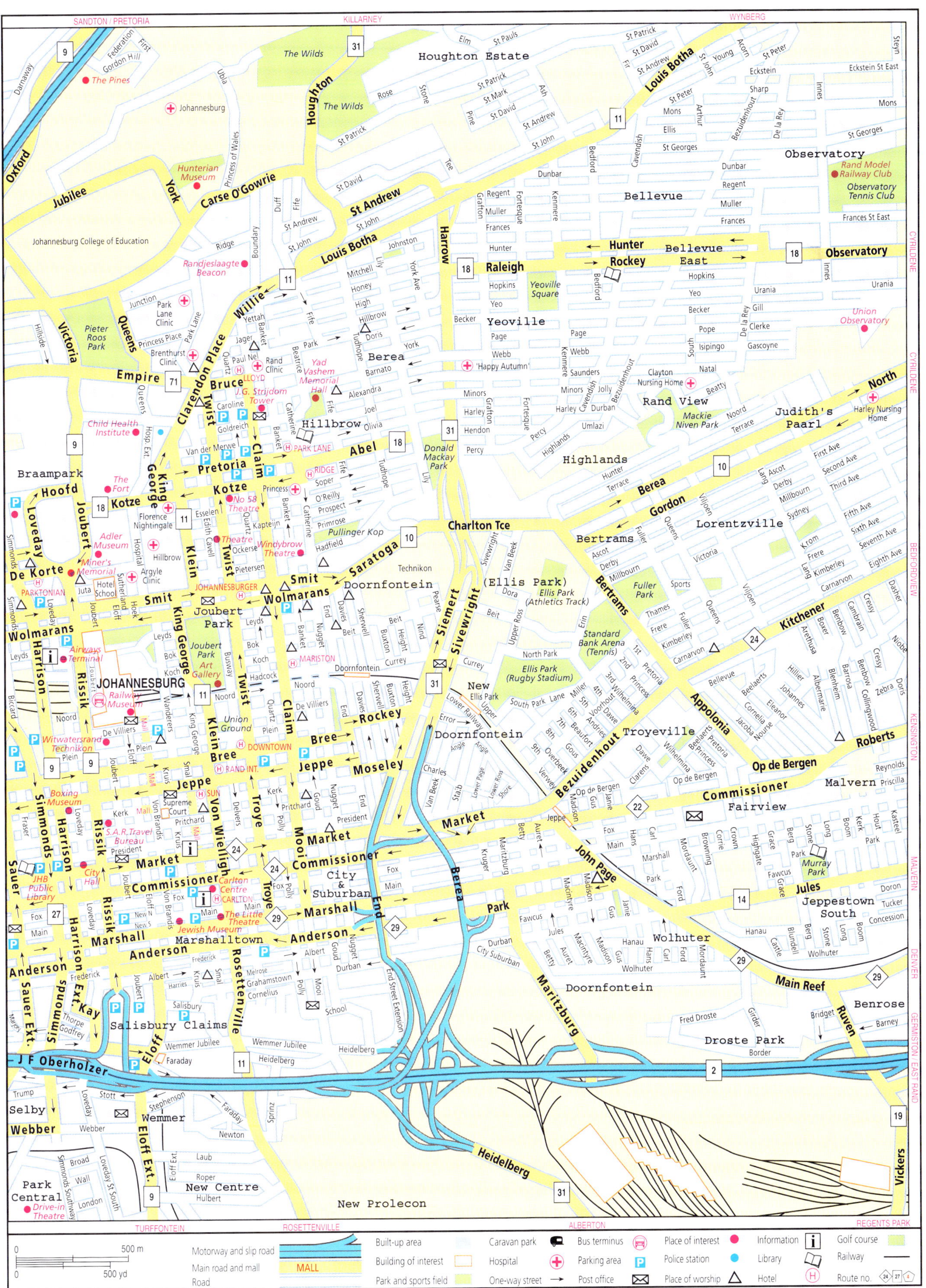

PRETORIA

Handsome Pretoria is noted for its stately, historic homes, the impressive Union Buildings (administrative seat of the South African government), its parks and gardens with their splendid wealth of indigenous flora, and for its tall jacaranda trees that transform the streets into a blaze of lilac each October/November, earning Pretoria its nickname. The city is the administrative capital of the country, as well as a centre of research and learning. Within its limits lie the Pretoria University; gigantic Unisa, the world's largest correspondence university; and Onderstepoort, an internationally renowned veterinary research institute.

Events and Festivals

Pretoria Show: international business exposition in **August.**
Spring Carnival: September celebration; live music and entertainment.
Jacaranda Festival: in **October** the city of Pretoria revels in the lilac glory of its many flowering trees.

Above: *Summer time in Pretoria is heralded by a glory of lilac blossoms as the many jacaranda trees begin to flower, covering city streets and walks with a fragrant, pastel-coloured carpet.*

MAIN ATTRACTIONS

Union Buildings: magnificent edifice designed by Sir Herbert Baker, on landscaped, terraced grounds that look out over the city from Meintjieskop.
Church Square: historic town square framed by beautiful old buildings such as the old Raadsaal (parliament), Palace of Justice and SA Reserve Bank.
Voortrekker Monument: construction on Monument Hill, 6km (4 miles) from the city, commemorating the Great Trek of the 1830 pioneers.
National Zoological Gardens: one of the world's largest; over 3500 exotic and indigenous species.
Transvaal Museum of Natural History: many extensive displays, including the impressive 'Life's Genesis' and the interesting Austin Roberts Bird Hall.
State Theatre: on completion in 1981, this imposing cultural complex, comprising five theatres and a public square, was the largest of its kind in the southern hemisphere.

PRETORIA	J	F	M	A	M	J	J	A	S	O	N	D
AV. TEMP. °C	23	22	21	18	15	11	12	14	18	20	21	22
AV. TEMP. °F	73	72	70	64	59	52	54	57	64	68	70	73
DAILY SUN hrs	9	8	8	8	9	9	9	10	10	9	9	9
RAINFALL mm	152	76	80	57	14	3	3	6	21	67	101	105
RAINFALL in	6	3	3.5	2.5	0.6	0.1	0.1	0.2	0.8	3	4	4.5

ACCOMMODATION

Centurion Lake Hotel ★★★★, 1001 Lenchen Avenue North, Centurion, tel: (012) 663-1825, fax: 663-2760.
Holiday Inn Crowne Plaza ★★★★, crn. Beatrix and Church streets, Arcadia, tel: (012) 341-1571, fax: 44-7534; centrally located.
Arcadia Hotel ★★★, tel: (012) 326-9311, fax: 326-1067; beautifully situated right at the foot of the impressive Union Buildings.
Bentley's Country Lodge ★★★, cnr. Main Street and Brits Road, Akasia, tel: (012) 542-1751, fax: 542-3487.
The Farm Inn ★★★, Lynwood Road, The Willows, tel: (012) 809-0266, fax: 809-0146; close to the city.
Madeleine Hotel, 562 Pretorius Street, tel: (012) 44-4281, fax: 341-7000; friendly establishment.
Panorama Inn, 706 Arcadia Street, tel: (012) 344-3010, fax: 343-8601.

USEFUL CONTACTS

HF Verwoerd Hospital, tel: (012) 354-1000.
Computicket, tel: (012) 326-4684.
International Embassies: all on code (012)

- Australia, tel: 342-3740
- France, tel: 43-5564, fax: 43-3481
- Germany, tel: 427-8900, fax: 343-9401
- Italy, tel: 43-5541, fax: 43-5547
- Netherlands, tel: 344-3910, fax: 343-9950
- Spain, tel: 344-3875, fax: 343-4891
- UK, tel: 43-3121, fax: 43-3207
- USA, tel: 342-1048, fax: 342-2299.

KEY TOURIST AREAS

PILANESBERG AND SUN CITY

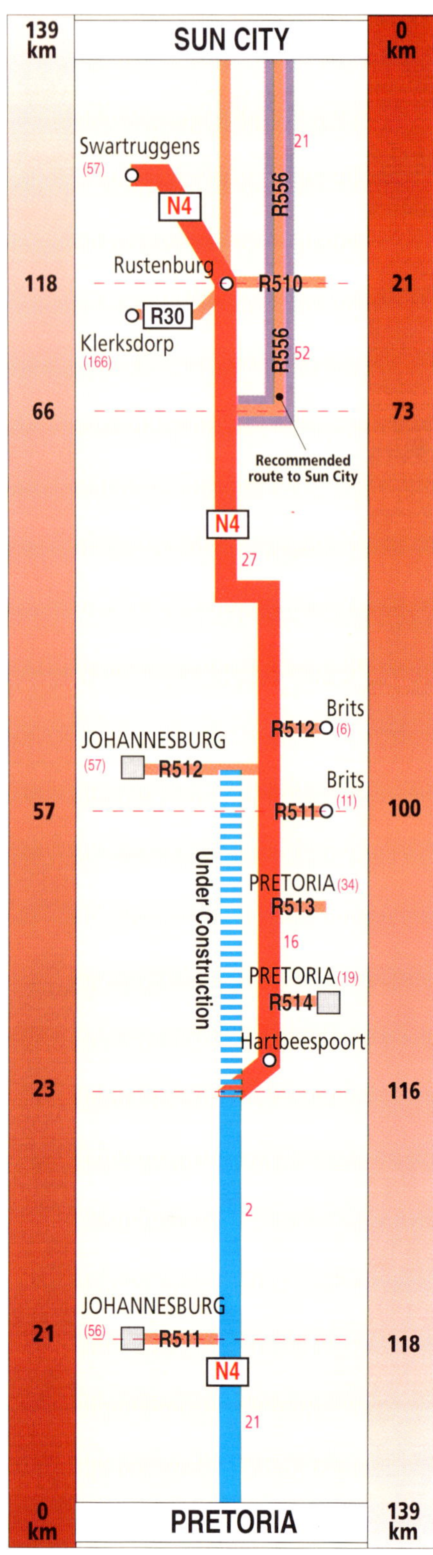

The dramatic Lost City and Sun City leisure resort, one of South Africa's most glittering tourist venues featuring casinos, bars, restaurants, theatres, nightclubs and shops, is set among the lush vegetation of beautifully landscaped grounds, in what before was little more than desert territory. Apart from the 31,500m² (339,063ft²) Valley of the Waves, a man-made water park with soft sand beaches, waterslides, cascades and 1.8m-high (5.9ft) waves, the complex also offers an Arizona Desert-style golf course where crocodiles lie in wait at the 13th hole, and another at the Gary Player Country Club, venue of the annual Million Dollar Golf Challenge.

Pilanesberg National Park north of Sun City has some 10,000 head of wildlife including the Big Five – buffalo, rhino (black and white), elephant, lion and leopard – and over 300 bird species. This game-rich habitat lies within four concentric mountain rings, the relics of an ancient volcano. In the centre of the bowl is Mankwe Lake, a favourite hippo haunt. The park is traversed by a network of game-viewing roads; guided walks and drives are conducted and hot-air balloon trips can be organized. This wonderful park is the result of 'Operation Genesis', a successful game-stocking venture. A visit to the aviary at Manyane Gate should not be missed.

Accommodation

Sun City complex
tel: (01465) 2-1000, fax: 2-1470.
The Cascades *****, opulent.
Palace of the Lost City *****, the ultimate in luxurious extravagance and splendour.
Sun City Cabanas ***, mainly family-oriented and affordable.
Sun City Main Hotel *****, superb five-star comfort.

Pilanesberg National Park
Bakubung Game Lodge ****, tel: (01465) 2-1861, fax: 2-1621, thatched rooms around a hippo pool in a private game reserve.
Kwa Maritane Game Lodge ****, tel: (01465) 2-1820, fax: 2-1268; luxurious accommodation in the African bush.

SUN CITY	J	F	M	A	M	J	J	A	S	O	N	D
AV. TEMP. °C	23	23	21	18	15	12	12	14	18	21	22	23
AV. TEMP. °F	73	73	70	64	59	54	54	57	64	70	72	73
DAILY SUN hrs	8	8	8	7	9	9	9	10	10	9	8	9
RAINFALL mm	138	98	76	57	17	8	5	7	17	53	98	111
RAINFALL in	5.5	4	3	2.5	0.7	0.3	0.2	0.3	0.7	2.5	4	4.5

USEFUL CONTACTS

Pilanesberg National Park, tel: (01465) 5-5356; for the real bush experience.
Sun International Group Central Reservations, tel: (011) 780-7443.

DISTANCE IN KM FROM SUN CITY	
Johannesburg	173
Pretoria	139
Rustenburg	48

Below: *The Palace of the Lost City rises dramatically out of the surrounding African bush, like the legendary temple of a mysterious civilization.*

KEY TOURIST AREAS

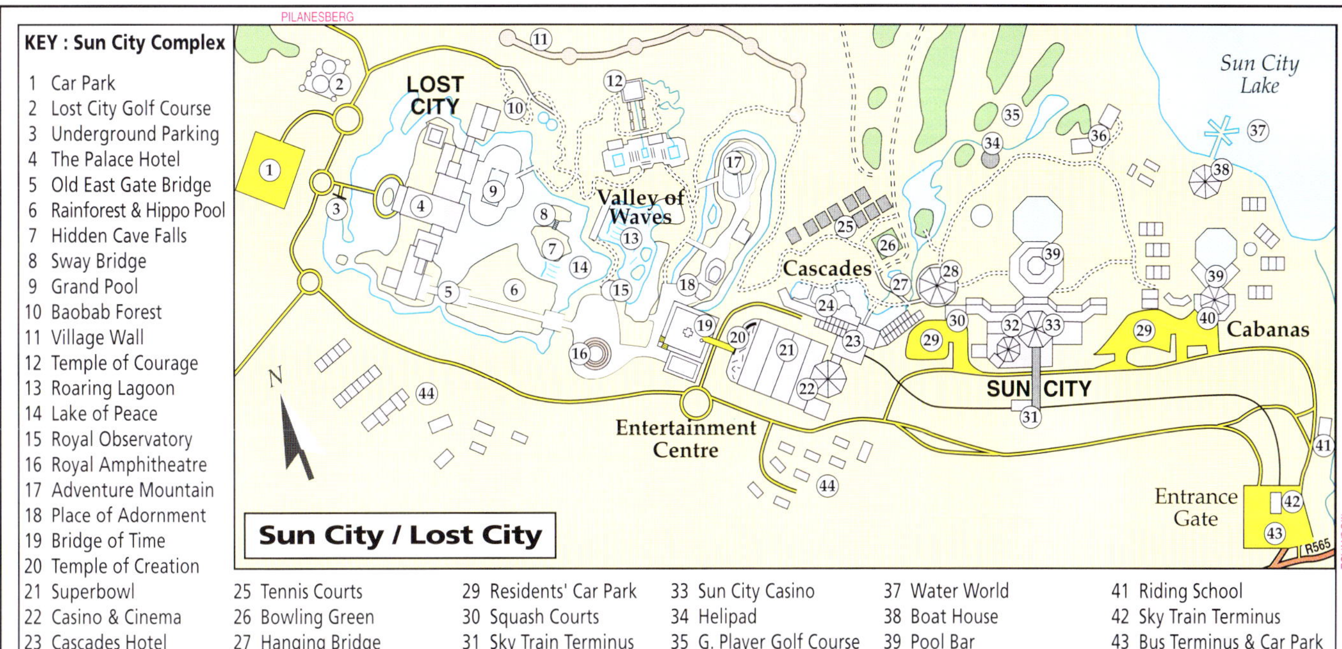

KEY : Sun City Complex

1 Car Park
2 Lost City Golf Course
3 Underground Parking
4 The Palace Hotel
5 Old East Gate Bridge
6 Rainforest & Hippo Pool
7 Hidden Cave Falls
8 Sway Bridge
9 Grand Pool
10 Baobab Forest
11 Village Wall
12 Temple of Courage
13 Roaring Lagoon
14 Lake of Peace
15 Royal Observatory
16 Royal Amphitheatre
17 Adventure Mountain
18 Place of Adornment
19 Bridge of Time
20 Temple of Creation
21 Superbowl
22 Casino & Cinema
23 Cascades Hotel
24 The Grotto
25 Tennis Courts
26 Bowling Green
27 Hanging Bridge
28 G. Player Country Club
29 Residents' Car Park
30 Squash Courts
31 Sky Train Terminus
32 Sun City Hotel
33 Sun City Casino
34 Helipad
35 G. Player Golf Course
36 18th Hole
37 Water World
38 Boat House
39 Pool Bar
40 Reception & Restaurant
41 Riding School
42 Sky Train Terminus
43 Bus Terminus & Car Park
44 Staff Village

PILANESBERG
LOST CITY
Valley of Waves
Cascades
Sun City Lake
Cabanas
SUN CITY
Entertainment Centre
Entrance Gate
R565
MOGWASE
N
Sun City / Lost City

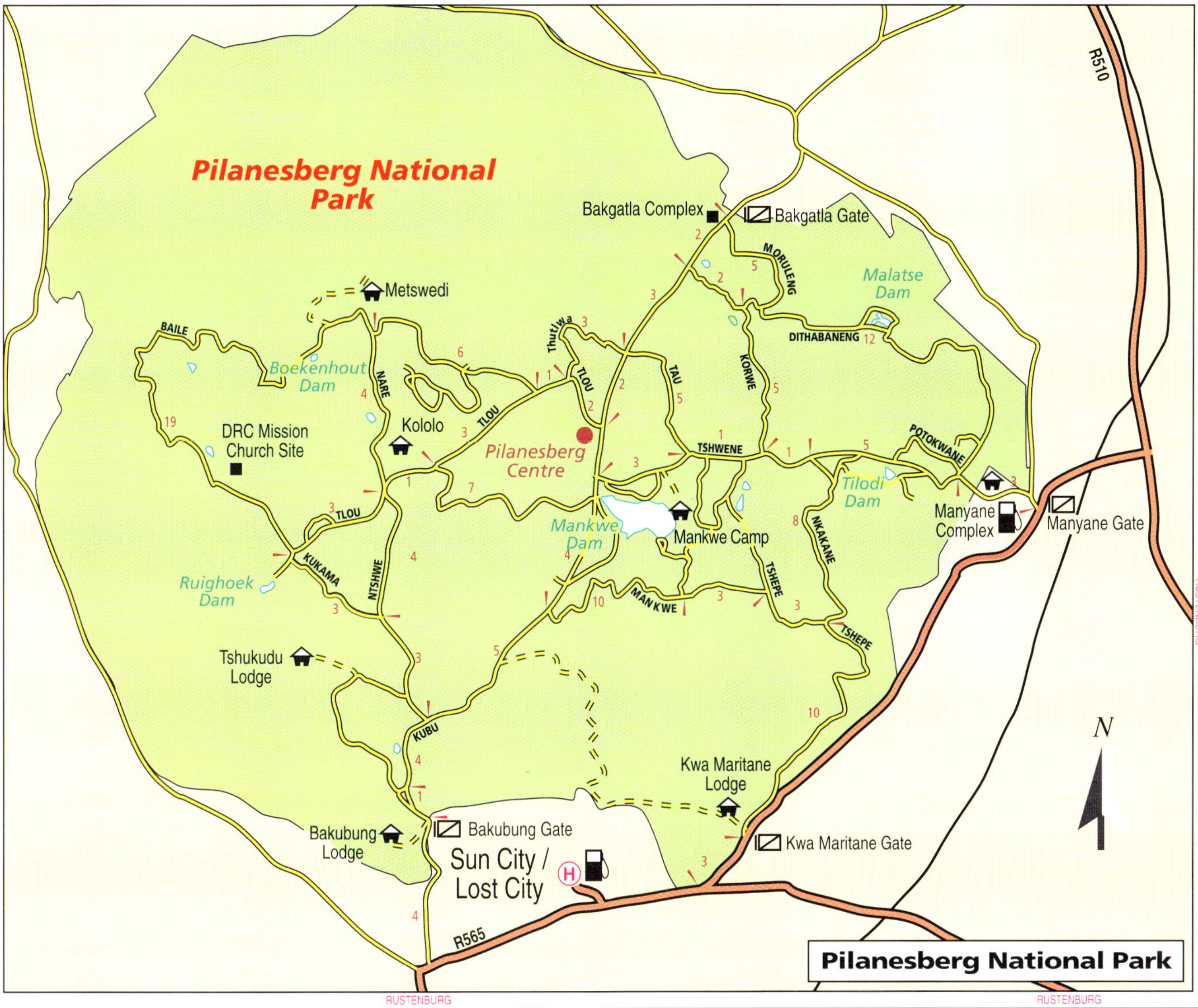

Pilanesberg National Park
Bakgatla Complex
Bakgatla Gate
Malatse Dam
Metswedi
BAILE
Boekenhout Dam
NARE
Kololo
DRC Mission Church Site
TLOU
Thutlwa
Pilanesberg Centre
TAU
KORWE
MORULENG
DITHABANENG
TSHWENE
POTOKWANE
Tilodi Dam
Manyane Complex
Manyane Gate
Mankwe Dam
Mankwe Camp
NKAKANE
TSHEPE
MANKWE
KUKAMA
NTSHWE
Ruighoek Dam
Tshukudu Lodge
KUBU
Kwa Maritane Lodge
Kwa Maritane Gate
Bakubung Lodge
Bakubung Gate
Sun City / Lost City
R565
R510
RUSTENBURG
N
Pilanesberg National Park

0 30 m 0 25 yd Sun City / Lost City

0 3 km 0 2 miles Pilanesberg National Park

Main road · Minor road · Distances · Track · National park · Water feature · Hotel · Camp · Park gate · Place of interest

KRUGER NATIONAL PARK

South Africa's premier wildlife sanctuary covers more than 20,000 km² (7720 sq miles) – an area about the size of Wales and larger than the state of Israel. Because this vast, wild expanse encompasses many different habitats, it is a haven for more varieties of wildlife than any other game reserve in Africa. Among the approximately 140 mammal species occurring here are the Big Five: lion (approximately 1500), elephant (about 8000), leopard (around 1000), buffalo (25,000), and rhino, both black and white. Other large wildlife populations include zebra, wildebeest, giraffe, hippo and crocodile, as well as some 500 bird species. If you are lucky, you may even spot a pack of the increasingly rare wild dogs.

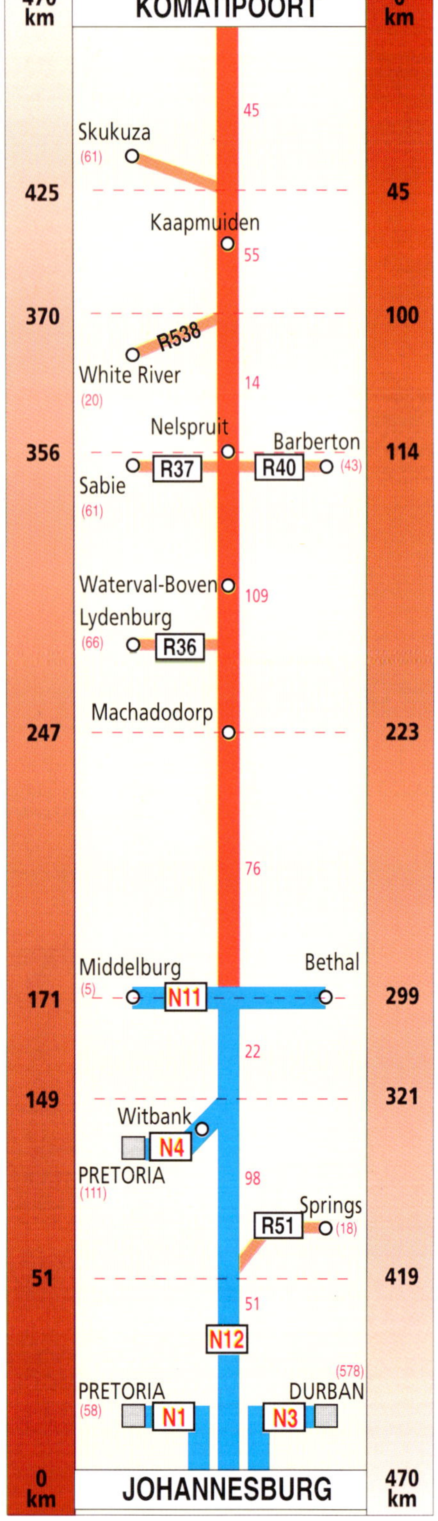

TRAVEL TIPS

An extensive network, consisting of about 880km (550 miles) of tarred surface and 1700km (1060 miles) of gravel road, traverses the park, providing effective access to all areas of the Kruger.

Should you experience any car trouble, vehicle breakdown services are available at Skukuza and Letaba camps.

A few general safety guidelines have to be observed by all visitors :

- Malaria treatment should be started prior to entering this area (consult your physician), and use insect repellent.
- Stay on the designated roads or tracks.
- Keep to the speed limit.
- Do not leave your vehicle.
- Don't injure, feed or disturb wildlife.
- Littering is an offence.
- Be sure to arrive at your rest camp by the stipulated time before sunset.

DISTANCE IN KM TO KRUGER NATIONAL PARK	
Bloemfontein	823
Cape Town	1827
Durban	780
Johannesburg	425
Port Elizabeth	1500

MAIN ATTRACTIONS

Olifants Camp: dramatically perched on a clifftop; the park's most magnificent viewing-point over the game-rich valley below.
Letaba Elephant Museum: an interesting exhibition at this camp.
Private game lodges: though generally very expensive, **MalaMala** (voted one of the world's finest safari destinations), **Sabi Sabi** and **Londolozi** are the ultimate in bushveld luxury.
Nwanetsi Lookout Point: magnificent viewpoint overlooking the Sweni River.
Mmphongolo drive: one of the best in the northern region.
Pafuri: in the far north is the best place in the park to view birds; superb scenery with a high density of baobab trees.
Stephenson-Hamilton Library: in Skukuza; interesting displays.
Night drives: well worth the cost; you may even spot a leopard.
Tshokwane Picnic Spot: highly recommended rest-stop where refreshments can be purchased.

ACCOMMODATION

Over 20 pleasant, clean and safe rest camps are located within the park. For all enquiries, contact the **National Parks Board: Pretoria**, tel: (012) 343-1991; **Cape Town**, tel: (021) 22-2810.

SATARA	J	F	M	A	M	J	J	A	S	O	N	D
AV. TEMP. °C	27	27	25	23	19	17	16	19	21	24	24	26
AV. TEMP. °F	81	81	77	73	66	63	61	66	70	75	75	79
DAILY SUN hrs	7	8	7	7	8	8	8	8	8	7	6	7
RAINFALL mm	51	91	42	25	7	15	8	9	16	38	59	76
RAINFALL in	2.5	4	2	1	0.3	0.6	0.3	0.3	0.6	1.5	2.5	3

Left: *Elephants should always be approached with caution. Displays of aggression such as a raised trunk and flapping ears should never be underestimated.*

Camp Gate & Entry Gate Timetable
OPEN
JAN FEB MAR APR MAY-JUL AUG-SEPT OCT NOV-DEC
04:30 5:30 5:30 6:00 6:00 6:00 5:30 4:30
CLOSE
JAN FEB MAR APR MAY-AUG SEPT OCT NOV-DEC
18:30 18:30 18:00 18:00 17:30 18:00 18:00 18:30
ENTRY GATES OPEN : JAN 5:30 NOV-DEC 5:30
PARK REGULATIONS
Speed Limit: Tarred rds-50 kph; Gravel rds 40 kph
Only leave car at selected viewpoints
Stay on road and do not feed animals
CAMP REGULATIONS
There may be no noise from 21:30 & 06:00
No roller-skating, skateboarding & cycling
No trading or advertising is permitted
Speed limit within rest camp is 10 km/h
No pets allowed & fire arms must be declared
MAIN CAMPSITE - Overnight accommodation & facilities for day visitors.
BUSHVELD CAMP - Overnight accommodation & camping.
PRIVATE CAMP - No facilities for day visitors, no entry without booking.
TRAIL BASE CAMP - Walking trails, no day visitor facilities, no entry without booking.
Kruger National Park
Northern Province
Mpumalanga
ZIMBABWE
MOZAMBIQUE
LEBOMBO MOUNTAINS
LEBOMBO MTN
DRAKENSBERG
Phalaborwa
Nelspruit
Hazyview
Lydenburg
Sabie
Graskop
Pilgrim's Rest
White River
Komatipoort
Ressano Garcia
Letaba
Olifants
Satara
Skukuza
Lower Sabie
Punda Maria
Shingwedzi
Mopani
Orpen
Crocodile Bridge
Berg-en-Dal
Malelane
Blyde River Canyon N.R.
Sabi Sand G.R.
Timbavati G.R.
Klaserie N.R.
Manyeleti G.R.
Umbabat N.R.
Thornybush G.R.
Tshukudu Game Lodge
Gustav Klingbiel N.R.
Ohrigstaddam N.R.
Mt Sheba N.R.
Sudwala Caves
God's Window
Bourke's Luck Potholes
National road & motorway
Principal road
Main road
Minor road
Distances
Scenic route
Mountain pass
Highland
National park
Other park
Park gate
Border post
Place of interest
Railway station
Peak in metres
Hotel
Camp
Battle site
Toll road
City
Major town
Town
Small town
Large village
Village
10 km
10 miles

MPUMALANGA

Mountainous terrain, misty forests, bushveld and endless views are the compelling features of this escarpment region far to the east of Gauteng, across the great Highveld plateau. For sheer scenic beauty, few parts of the southern African subcontinent can compare with the Great Escarpment, a spectacular wonderland of buttresses, strangely sculpted peaks and deep ravines. The Olifants and Crocodile rivers and a score of their tributaries run through verdant valleys. One tributary, the Blyde River, over centuries carved a canyon that now ranks as one of Africa's great scenic splendours.

MAIN ATTRACTIONS

Blyde River Canyon: a majestic gorge whose sheer cliff faces plunge to the water far below.
Bourke's Luck Potholes: a fantasia of hollowed-out rocks.
Pilgrim's Rest: town born out of the 1870 gold rush, now a quaint, living museum.
Jock of the Bushveld: plaques along former Lowveld transport routes commemorate this heroic dog, immortalized in the classic novel by Sir Percy FitzPatrick.
God's Window: for the most magnificent views of the area.
Mount Sheba: beautiful forest reserve high in the mountains.
Tzaneen: attractive town in the heart of the fertile Letaba district.
Magoebaskloof: large tracts of thick indigenous forest.
Long Tom Pass: spectacular pass between Sabie and Lydenburg.
Echo Caves: archaeological evidence of earlier inhabitants.

TRAVEL TIPS

The region has an excellent network of roads. Travelling from Johannesburg to Nelspruit and the escarpment, take the R22 and then the N4 near Witbank; from Pretoria take the N4 direct. The R40 leads from Nelspruit north into the escarpment. To reach the northern and northeastern territory, follow the N1 national highway from Pretoria; turn right at Pietersburg on the R71 for Tzaneen and the central region of the Kruger National Park (around Phalaborwa). If you intend travelling into the far northern region of the park, take the R524 at Louis Trichardt. Please note: this is a **malaria** area so ensure that the necessary precautions are taken before travelling into this area; alternatively consult your physician for advice.

ACCOMMODATION

Mount Sheba Hotel ★★★★, west of Pilgrim's Rest, tel: (013) 768-1241, fax: 768-1248; luxury hotel.
Sabi River Sun ★★★★, close to Paul Kruger Gate, tel: (013) 737-7311, fax: 737-7314; 18-hole golf course.
Pine Lake Sun ★★★★, White River, tel: (013) 751-5036, fax: 751-5134; on the edge of a lake; golf course.
Royal Hotel, Pilgrim's Rest, tel: (013) 768-1100, fax: 768-1188; for an unforgettable stay in a national monument; charming accommodation in authentic tin-roofed houses with antique furnishings.

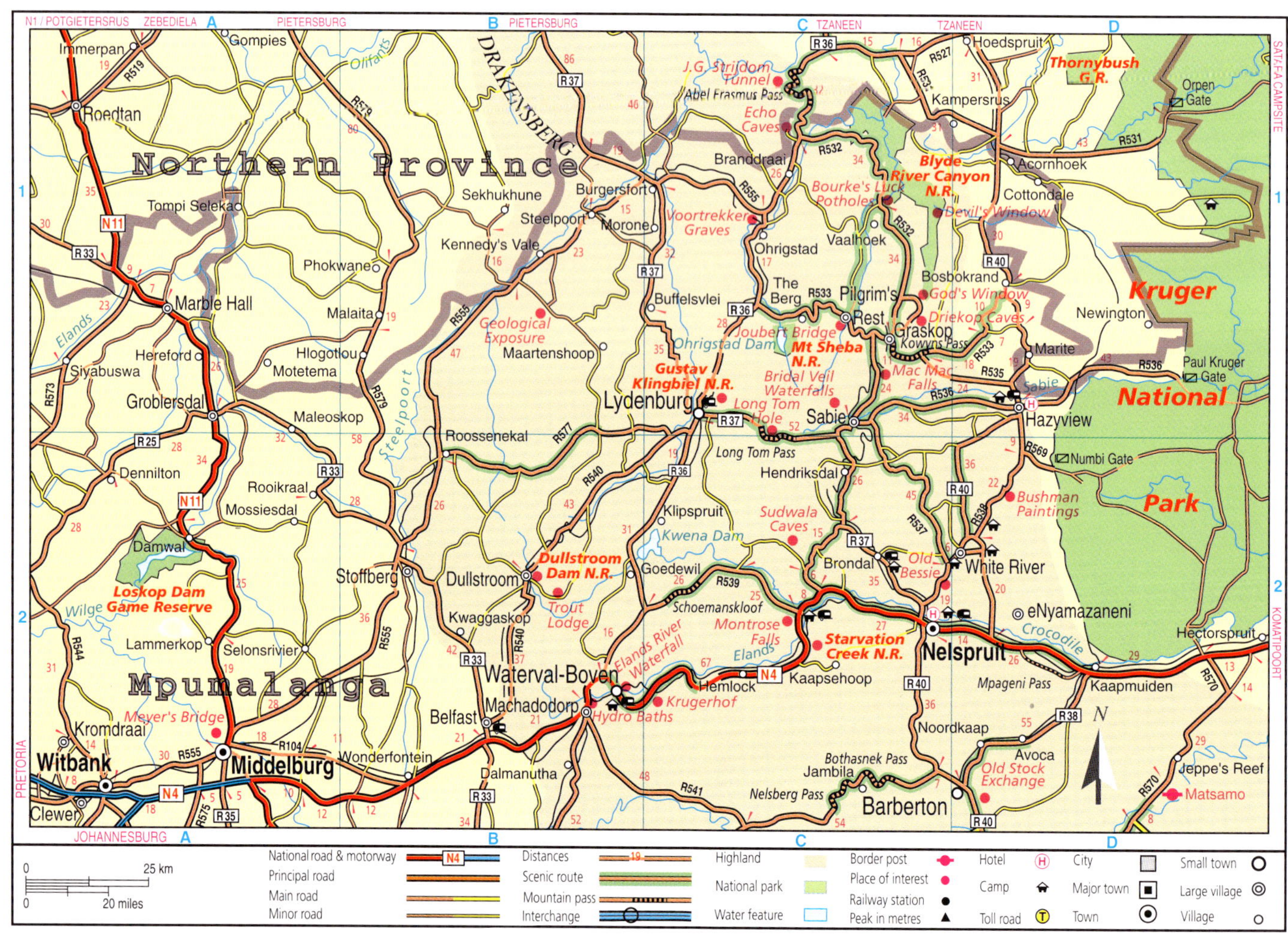

NELSPRUIT

The hot dry plains below the Great Escarpment are known as the Lowveld. The largest town in this grassland region of Mpumalanga and situated on the banks of the Crocodile River, Nelspruit is the centre of a fertile and beautiful agricultural area. It is an attractive and prosperous town of wide streets lined with poinciana trees that are ablaze with deep red blossoms during the summer months. This is the last major town en route to the Kruger National Park. Among Nelspruit's attractions are good hotels and restaurants, sophisticated shops and speciality outlets.

Accommodation

Cybele Forest Lodge ★★★★, on the R40, White River, tel: (013) 764-1823, fax: 764-1810; exclusive retreat surrounded by nature.
Hotel The Winkler ★★★★, tel: (013) 751-5068, fax: 751-5044; in the beautiful White River area.
Paragon Hotel ★★★, 19 Anderson Street, tel/fax: (013) 753-3205; pleasant, clean and comfortable.
Fig Tree Hotel ★★, 16 Anderson Street, tel: (013) 752-2955, fax: 753-3205; convenient location.
Lowveld Lodge, Kastings Street, White River, tel: (013) tel/fax: 750-0206; self-catering chalets.

MAIN ATTRACTIONS

Lowveld Botanic Gardens: on the banks of the Crocodile River, supporting over 500 indigenous species of flora.
Lowveld Herbarium: adjacent to the Gardens; of interest to the botanist as well as the layperson.
Sudwala Caves: dramatic cave formations and an interesting dinosaur park, about 40km (25 miles) northwest of Nelspruit.
Riverside Trail: self-guided 4km (2½-mile) hike along the Crocodile River, with some lovely waterfalls.
Farmstalls: roadside stalls around the town sell fresh fruit and curios.

WATERFALL ROUTE

There are several beautiful waterfalls in the Sabie/Graskop area some 50km (31 miles) north of Nelspruit. A visit to the waterfalls makes a lovely excursion, all of them are easily accessible; the roads are generally in very good condition, although dense fog patches may occur. Among the best falls to view are:
Bridal Veil: a delicate spray of water surrounded by a forest echoing with the call of many birds; 7km (4.2 miles) north of Sabie.
Mac-Mac: twin cascades plunge 56m (185ft) into a deep, green ravine.
Lone Creek: hidden some 68m (222ft) in a beautiful, misty forest.
Horseshoe: a national monument.
Berlin: plunges about 48m (158ft) into a deep pool.
Lisbon: picturesque double waterfall in a setting of special beauty.

USEFUL CONTACTS

Rob Ferreira Hospital, tel: (013) 741-3031.
Nelspruit Publicity, tel: (013) 755-1988.
Mpumalanga Tourist Board, tel: (013) 752-7001/2/3; tourist information.

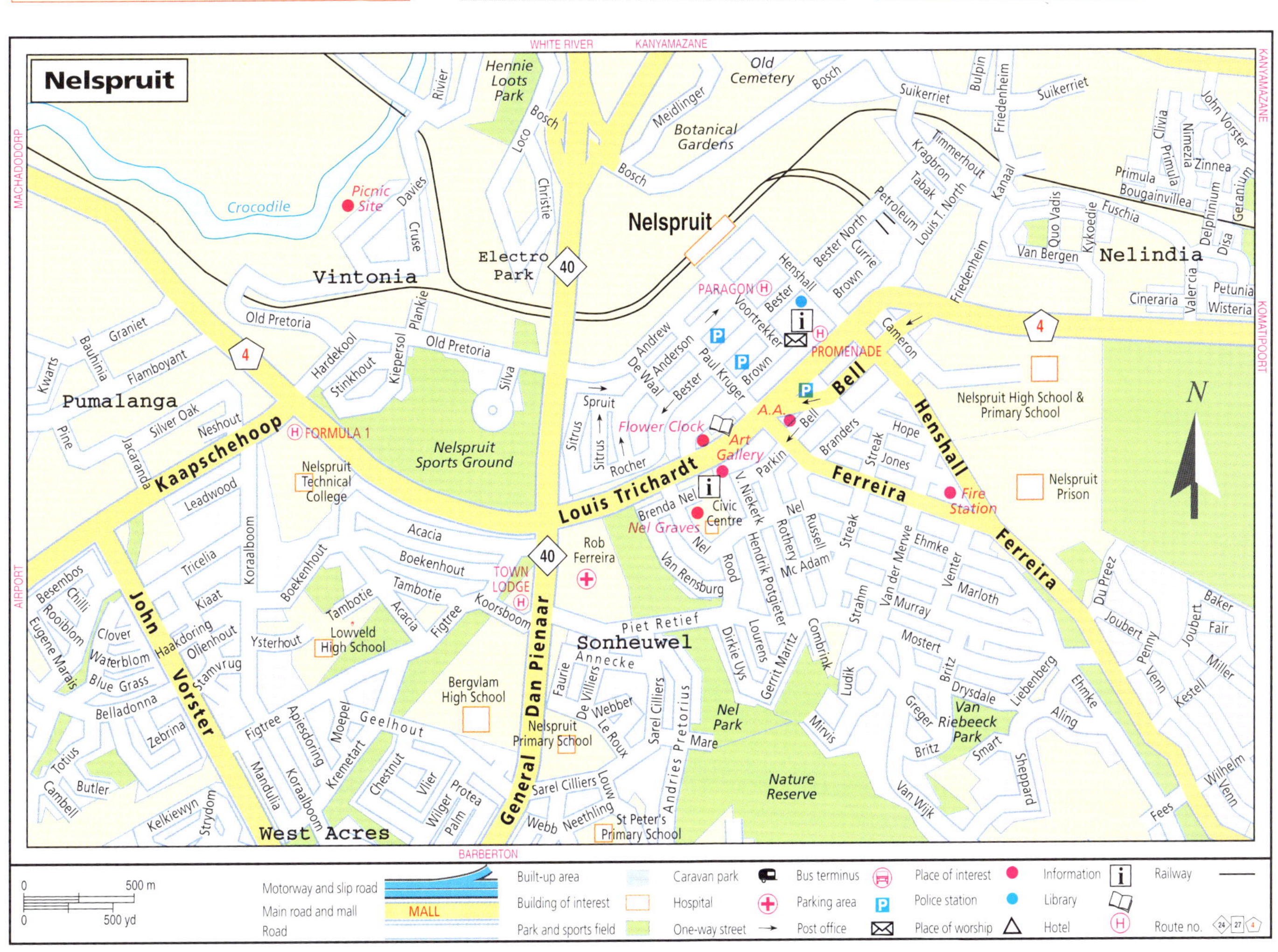

KWAZULU-NATAL NORTH COAST

Remarkable for its rich fauna and flora, northern KwaZulu-Natal boasts some of South Africa's finest game reserves (among them the Hluhluwe/Umfolozi Park, oldest of South Africa's many wildlife sanctuaries) and one of the world's great wetland and marine sanctuaries, the Greater St Lucia Wetland Park. Just north of Durban, along the Dolphin Coast that stretches for 90km (55 miles) up to the Tugela River mouth, lies the upmarket resort town of Umhlanga Rocks. Beyond lies the area historically known as Zululand, where Richards Bay is the largest city and industrial hub due to its deep-water port (the busiest in the country). The broad beaches, fringed by lush, tropical vegetation, attract sunbathers, anglers, divers and boating enthusiasts.

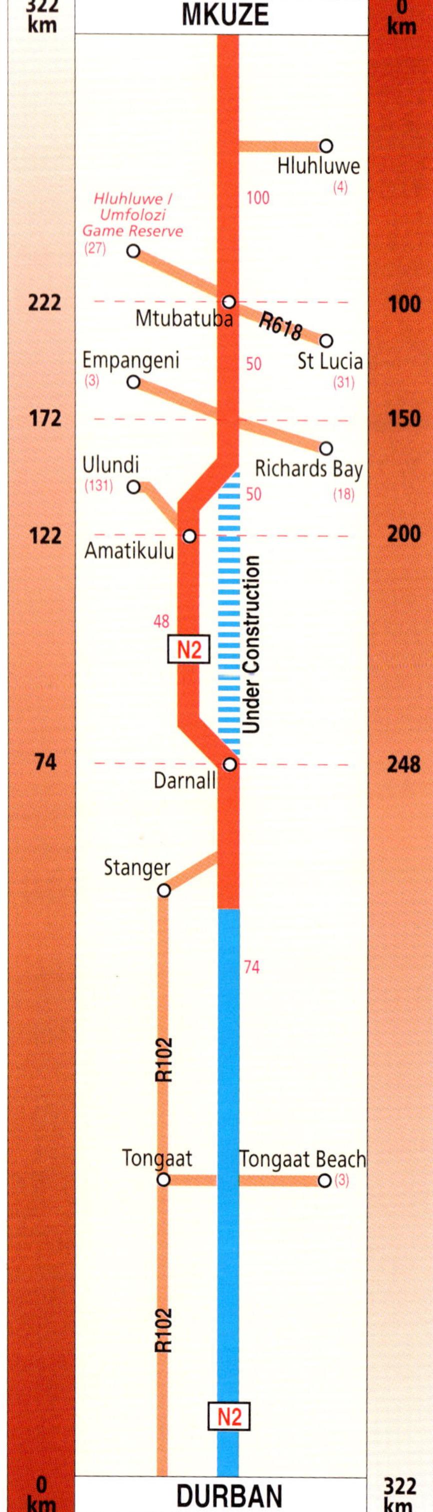

MAIN ATTRACTIONS

Beaches: some of the country's finest beaches are to be found north of Durban. These include Umhlanga Rocks, Tongaat, Ballito, Shaka's Rock, Salt Rock, Shelly Beach, North Beach (Margate) and Uvongo.
Natal Sharks Board: in Umhlanga; maybe witness the dissection of a shark and enjoy an informative audio-visual presentation.
Lake Sibaya: South Africa's largest natural freshwater lake.
The Greater St Lucia Wetland Park: many beautiful lakes, swamps, forests and marshlands surround the fauna-rich, shallow-water estuary of Lake St Lucia.
Maputaland Reserves: host some of the greatest concentrations of wildlife in the entire country.
The **Hluhluwe/Umfolozi Park** is famed for its rhino conservation programme and offers a haven for the Big Five.
Phinda Resource Reserve: luxury lodge, one of the best ecotourism destinations in the country.
Sodwana Bay: pristine marine wonderland, the best diving venue in the country.
Shakaland: model of a traditional Zulu village in the Nkwaleni Valley. Attractions here include culinary specialities, tribal dancing and traditional healers.

DISTANCE IN KM FROM ST LUCIA	
Durban	253
Hluhluwe/Umfolozi Park	58
Johannesburg	633

RICHARDS BAY	J	F	M	A	M	J	J	A	S	O	N	D
AV. TEMP. °C	25	25	25	23	20	18	17	19	20	21	23	25
AV. TEMP. °F	77	77	77	73	68	64	63	66	68	70	73	77
DAILY SUN hrs	7	7	7	8	8	7	8	8	7	6	7	7
RAINFALL mm	144	138	110	111	126	31	47	59	84	97	97	83
RAINFALL in	6	5.5	4.5	4.5	5	1	2	2.5	3.5	4	4	3.5
SEA TEMP. °C	24	24	24	23	22	21	20	20	20	21	21	23
SEA TEMP. °F	75	75	75	73	72	70	68	68	68	70	70	73

TRAVEL TIPS

The N2 runs parallel to, but out of sight of, the coast to the general vicinity of Richards Bay (about 2½ hours' drive north of Durban), and then sweeps inland to the Swaziland border. Major roads in Zululand are tarred; most of the minor ones (including those in the game reserves) are gravel and generally in a satisfactory condition.

USEFUL CONTACTS

Dolphin Coast Publicity Association, tel: (0322) 6-1997.
Isle of Capri, tel: (031) 37-7751, fax: 466-2434; offer educational tours, 1-hour deep-sea cruises, 1½-hour dinner-dance cruises and deep-sea fishing trips.
Natal Parks Board, Pietermaritzburg, tel: (0331) 47-1981.
Tourism KwaZulu-Natal, tel: (031) 304-7144.
Umhlanga Publicity, tel: (031) 561-4257.

Right: *The golden sands of St Lucia, washed by the warm Indian Ocean, make this a popular spot with watersports enthusiasts and sunbathers.*

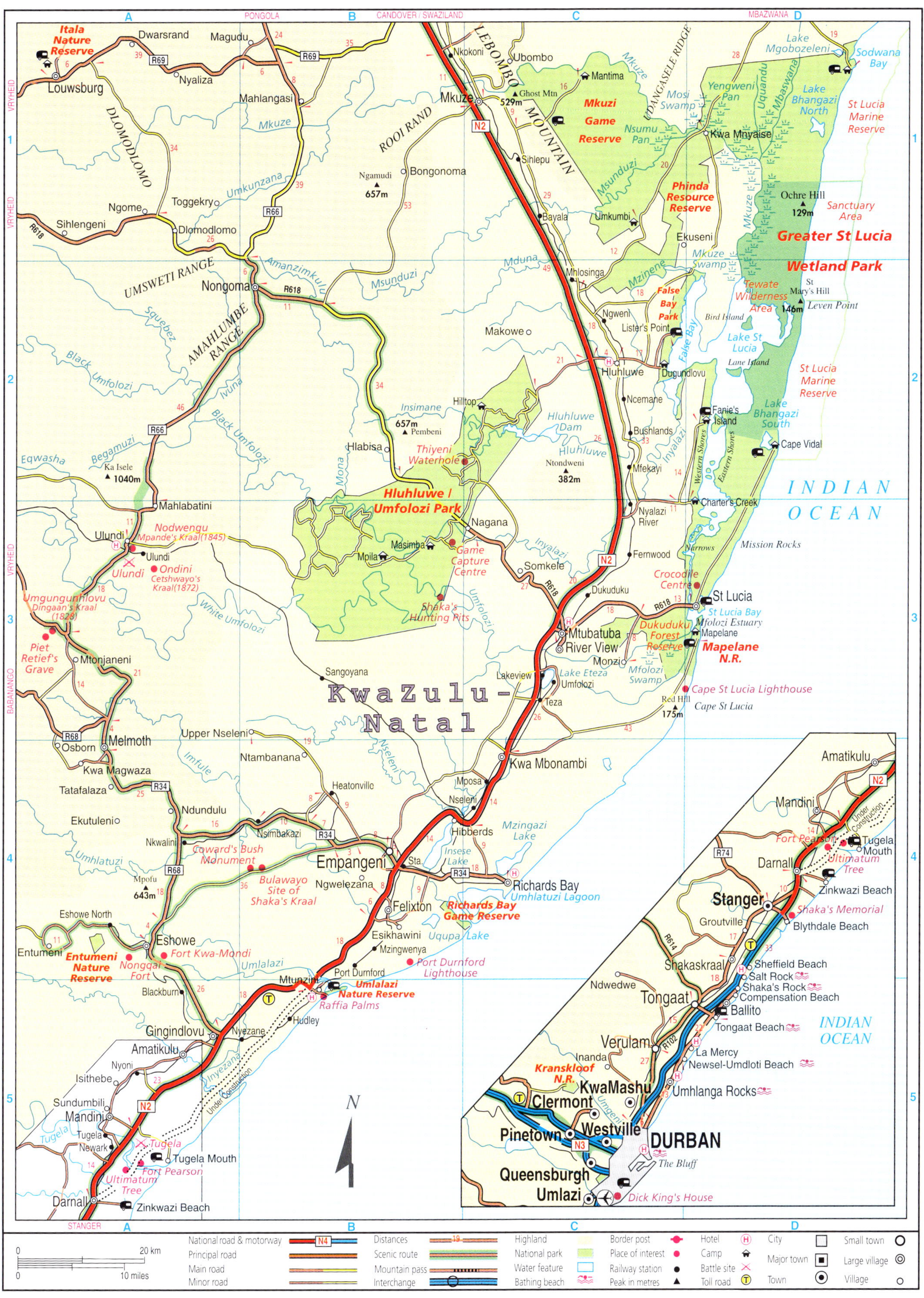

PONGOLA
CANDOVER / SWAZILAND
MBAZWANA
VRYHEID
BABANANGO
STANGER
Itala Nature Reserve
Dwarsrand
Magudu
Louwsburg
Nyaliza
Mahlangasi
DLOMODLOMO
Mkuze
Nkokoni
Ubombo
LEBOMBO MOUNTAIN
Ghost Mtn 529m
Mantima
Mkuzi Game Reserve
UDANGASELE RIDGE
Mosi Swamp
Nsumu Pan
Kwa Mnyaise
Lake Mgobozeleni
Sodwana Bay
Yengweni Pan
Lake Bhangazi North
St Lucia Marine Reserve
ROOI RAND
Ngamudi 657m
Bongonoma
Sihlepu
Umkunzana
Toggekry
Ngome
Sihlengeni
Dlomodlomo
Bayala
Umkumbi
Phinda Resource Reserve
Ochre Hill 129m
Sanctuary Area
Greater St Lucia Wetland Park
Ekuseni
Mkuze Swamp
UMSWETI RANGE
Nongoma
Amanzimkulu
Msunduzi
Mduna
Mhlosinga
Mzinene
False Bay Park
Tewate Wilderness Area
St Mary's Hill 146m
Leven Point
Bird Island
Squebez
AMAHLUMBE RANGE
Makowe
Ngweni
Lister's Point
Lake St Lucia
Lane Island
Black Umfolozi
Hluhluwe
Dugandlovu
Ivuna
Insimane
Hilltop
Hluhluwe Dam
Ncemane
Fanie's Island
Lake Bhangazi South
657m Pembeni
Bushlands
Eqwasha
Begamuzi
Ka Isele 1040m
Hlabisa
Thiyeni Waterhole
Hluhluwe
Ntondweni 382m
Mfekayi
Inyalazi
Western Shores
Eastern Shores
Cape Vidal
INDIAN OCEAN
Mahlabatini
Mona
Hluhluwe / Umfolozi Park
Nagana
Nyalazi River
Charter's Creek
Ulundi
Nodwengu
Mpande's Kraal (1845)
Masimba
Mpila
Game Capture Centre
Somkele
Fernwood
Narrows
Mission Rocks
Ondini
Cetshwayo's Kraal (1872)
Umgungundlovu
Dingaan's Kraal (1828)
White Umfolozi
Shaka's Hunting Pits
Umfolozi
Dukuduku
Crocodile Centre
St Lucia
St Lucia Bay
Mfolozi Estuary
Mapelane
Piet Retief's Grave
Mtonjaneni
Mtubatuba
River View
Dukuduku Forest Reserve
Mapelane N.R.
Monzi
Sangoyana
Lakeview
Lake Eteza
Umfolozi
Mfolozi Swamp
Cape St Lucia Lighthouse
Red Hill 175m
Cape St Lucia
KwaZulu-Natal
Teza
Melmoth
Osborn
Upper Nseleni
Kwa Magwaza
Ntambanana
Nseleni
Imfule
Kwa Mbonambi
Tatafalaza
Heatonville
Mposa
Ndundulu
Ekutuleni
Nkwalini
Ntimbakazi
Hibberds
Mzingazi Lake
Coward's Bush Monument
Umhlatuzi
Empangeni
Insese Lake
Mpofu 643m
Bulawayo Site of Shaka's Kraal
Ngwelezana
Richards Bay
Umhlatuzi Lagoon
Eshowe North
Felixton
Richards Bay Game Reserve
Entumeni
Entumeni Nature Reserve
Eshowe
Fort Kwa-Mondi
Esikhawini
Mzingwenya
Uqupa Lake
Nongqai Fort
Umlalazi
Port Durnford
Port Durnford Lighthouse
Blackburn
Mtunzini
Umlalazi Nature Reserve
Raffia Palms
Hudley
Gingindlovu
Nyezane
Amatikulu
Inyezane
Nyoni
Isithebe
Under Construction
Sundumbili
Mandini
Tugela
Newark
Tugela Mouth
Fort Pearson
Ultimatum Tree
Darnall
Zinkwazi Beach
N
Amatikulu
Mandini
Fort Pearson
Tugela Mouth
Ultimatum Tree
Darnall
Zinkwazi Beach
Stanger
Shaka's Memorial
Groutville
Blythdale Beach
Shakaskraal
Sheffield Beach
Salt Rock
Shaka's Rock
Ndwedwe
Tongaat
Compensation Beach
Ballito
Tongaat Beach
INDIAN OCEAN
Verulam
La Mercy
Inanda
Newsel-Umdloti Beach
Kranskloof N.R.
KwaMashu
Umhlanga Rocks
Clermont
Umgeni
Pinetown
Westville
DURBAN
The Bluff
Queensburgh
Umlazi
Dick King's House
20 km
10 miles
National road & motorway
Principal road
Main road
Minor road
Distances
Scenic route
Mountain pass
Interchange
Highland
National park
Water feature
Bathing beach
Border post
Place of interest
Railway station
Peak in metres
Hotel
Camp
Battle site
Toll road
City
Major town
Town
Small town
Large village
Village

KWAZULU-NATAL SOUTH COAST

The southern coast of KwaZulu-Natal is a lush tropical wonderland of wide, unspoilt beaches lapped by the warm aquamarine waters of the Indian Ocean. A string of friendly little towns and hamlets, each with its own attractions, lines this wonderful coastline, offering accommodation and a selection of restaurants. Although there is no visible distinction, the coast south of Durban is divided into two sections: the area from Amanzimtoti, just south of Durban, to Mtwalume is known as the Sunshine Coast, that from Hibberdene to Port Edward is called the Hibiscus Coast; both offer outstanding holiday venues.

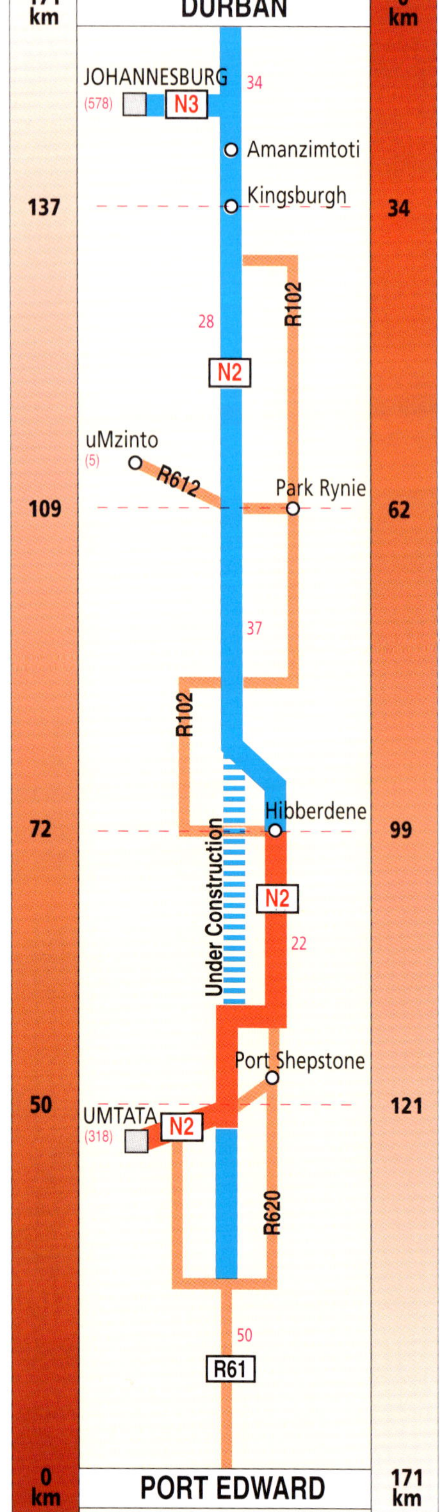

MAIN ATTRACTIONS

Sunshine Coast
Kingsburgh: five seaside resorts popular for their white sands and shark-protected bathing.
Umkomaas: a championship golf course and floodlit tidal pool.
Scottburgh: a charming beach, and fascinating Crocworld nearby.
Vernon Crookes Nature Reserve: lush sanctuary for various antelope.
Hibiscus Coast
Hibberdene: lagoon, woodland-fringed beaches, amusement park.
uMzumbe: excellent family hotel; rock and surf angling.
Banana Beach: safe bathing and very good surfing.
Bendigo: four seaside resorts geared towards holiday-makers.
Umtentweni: for a quiet getaway.
Port Shepstone: at the mouth of the Umzimkulu River; offers excellent bowling greens and one of South Africa's best golf courses.
Oribi Gorge Nature Reserve: some 20km (14 miles) inland from Port Shepstone – a striking canyon carved through layers of sandstone by the Umzimkulwana River.
Uvongo: lively little resort in an idyllic tropical setting.
Margate: very popular seaside town, but it can get crowded.
Ramsgate: magnificent lagoon and a long beach.
Port Edward: charming town in the former Transkei, with a pleasant beach; close to the Wild Coast Sun.

Above: *Scottburgh is a popular holiday resort on the Sunshine Coast. The lovely beach offers safe bathing, as well as some fine angling spots.*

USEFUL CONTACTS

Hospital GJ Crookes, Scottburgh, tel: (0323) 2-1300.
Hibiscus Coast Publicity Association, Margate, tel: (03931) 2-2322.
Sunshine Coast Publicity Association, Scottburgh, tel: (0323) 2-1364.

TRAVEL TIPS

Towns and resorts are linked to Durban by the N2 as far as Port Shepstone, while the R61 leads to Port Edward. Both roads are in good condition, though inland roads can be a little rough and caution is advised.

DISTANCE IN KM FROM PORT SHEPSTONE	
Durban	121
Richards Bay	311
Umtata	312

KEY TOURIST AREAS

DURBAN AND PIETERMARITZBURG

The city of Durban is the country's third-largest metropolis, and its foremost seaport (in fact, it has the biggest and busiest harbour in Africa). With its fine beaches and tourist amenities, Durban is a popular holiday destination in South Africa, especially due to its excellent watersports facilities: its beaches offer some of the best surfing venues in the country, and deep-sea game-fishing trips, scuba diving and sailing trips are all readily available to the tourist.

Accommodation

Royal Hotel *****, 267 Smith Street, tel: (031) 304-0331, fax: 307-6884; one of the best, offering luxury and excellent service.
Holiday Inn Crowne Plaza Durban ****, 63 Snell Parade, tel: (031) 37-1321, fax: 332-5527; large resort hotel with an international business centre; three restaurants and two bars.
Beach Hotel ***, Marine Parade, tel: (031) 37-5511, fax: 37-5409; conveniently situated on the Golden Mile beachfront.
Holiday Inn Garden Court (Marine Parade) ***, next to the Edward Hotel, tel: (031) 37-3341, fax: 37-5929; stylish and comfortable, with reliable service.
Balmoral Hotel, 125 Marine Parade, tel: (031) 368-5940, fax: 368-5955; situated right across the road from the beach.
Sandhurst Hotel, 202 Currie Road, tel: (031) 21-4241, fax: 21-4243; a 78-room hotel, located 5km (3 miles) from the beach on the bus route.

Travel Tips

Durban is linked to all other major South African centres by a network of national roads. The N2 leads south and then east along the coast, through Port Elizabeth to Cape Town. The N3 takes the traveller northwest through Pietermaritzburg and Harrismith to Johannesburg.

Events and Festivals

Durban International Film Festival: held in **January**.
Comrades Marathon: famous marathon in **June** (Durban to Pietermaritzburg the one year, vice versa the following one).
Rothman's July Handicap: prestigious horseracing event in **July**.
Gunston 500: world-renowned annual surfing contest held in the Bay of Plenty in **July**.

Useful Contacts

Addington Hospital, tel: (031) 332-2111.
Sea Rescue Services, tel: (031) 37-2200.
Durban Tourism, Tourist Junction Building, tel: (031) 304-4934.
SATOUR, tel: (031) 305-2091.
Timeless Afrika (run by the Zululand–Thukela Marketing Authority), tel: (031) 307-3800, fax: 307-3822.
Sea World and the Oceanographic Research Centre, tel: (031) 37-3536; for information about show times.
***Sarie Marais* Cruises**, tel: (031) 305-4022, fax: 25-8788; offer interesting harbour and dinner-dance cruises.

DURBAN	J	F	M	A	M	J	J	A	S	O	N	D
AV. TEMP. °C	24	25	24	22	19	17	16	17	19	20	22	23
AV. TEMP. °F	75	77	75	72	66	63	61	63	66	68	72	73
DAILY SUN hrs	6	7	7	7	7	7	7	7	6	5	5	6
RAINFALL mm	135	114	124	87	64	26	44	58	65	89	104	108
RAINFALL in	5.5	4.5	5	3.5	3	1	2	2.5	3	4	4.5	4.5
SEA TEMP. °C	24	25	24	23	21	20	19	19	20	21	22	23
SEA TEMP. °F	75	77	75	73	70	68	66	66	68	70	72	73

Below: *The Paddling Pools form part of Durban's sparkling Golden Mile which is lined with colourful markets, many restaurants, walkways and fountains.*

Main Attractions

Golden Mile: fabulous holiday playground stretching for 6km (4 miles) along the sandy Indian Ocean shoreline, with everything the entertainment-seeking tourist could desire.
Pietermaritzburg: quaint colonial-style town with fine architecture and very interesting museums.
Sea World: on the Golden Mile, popular aquarium–dolphinarium.
Fitzsimon's Snake Park: home to many indigenous and exotic species, as well as crocodiles.
Victoria Street Indian Market: colourful and exotic place of bargain and barter, housed in a huge domed building.
Umgeni River Bird Park: rated third best of the world's bird parks; has approximately 300 local and exotic species.
Mahatma Gandhi Museum: dedicated to the memory of this great leader.
The Wheel: very lively and glitzy modern shopping complex, with many tempting restaurants and live entertainment.
Port Natal Maritime Museum: on the Victoria Embankment; interesting exhibits for young and old.

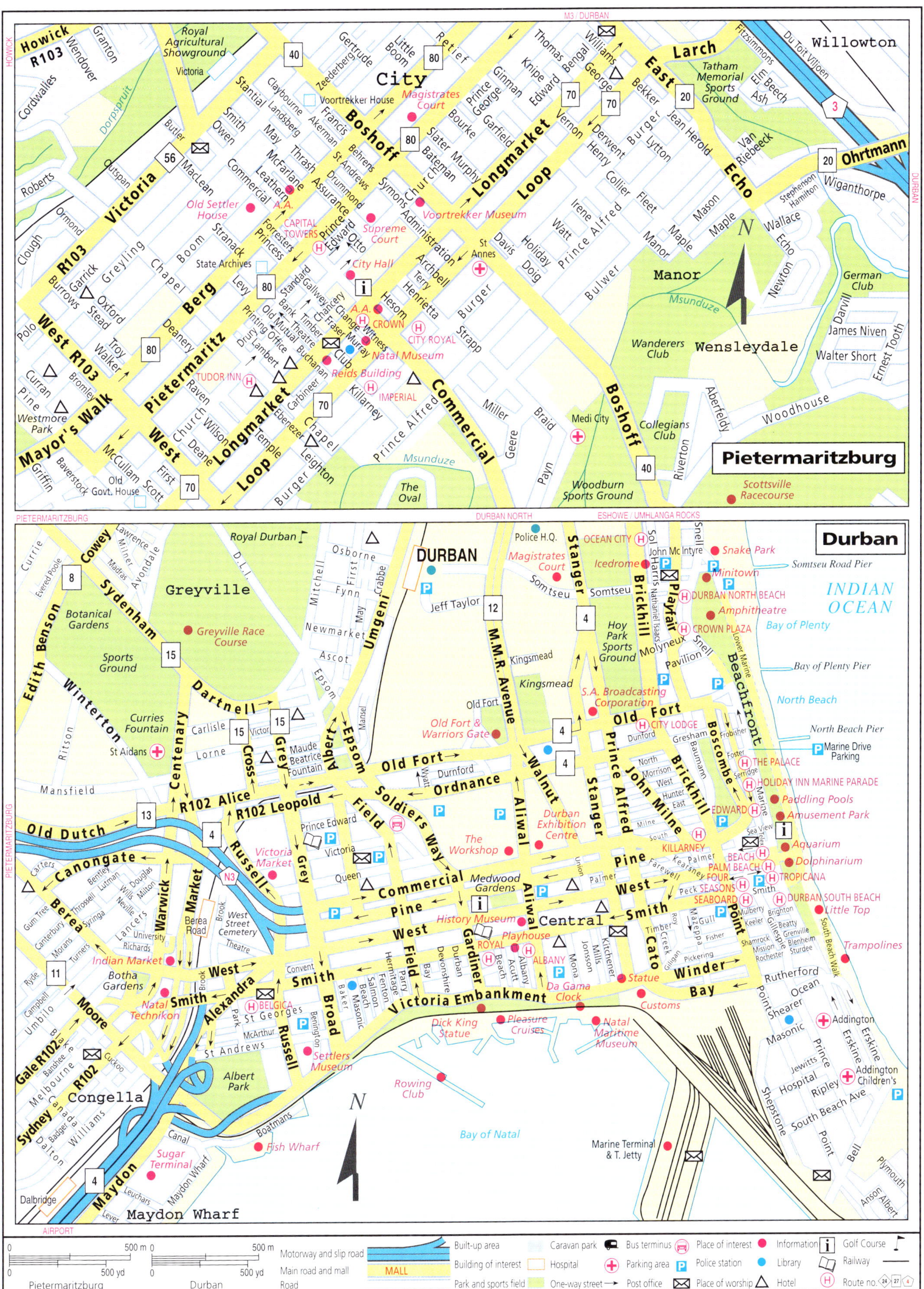
Pietermaritzburg
Royal Agricultural Showground
City
Magistrates Court
Voortrekker House
Old Settler House
Voortrekker Museum
Supreme Court
City Hall
State Archives
A.A.
CAPITAL TOWERS
CROWN
CITY ROYAL
Natal Museum
Reids Building
IMPERIAL
TUDOR INN
Westmore Park
Old Govt. House
The Oval
Medi City
Woodburn Sports Ground
Collegians Club
Wanderers Club
Wensleydale
Manor
Msunduze
Tatham Memorial Sports Ground
German Club
Scottsville Racecourse
Willowton
Howick
R103
Victoria
Boshoff
Longmarket
Loop
Church
Commercial
Berg
Pietermaritz
West
Mayor's Walk
Prince Alfred
Larch
East
Echo
Ohrtmann
Durban
DURBAN
Royal Durban
Greyville
Greyville Race Course
Botanical Gardens
Sports Ground
Curries Fountain
St Aidans
Maude Beatrice Fountain
Police H.Q.
Magistrates Court
OCEAN CITY
Snake Park
Icedrome
Minitown
DURBAN NORTH BEACH
Amphitheatre
CROWN PLAZA
Hoy Park Sports Ground
Kingsmead
S.A. Broadcasting Corporation
Old Fort & Warriors Gate
CITY LODGE
THE PALACE
HOLIDAY INN MARINE PARADE
Paddling Pools
Amusement Park
EDWARD
Aquarium
Dolphinarium
KILLARNEY
BEACH
PALM BEACH
TROPICANA
FOUR SEASONS
SEABOARD
DURBAN SOUTH BEACH
Little Top
Trampolines
Durban Exhibition Centre
The Workshop
Victoria Market
Medwood Gardens
History Museum
Playhouse
ROYAL
ALBANY
Central
Statue
Customs
Da Gama Clock
Indian Market
Botha Gardens
Natal Technikon
BELGICA
West Street Cemetery
Berea Road
Settlers Museum
Albert Park
Congella
Dick King Statue
Pleasure Cruises
Natal Maritime Museum
Rowing Club
Bay of Natal
Fish Wharf
Sugar Terminal
Marine Terminal & T. Jetty
Maydon Wharf
Addington
Addington Children's
INDIAN OCEAN
Bay of Plenty
Somtseu Road Pier
Bay of Plenty Pier
North Beach
North Beach Pier
Marine Drive Parking
Victoria Embankment
Old Dutch
Canongate
R102 Alice
R102 Leopold
Old Fort
Ordnance
Soldiers Way
Pine
Smith
West
Winder
Bay
Point
M.M.R. Avenue
Umgeni
Snell
Beachfront
0 500 m 0 500 yd Pietermaritzburg
0 500 m 0 500 yd Durban
Motorway and slip road
Main road and mall
Road
MALL
Built-up area
Building of interest
Park and sports field
Caravan park
Hospital
One-way street
Bus terminus
Parking area
Post office
Place of interest
Police station
Place of worship
Information
Library
Hotel
Golf Course
Railway
Route no.

DRAKENSBERG MOUNTAIN RESORTS

South Africa's highest mountain range, the Drakensberg is a massive and strikingly beautiful rampart of deep gorges, pinnacles and saw-edged ridges, caves, overhangs and balancing rocks. In the winter months its upper levels lie deep in snow, but clustered among the foothills far below, in undulating grassland, is a score of resort hotels created and maintained for family holiday-makers. People come for the fresh, clean mountain air; for the walks, climbs and drives; for the gentler sports (trout fishing, golf, bowls and horseback riding); and for casual relaxation in the most exquisite surrounds. Particularly recommended are the northern (Mont-Aux-Sources) and central Drakensberg areas (Giant's Castle to Cathedral Peak).

578 km | JOHANNESBURG | 0 km

(2) Heidelberg — Nigel (12)

121

457 | Villiers | 121

153

304 | Harrismith | 274

N5 Bethlehem

35

269 | Van Reenen | 309

Ladysmith N11 (20)

R616

Bergville

The Natal Drakensberg Park

104

R74

165 | Estcourt | 413

The Natal Drakensberg Park

86

Mooi River

Howick

79 | PIETERMARITZBURG | 499

The Natal Drakensberg Park

N3

79

0 km | DURBAN | 578 km

Accommodation

Cathedral Peak Hotel ***, Winterton, tel/ fax: (036) 488-1888; set amid some spectacular peaks.
Drakensberg Sun Hotel ***, in the central Drakensberg region, tel: (036) 468-1000, fax: 468-1224; wonderful views.
Little Switzerland Hotel ***, between Bergville and Harrismith, tel: (036) 438-6220, fax: 438-6222; view of the spectacular Amphitheatre.
Sani Pass Hotel ***, Himeville, tel: (033) 702-1320, fax: 702-0220; 800ha (1977 acres) at the foot of Sani Pass.
Champagne Castle, tel: (036) 468-1063, fax: 468-1306; guided walks; golf course.
Royal Natal National Park Hotel, Mont-Aux-Sources, tel: (036) 438-6200, fax: 438-6101; beautiful hiking resort in a lovely setting.

MAIN ATTRACTIONS

Royal Natal National Park: an extensive and beautiful floral and wildlife sanctuary. Excursions are offered to the imposing Mont-Aux-Sources plateau and its giant, natural Amphitheatre, as well as to the spectacular Tugela Falls, the country's highest waterfall.
Giant's Castle Game Reserve: in the central Drakensberg, dominated by the Giant's Castle and Injesuthi buttresses, a scenic wonderland famous for its Bushman rock art and raptor conservation programmes.
Ndedema Gorge: 'place of rolling thunder'; a magnificent gorge renowned for its rock art.
Himeville Nature Reserve: in the southern Drakensberg; a paradise for trout fishermen.
Drakensberg Boys Choir School: in the foothills of beautiful Champagne Castle; the world-famous choir performs for the public on Wednesday afternoons.

ESTCOURT	J	F	M	A	M	J	J	A	S	O	N	D
AV. TEMP. °C	21	21	20	17	13	10	11	13	16	18	19	21
AV. TEMP. °F	70	70	68	63	55	50	52	55	61	64	66	70
DAILY SUN hrs	7	7	7	7	8	8	9	9	8	7	7	7
RAINFALL mm	147	87	74	47	10	6	6	26	37	66	94	129
RAINFALL in	6	3.5	3	2	0.4	0.2	0.2	1	1.5	3	4	5.5

USEFUL CONTACTS

Mountain Rescue Club (via the Natal Parks Board – stationed at Monk's Cowl), tel: (036) 468-1103.
Basotho Cultural Village, Witsieshoek, tel: (05861) 31794.
Drakensberg Tourism, tel: (036) 448-1557.
Drakensberg Boys Choir School, tel: (036) 468-1012, except during school holidays.
Wildways Mountaineering & Guiding Services, Mooiriver, tel: (0333) 3-7496.

Below: *Impressive Giant's Castle, just one of the spectacular formations to be found in the beautiful Drakensberg Mountain range.*

Free State
KwaZulu-Natal
LESOTHO
DRAKENSBERG
Harrismith
Walton
Swinburne
Van Reenen
Oban
Guest Farm
De Beers Pass
Van Reenen's Pass
1944m Lions Rump
Brakwal
Colworth
Kerkenberg
Sterkfontein Dam
Sterkfontein Dam N.R.
Phuthaditjhaba
Rock Paintings
Babangiboni 2329m
Hlolela 2188m
Northern Berg Resorts
Little Switzerland
The Cavern Berg Resort
Oliviershoek Pass
Kilburn Dam
Rugged Glen N.R.
Hlalanathi Berg Resort
Mont-Aux Sources Hotel
Hotel
Witsieshoek Mountain Resort
Tendele
Royal Natal National Park
3282m
Mont-Aux-Sources
Woodstock Dam
M'Weni
Geluksburg
Sand River Valley
Vente rspruit
Besters
Smith's Crossing
Pepworth
Matiwane
Craigsforth
Biggarsberg
Karel Pieter Landman's House
Wasbank
Wesselsnek
Elandslaagte
Lombardskop
Ladysmith
Rensburg
Wagon Hill
Umbulwana
Pieters
Spioenkop Dam N.R.
Spioenkop Dam
Bergville
Eversholt
Roosboom
Little Tugela
Tugela
Toll House and Bridge
Colenso
Winterton
Mlamboni
Cathedral Peak 3004m
Cathedral Peak Hotel
Zunckels
3280m Cleft Peak
Khubedu
Tlangaku
Sengu
Cathkin Park Hotel
The Nest
Drakensberg Sun
Ndedema Gorge
Voortrekker Memorial
Sports Club
Dragon Peaks
Champagne Castle Hotel
3181m Cathkin Peak
Monk's Cowl
Champagne Castle 3377m
Central Berg Resorts
Loskop
Draycott
Frere
Chieveley
Bloukrans Monument
Winston Churchill
Bloukrans
Old Mill & Voortrekker House
Weenen
Weenen G.R.
Ennersdale
Estcourt
Saailaer
Little Bushmans
Wagendrift N.R.
Moremohol
Motsitseng
Injasuti
Ntabamhlope
White Mountain Resort
3450m Mafadi
New Beacon Hill
Willow Grange
Griffins Hill
Lowlands
Middelrus
A1
Mokhotlong
3330m Popple Peak
Bushmans
Rockmount
Giant's Castle
Sangebethu
Hidcote
South Downs
The Grove
Mooi
Mnuamvubu
The Natal Drakensberg Park
Ncibidwane
Hlatikul
Mt Lebanon 2126m
Mooi River
Craigieburn Dam
Craigieburn N.R.
Giant's Castle 3314m
Little Mooi
Rietvlei
Mount Alida
A14
Masenkeng
Mokhotlong
Redcliffe
Rosetta
Umvoti
Thabana Ntlenyana 3482m
Redi 3298m
Kamberg
Nottingham Road
Karkloof
Sehonghong
Loteni
Curry's Post
Sani
Vergelegen
Nottingham
Umgeni Vlei N.R.
Balgowan
Lions
Pitsang
Umkomaas
Lower Loteni
Mkhomazi
Karkloof Falls
Mashai
Sani Pass
Lidgetton
Lions River
Karkloof N.R.
Dargle
3257m Hodgson's Peak
Umkomanazana
Umgeni
Howick
Howick Falls
Merrivale
Everglades Hotel
Midmar Public Resort N.R.
Midmar Dam
Albert Falls Public Resort N.R.
The Natal Drakensberg Park
Phoiela
Sani Pass Hotel
1967m Mpendle
Mpendle
Otto's Bluff
Thamatuwe 3431m
Cobham
Queen Elizabeth N.P.
Drakensberg Garden Hotel
Old Prison Building
Himeville N.R.
Himeville
Hilton
PIETERMARITZBURG
Raisethorpe
Sweet Waters
Henley Dam
Msunduzi
Taylors
Underberg
Pevensey
Deepdale
Elandskop
Edendale
Natal Lion Park
Bushman's Nek Hotel
2495m Watershed
Ngwangwane
Umzimkulu
Bulwer
Lurane
Ashburton
Umlazi
Thornville
Sehlabathebe National Park
Enda...ana
Coleford N.R.
Sizanenjana
Ncwadi
Illovo
Umlaas Road
Nelsrus
KESTELL
BETHLEHEM / KESTELL
WARDEN
NEWCASTLE
GREYTOWN
NEW HANOVER
DURBAN
RICHMOND
DONNYBROOK
KINGSCOTE
N5
N3
N11
N4
R57
R712
R74
R616
R600
R103
R602
R614
R33
R617
R622
R626
R612
N
0 20 km
0 10 miles
National road & motorway
Principal road
Main road
Minor road
Distances
Scenic route
Mountain pass
Interchange
Highland
National park
Water feature
Lodge / resort
Nest
Border post
Place of interest
Railway station
Peak in metres
Hotel
Camp
Battle site
Toll road
City
Major town
Town
Small town
Large village
Village

HISTORIC BATTLEFIELDS

For most of the 19th century, the KwaZulu-Natal midlands region was a bloody battlefield, as Zulu, Boer and Briton fought for territorial supremacy. Military enthusiasts – indeed anyone interested in the region's turbulent past – will find the Battlefields Route (which includes the sites of Blood River, Isandhlwana, Rorke's Drift, Ulundi, Majuba Hill, Talana, Elandslaagte, Tugela Heights, Colenso, Ladysmith and Spioenkop) fascinating. Some of the most dramatic confrontations occurred in the triangular area bounded by Estcourt in the south, Volksrust in the north, and Vryheid to the east.

TRAVEL TIPS

Tour by Greyhound coach or embark on self-guided drives (Walk 'n Talk audio cassettes available). Call the local publicity association or the curator of the **Talana Museum**, tel: (0341) 2-2654, for information.

THE BATTLE ROUTE

Blood River (1838): the final and decisive clash between the Zulus and the Voortrekker pioneers during the Boer migration into Natal. Raw courage proved no match for superior firepower – more than 3000 Zulus perished on the field; the Boer losses amounted to three wounded.
Isandhlwana (1879): part of a British invading force, under Lord Chelmsford's overall command, was annihilated by 24,000 Zulu *impi* (warriors); only a handful of the 1000-plus redcoats survived.
Rorke's Drift (1879): a bitterly fought skirmish in which a small British garrison held out against wave after wave of Zulu *impi*. This dramatic battle was much publicized by the British press; between them, the defenders earned 11 Victoria Crosses.
Majuba Hill (1881): final battle of the brief Anglo-Transvaal war, in which a Boer force of part-time soldiers drove the British regulars from the slopes of the high hill, inflicting severe casualties. The British commander, Sir George Colley, is thought to have committed suicide during the retreat.
Spioenkop (1891): the Anglo-Boer War's bloodiest battle, savagely fought between Boer and Briton for control of the strategic hill on the route leading to the besieged Ladysmith. Casualties were high on both sides; the Boers eventually prevailed.

WILD COAST

Just South of Port Edward, between the Umtamvuna River and the Great Kei further south, stretches the Wild Coast. This beautiful region was formerly part of the independent homeland of Transkei, but has now been incorporated into the Eastern Cape province. The sandy bays and rocky coves along this spectacular coast, although often difficult to access from the main road, are becoming increasingly popular. The scenery is breathtaking and the fishing along this coast is reputed to be excellent, from flimsy mackerel to shark weighing 450kg (990lb).

Accommodation

Wild Coast Sun and Casino *****, Mzamba, tel: (039) 305-9111, fax: 305-2778; glitz and glamour.
Trennery's Hotel, tel: (0471) 2-5344; beautifully situated on the Great Kei River, in Kentani district.

Travel Tips

The N2 bisects this region, passing north to south from Port Shepstone through Kokstad, Mount Frere, Umtata and Butterworth, where grocery supplies and petrol can be obtained. The gravel roads leading down to the coast can be rather taxing on both vehicle and driver. Beware of straying animals.

Above: *The strange detached cliff known as the Hole-in-the-Wall, is a well-known spot not far from Coffee Bay, on the beautiful Wild Coast.*

Main Attractions

Wild Coast Sun: an extravagant, luxury hotel-casino complex situated right on the beachfront.
Hole-in-the-Wall: 1½ hours' walk south of Coffee Bay stands a massive, detached cliff with a small arched opening through which the surf thunders.
Mazeppa Bay: palm trees line three wide beaches; the scuba diving and snorkelling are good and the fishing is excellent.
Qora Mouth: a good beach with interesting rock pools, close to the hotel. The Dwesa and Cwebe nature reserves offer a combination of forest, grassland and rocky coastline that is populated by many birds and small mammals. Shell collecting is reputed to be very good here.
Fishing: fish caught along this coast range from kob, blacktail bronze bream and shad to barracuda and trophy-sized sharks.

Eastern Cape
Port Edward
DURBAN
UMTATA
Queenstown
EAST LONDON

INDIAN OCEAN

0 25 km
0 10 miles

National road & motorway N4
Principal road
Main road
Minor road
Distances
Scenic route
Mountain pass
Interchange
Highland
National park
Water feature
Bathing beach
Border post
Place of interest
Railway station
Peak in metres
Hotel
Camp
Battle site
Toll road
City
Major town
Town
Small town
Large village
Village

EASTERN CAPE

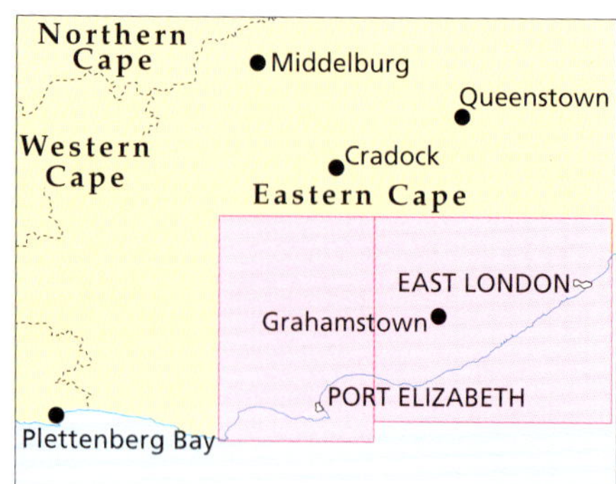

The Eastern Cape's shoreline extends from the KwaZulu-Natal border southwards to the Storms River mouth, incorporating the previously independent 'homelands' of Transkei and Ciskei. This beautiful region has an extremely turbulent history. It was here that 19th-century white settlers and black tribesmen fought bitterly for territorial possession, a confrontation that began in 1820 with the arrival in Algoa Bay of some 4000 British immigrants.

USEFUL CONTACTS

Eastern Cape Tourism Board, Port Elizabeth, tel: (041) 55-7761. Wild Coast region, tel: (0471) 31-2885.
Grahamstown Tourism, tel: (0461) 2-3241, fax: 2-3266.
NSRI (Sea Rescue), tel: (041) 55-6011.
Computicket, tel: (041) 34-4550.
Accommodation Bureau, tel: (041) 35-3248.

ACCOMMODATION

Fish River
Tsolwana Game Park and **Great Fish River Reserve**; for bookings at either reserve , tel: (0401) 95-2115, fax: 9-2756.
Hogsback
Hogsback Inn ★★, tel: (045) 962-1006, fax: 962-1015; surrounded by forest; beautiful nature walks and prolific birdlife.

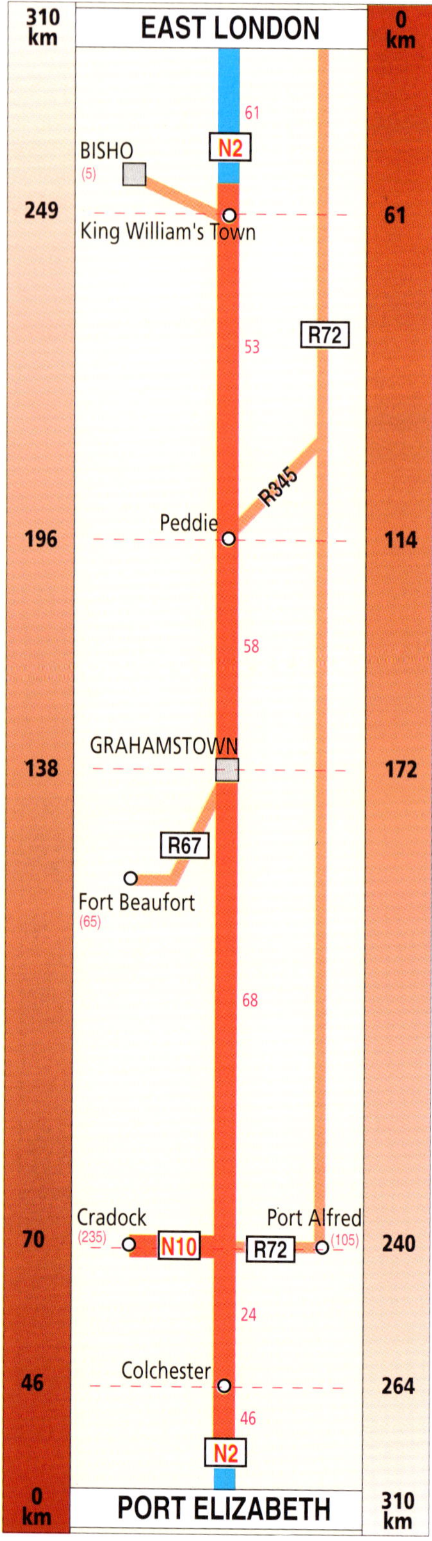

TRAVEL TIPS

The N2 leads west to Cape Town and northeast to Durban. The R32 links Port Elizabeth with Cradock. Wild Coast resorts are accessible via subsidiary (often gravel) roads leading off the N2. Beware of potholes, hairpin bends and straying animals.

P.E.	J	F	M	A	M	J	J	A	S	O	N	D
AV. TEMP. °C	21	21	20	18	16	14	14	14	15	17	18	20
AV. TEMP. °F	70	70	68	64	61	57	57	57	59	63	64	68
DAILY SUN hrs	9	8	7	7	7	7	7	8	7	8	9	7
RAINFALL mm	41	39	55	57	68	61	54	75	70	59	49	34
RAINFALL in	2	2	2.5	2.5	3	2.5	2.5	3	3	2.5	2	1.5
SEA TEMP. °C	21	21	20	19	17	16	16	16	17	18	19	21
SEA TEMP. °F	70	70	68	66	63	61	61	61	63	64	66	70

Right: *Every July Grahamstown swarms with visitors during the colourful National Arts Festival.*

MAIN ATTRACTIONS

Jeffreys Bay: a surfer's paradise.
Grahamstown: academic and cultural centre; hosts acclaimed National Arts Festival each July.
Great Fish River Reserve: home to hippo, buffalo and black rhino.
Tsolwana Game Reserve: truly magnificent mountain reserve.
Hogsback: northwest of King William's Town, set among the exquisite forests which provided the inspiration for JRR Tolkien's novel, *The Hobbit*.
Port Alfred: pretty resort town at the mouth of the Kei River.

Bedford
Adelaide
Liddleton
Amherst
Hogsback
Upper Tyume
St Matthew's
Gaika's Grave
Gladstone
Bethel
Komga
Tanga
Keiskammahoek
Fort Beaufort
Alice
Fort Hare
King William's Town
BISHO
Zwelitsha
Mdantsane
Beacon Bay
EAST LONDON
Peddie
GRAHAMSTOWN
Port Alfred
Settler's Church
Kenton on Sea
Bushmans River Mouth
Alexandria
Bathurst
Great Fish Point
Keiskamma Point
Cape Padrone
INDIAN OCEAN

Scale: 0 – 20km; 0 – 10 miles

National road & motorway; Principal road; Main road; Minor road; Distances; Scenic route; Mountain pass; Interchange; Highland; National park; Water feature; Bathing beach; Border post; Place of interest; Railway station; Peak in metres; Hotel; Camp; Battle site; Toll road; City; Major town; Town; Small town; Large village; Village

PORT ELIZABETH

Known as the 'friendly city' and also as the 'windy city', Port Elizabeth is the economic hub of the Eastern Cape, much of its industrial activity revolving around the vehicle assembly sector and related concerns. P.E., as it is most often called, is also a major tourist centre. Set on the shores of Algoa Bay, the country's fifth-largest city has some excellent beaches, many historic buildings, sophisticated shopping centres, good hotels and restaurants. Port Elizabeth owes its origins to the 4000 British settlers who landed here in 1820.

MAIN ATTRACTIONS

Beaches: Port Elizabeth has four major beaches: King's, Humewood, Hobie and Pollok, each with its own special attractions.
Oceanarium and Museum Complex: at Humewood; see the performing dolphins and seals and visit the Aquarium and Snake Park.
Nature rambles: in and around P.E. lie **St George's Park** and the **Pearson Conservatory, Settler's Park**, the **Island Conservation Area** and the beautifully tended **Van Staden's Wildflower Reserve.**
Addo Elephant National Park: this park, located about 72km (45 miles) northeast of the city, was created in 1931 to protect the few remaining survivors of the once-prolific herds of Cape elephant. The sanctuary offers good game-viewing and comfortable accommodation.
Donkin Heritage Trail: a steeply winding historical walking tour.
Fort Frederick: building of historical significance built in 1799; located on Belmont Terrace, overlooking the Baakens River estuary.

Accommodation

Marine Protea Hotel ★★★★, tel: (041) 53-2101, fax: 53-2076; on the Summerstrand beachfront.
City Lodge ★★★, tel: (041) 56-3322, fax: 56-3374; on Humewood beach.
Holiday Inn Garden Court King's Beach ★★★, tel: (041) 52-3720, fax: 55-5754; overlooks King's Beach.
Beach Hotel ★★★, tel/fax: (041) 53-2161; close to the Oceanarium and Hobie Beach.
Edward Hotel ★★, tel/fax: (041) 56-2056, fax: 56-4925; Edwardian-style; overlooks Donkin Memorial.

USEFUL CONTACTS

St George's Hospital, tel: (041) 33-7921.
Automobile Association, tel: (041) 34-1313.
Computicket, tel: (041) 34-4550.
Port Elizabeth Museum, tel: (041) 56-1051.
Port Elizabeth Tourism, tel: (041) 56-0773.

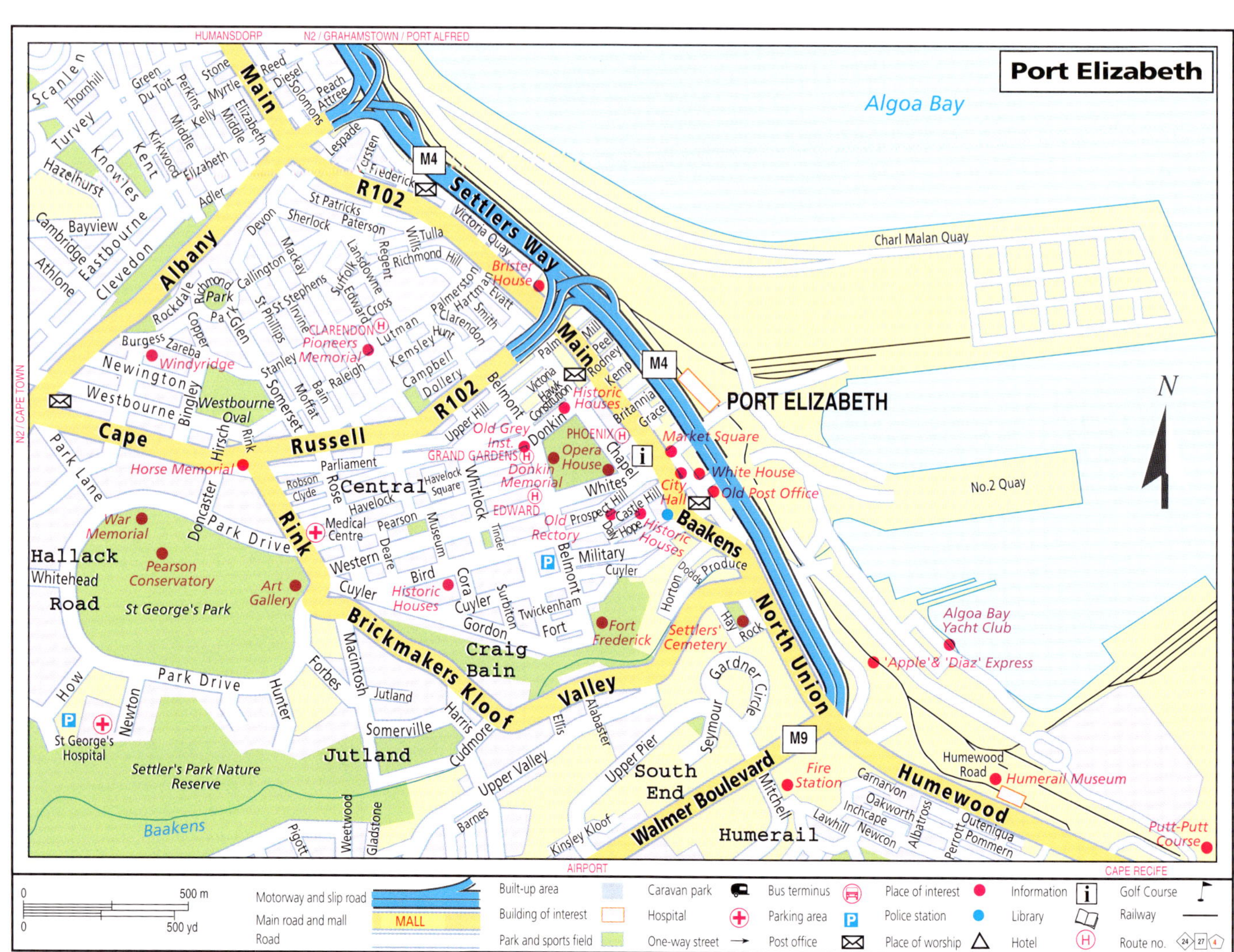

EAST LONDON

Situated at the mouth of the Buffalo River, the river port of East London combines the charm of a relatively small community with all the essential amenities of a large city. Its attractions are of the quiet, undemanding, family-orientated kind: it has fine beaches, pleasant parks and gardens, good hotels and restaurants, and some entertaining nightlife in the summer months, especially in the seafront area. The principal thoroughfare, Oxford Street, is lined with a variety of modern shops, many of which cater to the tourist trade. The port serves the industries of the Eastern Cape and the Free State.

MAIN ATTRACTIONS

Superb beaches: most popular and accessible is Orient Beach.
East London Museum: Oxford Street; exhibits include the first coelacanth (a species of fish hitherto considered extinct) and the world's only dodo egg.
Aquarium: over 400 species.
Queen's Park Botanical Gardens: splendour of indigenous flora.
Ann Bryant Gallery: fine local paintings and sculptures.
Hiking trails: a choice of walks from the 4-day Shipwreck Trail to the 2-hour Umtiza Trail lead nature lovers along unspoilt beaches, through nature reserves, or into the Amatola mountains to the northwest of East London.

ACCOMMODATION

Holiday Inn Garden Court East London ***, cnr. John Bailey and Moore Streets, tel: (0431) 2-7260, fax: 43-7360; on beachfront.
Kennaway Hotel ***, tel: (0431) 2-5531, fax: 2-5531; close to the city centre and the beaches.
Esplanade Hotel **, tel: (0431) 2-2518, fax: 2-3679; conveniently situated on the main beachfront.
Kidds Beach Hotel, Main Road, Kidds Beach, tel: (0432) 81-1715, fax: 81-1852; country hotel five minutes from the beachfront.
Blue Lagoon Hotel, Blue Bend Place, Beacon Bay, tel: (0431) 47-4821, fax: 47-2037; very close to the beach.
The Hornbills, 28 Lotus Avenue, Bonza Bay, tel/fax: (0431) 47-1789; bed and breakfast establishment.

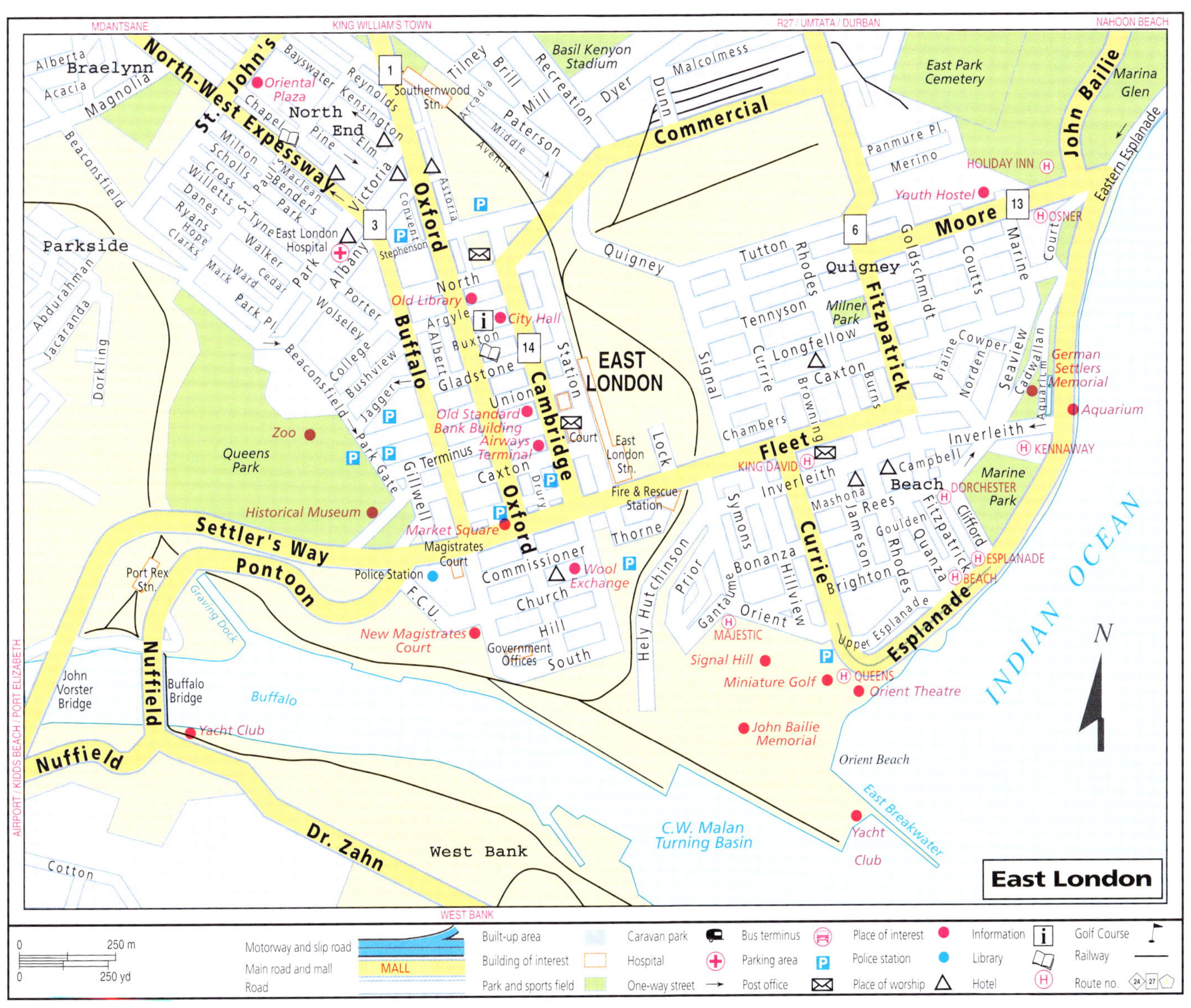

Beaufort West
Cradock
Western Cape
Eastern Cape
Oudtshoorn
George
Plettenberg Bay
PORT ELIZABETH
Mossel Bay
Knysna

GARDEN ROUTE

The Western Cape coastal terrace, extending from the Storms River and the Tsitsikamma area in the east to Mossel Bay in the west, is known as the Garden Route. This is an enchanting shoreline of lovely bays and coves, high cliffs and wide estuaries, with a hinterland of mountains, spectacular passes, rivers, waterfalls and wooded ravines. The lagoons and lakes around Knysna and Wilderness are magical stretches of water. The attractions are many: good hotels and eating places, pleasant villages and resorts, and a warm ocean that beckons bather, yachtsman and angler alike. Further inland are the town of Oudtshoorn and its surrounding ostrich farms, as well as the magnificent Cango Caves.

378 km | PORT ELIZABETH | 0 km
R368
32
N2
Uitenhage (24)
R334
346 | 32
Jeffreys Bay (9)
46
Cape St Francis (22)
R330
300 | Humansdorp | 78
Oudtshoorn (254) R62
143
Nature's Valley
157 | R102 | 221
14
143 | Plettenberg Bay | 235
37
106 | Knysna | 272
61
Oudtshoorn (59)
N12
George
45 | 333
Oudtshoorn (83) R328
45
N2
0 km | MOSSEL BAY | 378 km

ACCOMMODATION

Wilderness
Karos Wilderness Hotel ★★★★, tel: (044) 877-1110, fax: 887-1910; surrounded by unspoilt nature; heated pools.
Fairy Knowe Hotel ★★, tel: (044) 877-1100, fax: 877-0364; on the banks of the Touw River.
Baywater Village, tel: (04455) 3-2008, fax: 3-2688; serviced chalets.

Knysna
Brenton-on-Sea Hotel ★★★, tel: (0445) 81-0081, fax: 81-0026; 15km (9 miles) from Knysna.

Plettenberg Bay
Beacon Island Hotel ★★★, tel: (04457) 3-1120, fax: 3-3880; smart hotel in a unique setting.
Formosa Bay Hotel, tel: (04457) 3-2060, fax: 3-3343; estate on N2.
Stromboli's Inn ★★★, tel: (04457) 7710, fax: 7823; between Wilderness and Tsitsikamma.

Sedgefield
Lake Pleasant Hotel ★★★, tel: (04455) 3-1313, fax: 3-2040; bass lake.

Oudtshoorn
Riempie Estate Hotel ★★★, tel: (0443) 22-6161, fax: 22-6772; close to Highgate Ostrich Farm.

MOSSEL BAY	J	F	M	A	M	J	J	A	S	O	N	D
AV. TEMP. °C	21	21	20	18	17	16	15	15	16	17	18	20
AV. TEMP. °F	70	70	68	64	63	61	59	59	61	63	64	68
DAILY SUN hrs	7	7	7	7	7	7	7	7	7	7	7	7
RAINFALL mm	28	31	36	40	37	31	32	36	39	38	34	28
RAINFALL in	1	1	1.5	2	1.5	1	1	1.5	2	1.5	1.5	1
SEA TEMP. °C	22	22	20	19	18	16	16	16	16	17	19	21
SEA TEMP. °F	72	72	68	66	64	61	61	61	61	63	66	70

MAIN ATTRACTIONS

Tsitsikamma National Park and **Otter Trail:** an 80km (50-mile) strip of superb coastline and large offshore marine reserve.
Storms River Mouth: dramatic scenery at this spectacular site; spend a night in the chalets.
Plettenberg Bay: fashionable holiday resort with beautiful beaches.
Mossel Bay: excellent beaches and the Bartolomeu Dias Museum.
Goukamma Nature Reserve: short distance west of Knysna; unspoilt nature and wonderful birdlife.
Garden of Eden: a beautiful forest area; many of its trees are labelled.
Knysna: charming little resort town with an attractive lagoon.
Wilderness Lake Area: superb scenery and prolific birdlife.
Oudtshoorn: famous for its fascinating ostrich farms.
Cango Caves: complex of caverns ranked among the most remarkable of Africa's many natural wonders.
Bungi jumping: only the brave will attempt the awesome jump off Gourits River bridge.

DISTANCE IN KM FROM GEORGE	
Bloemfontein	773
Cape Town	438
Durban	1319
Johannesburg	1171
Port Elizabeth	335

Left: *The Tsitsikamma Trail offers hikers an opportunity to enjoy the serene countryside.*

USEFUL CONTACTS

Tsitsikamma National Park, tel: (042) 541-1607, fax: 541-1629.
Oudtshoorn Publicity Association, tel: (0443) 22-2228.
Mossel Bay Marketing Association, tel: (0444) 91-2202.
Plettenberg Bay Info, tel: (04457) 3-4065.

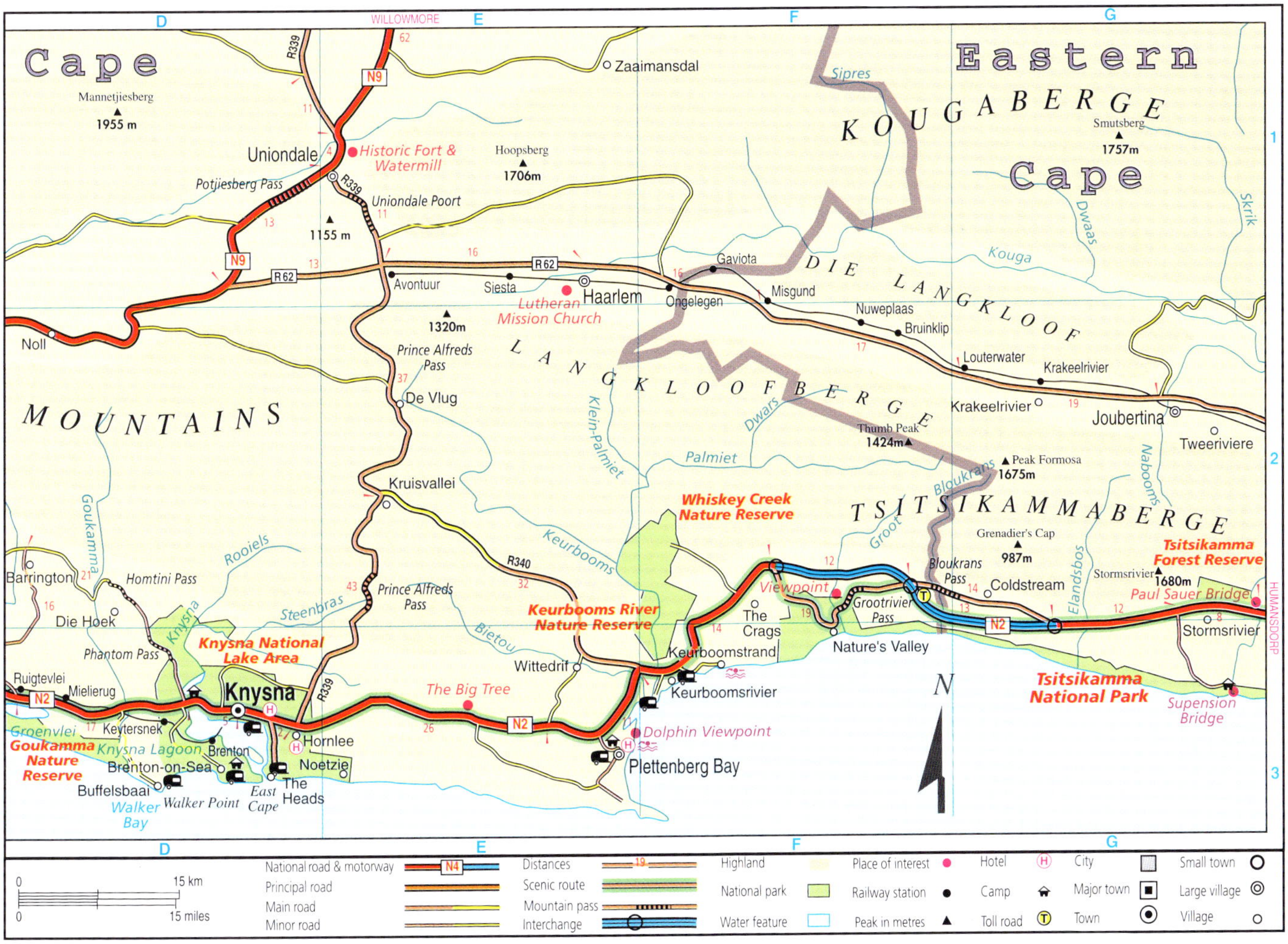

GEORGE

This pleasant little town, which was named after England's King George III, has some 75,000 inhabitants, lies at the foot of the Outeniqua Mountains and is the Garden Route's principal urban centre. The surrounding countryside is devoted to general farming, forestry and the cultivation of hops. The town is linked to Knysna by the main Garden Route highway. George is also the aerial gateway to the region.

Above: *The Van Kervel Gardens near George – a tranquil haven of lush vegetation, still waters and rich birdlife, overlooked by the Outeniqua range.*

MAIN ATTRACTIONS

Outeniqua Choo-Tjoe: this old steam train will take you on a scenic day trip to Knysna.
George Museum: in the Old Drostdy; noted for its antique musical instruments.
Churches: visit St Mark's, South Africa's smallest cathedral; the Dutch Reformed church, completed in 1842, has a fine hardwood interior; and St Peter and St Paul is the oldest Roman Catholic church in the country.
Beaches: excellent bathing, fishing and sun-worshipping at Herold's and Victoria bays.

USEFUL CONTACTS

George Information Bureau, 124 York Street, tel: (044) 863-9295, fax: 73-5228; tourist information and advice.

ACCOMMODATION

Fancourt Hotel *****, tel: (044) 70-8282, fax: 70-7605; elegant, with excellent golfing facilities.
Far Hills Protea Hotel ***, tel: (044) 71-1295, fax: 71-1951; overlooks the Outeniqua mountains.
Hoogekraal Country House, tel: (044) 79-1277, fax: 79-1300; well-kept 18th-century homestead; SATOUR-acclaimed.

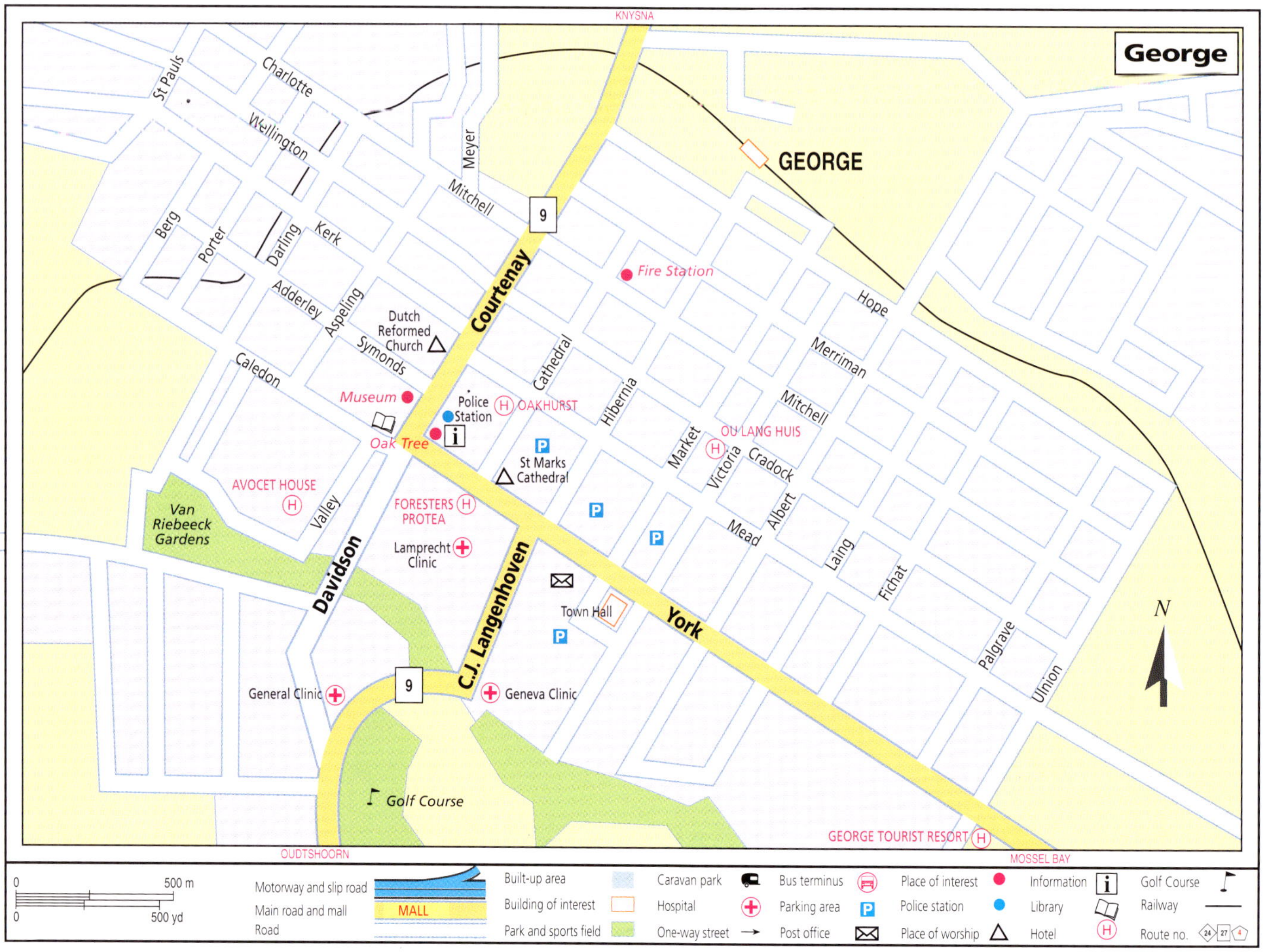

George

KNYSNA
GEORGE
Charlotte
St Pauls
Wellington
Meyer
Mitchell
Berg
Porter
Darling
Kerk
Courtenay
Fire Station
Adderley
Aspeling
Dutch Reformed Church
Symonds
Caledon
Cathedral
Hope
Merriman
Hibernia
Museum
Police Station
OAKHURST
Oak Tree
St Marks Cathedral
Mitchell
Market
OU LANG HUIS
Victoria
Cradock
AVOCET HOUSE
Van Riebeeck Gardens
Valley
FORESTERS PROTEA
Lamprecht Clinic
Mead
Albert
Davidson
C.J. Langenhoven
Town Hall
York
Laing
Fichat
Palgrave
Union
General Clinic
Geneva Clinic
Golf Course
GEORGE TOURIST RESORT
OUDTSHOORN
MOSSEL BAY

0 500 m
0 500 yd
Motorway and slip road
Main road and mall — MALL
Road
Built-up area
Building of interest
Park and sports field
Caravan park
Hospital
One-way street
Bus terminus
Parking area
Post office
Place of interest
Police station
Place of worship
Information
Library
Hotel
Golf Course
Railway
Route no.

KNYSNA

Knysna is celebrated for its locally brewed draught ale (Mitchell's), its fresh oysters, and the fine furniture made from the area's hardwoods. The biggest drawcard, however, is Knysna Lagoon: a stretch of water guarded by two sandstone cliffs known as The Heads. The lagoon, popular with boating enthusiasts, waterskiers and anglers, harbours a variety of fish and water-birds, 'pansy shells' and a rare species of sea horse. Cabin cruisers and houseboats may be hired; the John Benn, *a 20-ton pleasure boat, leaves from the jetty each morning (sightseeing, live entertainment, wining and dining on board).*

USEFUL CONTACTS

Knysna Hospital, tel: (0445) 2-3123.
Knysna Tourism, tel: (0445) 82-5510.
Featherbed Bay Nature Reserve, tel: (0445) 2-1693; free ferry ride across the bay to the lovely reserve, where you can hike, picnic or dine in style at the restaurant.

KNYSNA	J	F	M	A	M	J	J	A	S	O	N	D
AV. TEMP. °C	21	21	20	18	17	16	15	15	16	17	18	20
AV. TEMP. °F	70	70	68	64	63	61	59	59	61	63	64	68
DAILY SUN hrs	7	7	7	7	7	7	7	7	7	7	7	7
RAINFALL mm	28	31	36	40	37	31	32	36	39	38	34	28
RAINFALL in	1	1	1.5	2	1.5	1	1	1.5	2	1.5	1.5	1
SEA TEMP. °C	22	22	20	19	18	16	16	16	16	17	19	21
SEA TEMP. °F	72	72	68	66	64	61	61	61	61	63	66	70

ACCOMMODATION

Old Drift Forest Lodges ***, tel/fax: (0445) 2-1994; comfortable, self-catering log chalets in a beautiful forest setting; a paradise for birdwatchers.
Belvidere Manor, tel: (0445) 387-1055, fax: 387-1059; historic home at the edge of the lagoon; dates back to 1834.
Under Milk Wood, tel: (0445) 2-2385, fax: 2-2494; self-catering holiday log cabins situated right on lovely Knysna Lagoon.
Overlander's Lodge, tel: (0445) 82-5920; convenient, affordable backpackers' accommodation.

MAIN ATTRACTIONS

Knysna Heads: two imposing promontories which guard the entrance to Knysna Lagoon and provide good views of the surrounding area.
Royal Hotel: Prince Alfred and George Bernard Shaw stayed here.
Millwood Museum: local history, gold mining and timber industry.
Fresh oysters: try some, sprinkled with fresh lemon juice or hot chilli sauce, at the Knysna Oyster Co.
Crab's Creek: a restaurant on the water's edge; sit under umbrellas and enjoy the prolific birdlife.
Noetzie: stroll past the five castles on the sea (please note that they are private residences).
Knysna Forest: together with the Tsitsikamma Forest, forms the largest expanse of indigenous high forest in South Africa.
Die Ou Fabriek: arts and crafts on offer in the garden of Craft House.

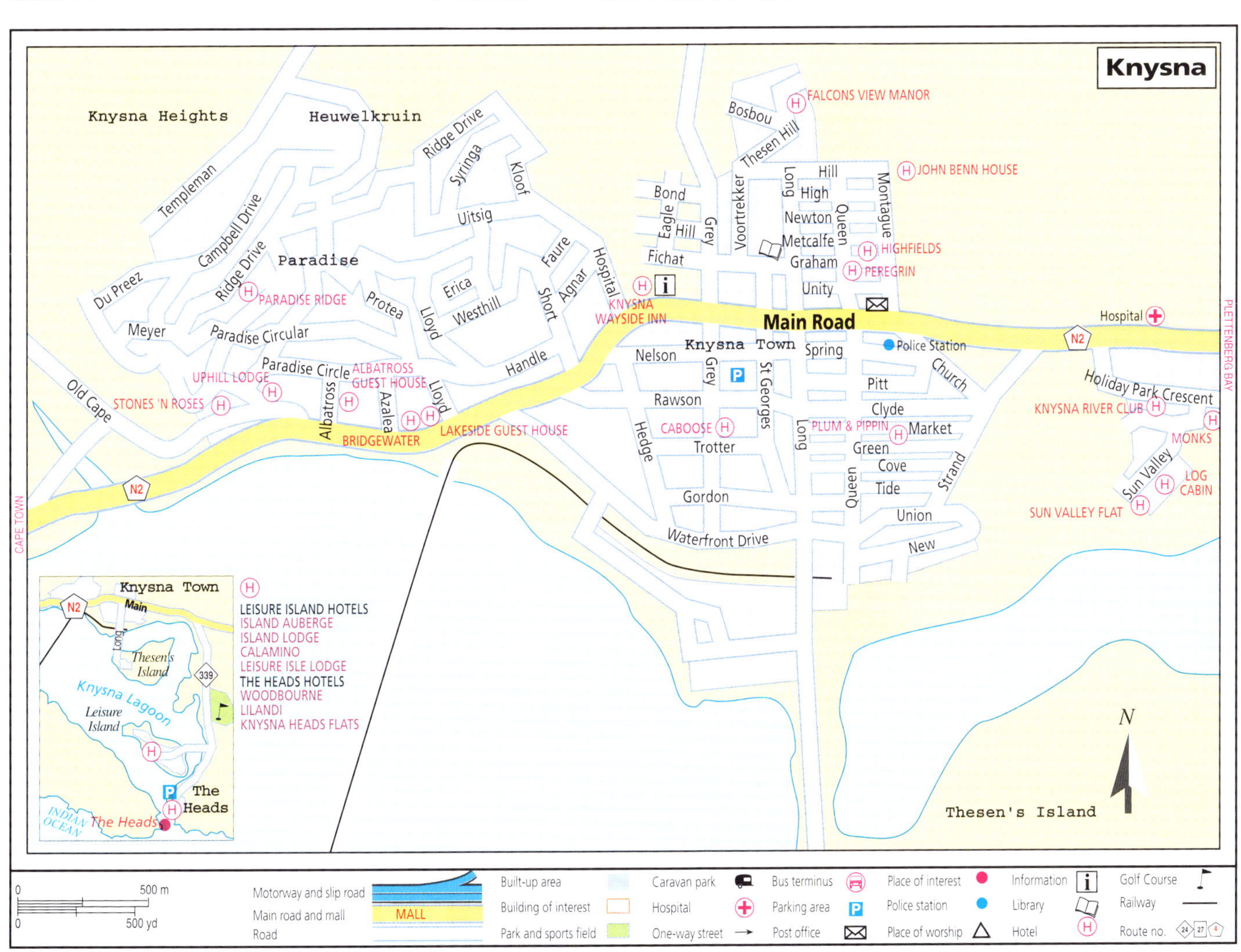

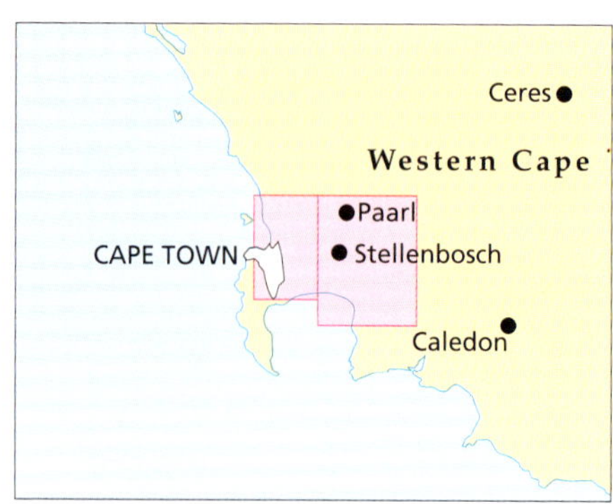

CAPE WINELANDS

Within easy reach of Cape Town lie a number of superb vineyards, some of which have achieved international acclaim. Begin your tour in elegant Constantia, on the eastern slopes of the mountain, with its four choice estates. But quaint country towns such as Stellenbosch, Paarl, Grabouw, Franschhoek and Somerset West, with their stately Cape-Dutch homes, form the hub of South Africa's wine-making industry.

MAIN ATTRACTIONS

Stellenbosch: hub of the wineland region; a picturesque town that prides itself on its lovely historic buildings and oak-lined avenues.
Franschhoek: founded by French Huguenots between 1680 and 1690. Protestant settlers were forbidden to form independent communities and, through intermarriage, lost much of their cultural heritage, but they left an indelible mark on the local wine-growing industry.
Paarl: original farming settlement established in 1720; visit a number of splendid wine estates in the vicinity of this little town.
Somerset West: the beautiful big homestead of Vergelegen estate was built by an early Cape governor and completed in 1701.

Right: *The wide and fertile Hex River Valley supports some 200 farms. By late autumn the surrounding mountains are often dusted with snow.*

DISTANCE IN KM FROM CAPE TOWN	
Constantia	10
Franschhoek	57
Paarl	58
Stellenbosch	42

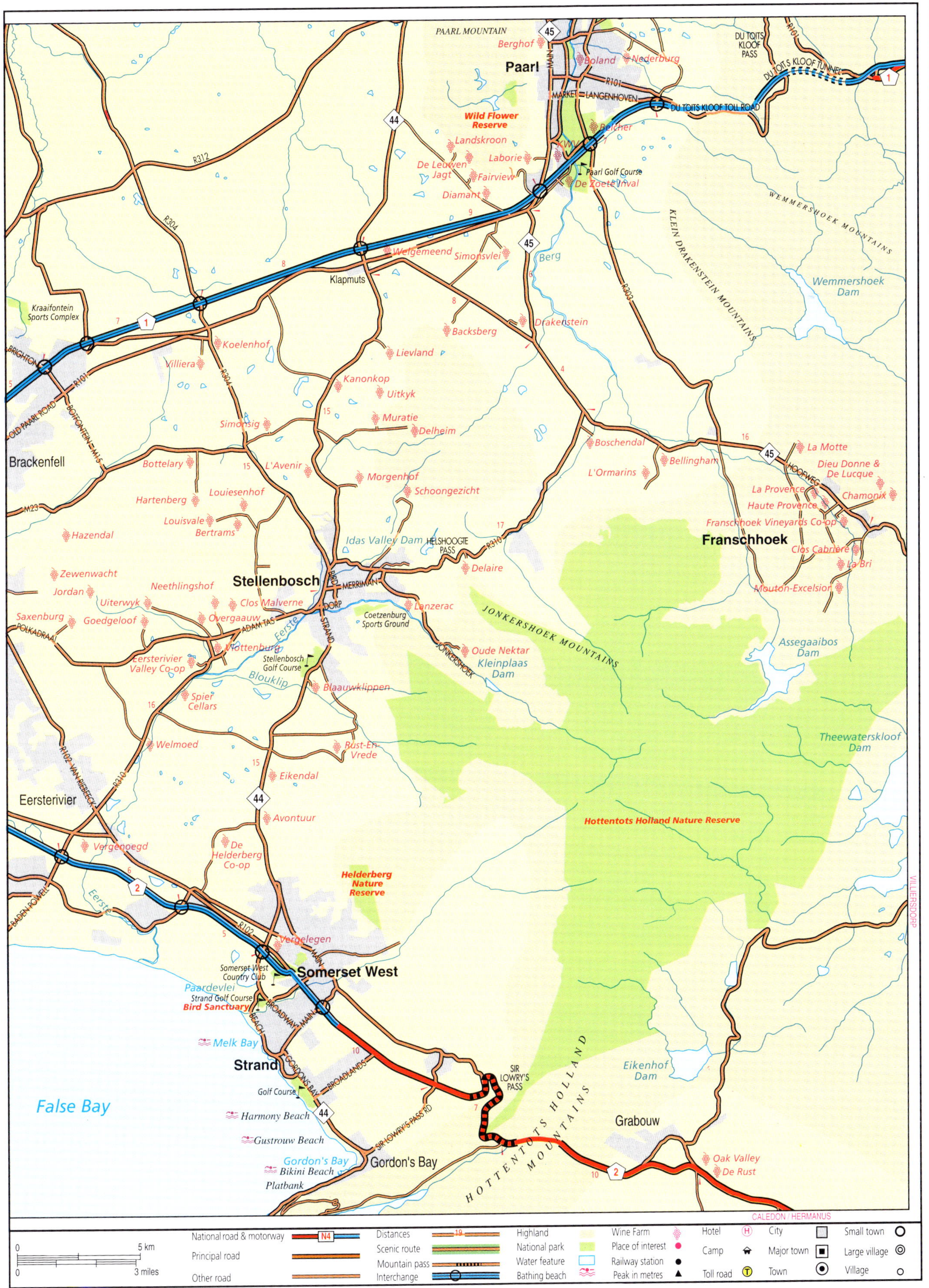
PAARL MOUNTAIN
Berghof
Paarl
Boland
Nederburg
DU TOITS KLOOF PASS
DU TOITS KLOOF TUNNEL
DU TOITS KLOOF TOLL ROAD
Wild Flower Reserve
Landskroon
Laborie
De Leuwen Jagt
Fairview
Diamant
Belcher
Paarl Golf Course
De Zoete Inval
WEMMERSHOEK MOUNTAINS
KLEIN DRAKENSTEIN MOUNTAINS
Welgemeend
Simonsvlei
Berg
Klapmuts
Wemmershoek Dam
Kraaifontein Sports Complex
Backsberg
Drakenstein
Koelenhof
Lievland
Villiera
Kanonkop
Uitkyk
Muratie
Delheim
Simonsig
Brackenfell
Bottelary
L'Avenir
Boschendal
Bellingham
L'Ormarins
La Motte
Dieu Donne & De Lucque
La Provence
Chamonix
Haute Provence
Franschhoek Vineyards Co-op
Franschhoek
Clos Cabrière
La Bri
Mouton-Excelsior
Morgenhof
Schoongezicht
Hartenberg
Louiesenhof
Louisvale
Bertrams
Hazendal
Idas Valley Dam
HELSHOOGTE PASS
Delaire
Zewenwacht
Jordan
Neethlingshof
Stellenbosch
Uiterwyk
Clos Malverne
Saxenburg
Goedgeloof
Overgaauw
Lanzerac
Coetzenburg Sports Ground
JONKERSHOEK MOUNTAINS
Oude Nektar
Kleinplaas Dam
Assegaaibos Dam
Vlottenburg
Eersterivier Valley Co-op
Stellenbosch Golf Course
Blouklip
Eerste
Blaauwklippen
Spier Cellars
Welmoed
Rust-En-Vrede
Theewaterskloof Dam
Eikendal
Eersterivier
Avontuur
Hottentots Holland Nature Reserve
Vergenoegd
De Helderberg Co-op
Helderberg Nature Reserve
VILLIERSDORP
Vergelegen
Somerset West Country Club
Somerset West
Paardevlei
Strand Golf Course
Bird Sanctuary
Melk Bay
Strand
SIR LOWRY'S PASS
HOTTENTOTS HOLLAND MOUNTAINS
Eikenhof Dam
False Bay
Golf Course
Harmony Beach
Grabouw
Gustrouw Beach
Gordon's Bay
Bikini Beach
Gordon's Bay
Platbank
Oak Valley
De Rust
CALEDON / HERMANUS
0 5 km
0 3 miles
National road & motorway
Principal road
Other road
Distances
Scenic route
Mountain pass
Interchange
Highland
National park
Water feature
Bathing beach
Wine Farm
Place of interest
Railway station
Peak in metres
Hotel
Camp
Toll road
City
Major town
Town
Small town
Large village
Village

STELLENBOSCH AND PAARL

Charming Stellenbosch, less than an hour's drive from Cape Town, lies in the Eerste River Valley. The town is very proud of its heritage – a fact that is evident in the original watering system, old churchyards and well-maintained gabled buildings along the oak-lined streets. Stellenbosch is a leading centre of learning; university and town integrate harmoniously. Paarl, the biggest of the wineland towns, began as a farming and wagon-building settlement in 1720 and was named after the granite rock that resembles a giant pearl on the overlooking mountain. Both the mountain and its surrounds are maintained as a nature reserve; there's a circular route to the top.

Accommodation

Grande Roche Hotel *****, tel: (021) 863-2727, fax: 863-2220; elegant hotel with award-winning Bosman's Restaurant.
Lanzerac Manor and Winery ****, tel: (021) 887-1132, fax: 887-2310; superb facilities, elegantly refurbished; wine made on the premises.
D'Ouwe Werf ***, tel: (021) 887-4608, fax: 887-4626; tradition and atmosphere combined.
Roggeland Country House, tel: (021) 868-2501, fax: 868-2113; internationally acclaimed.

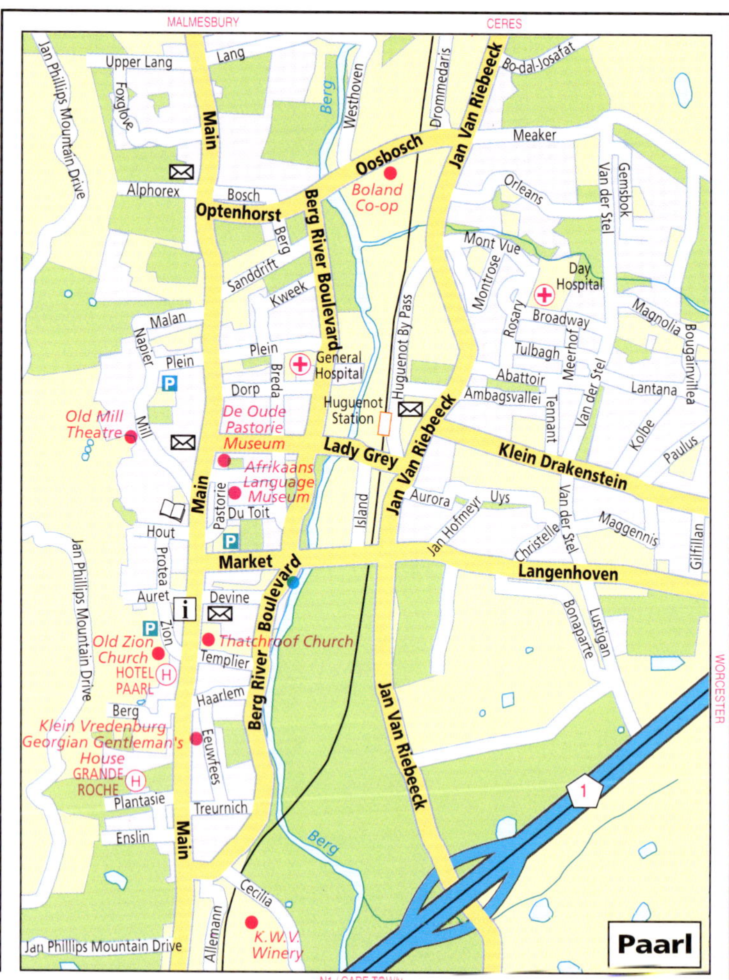

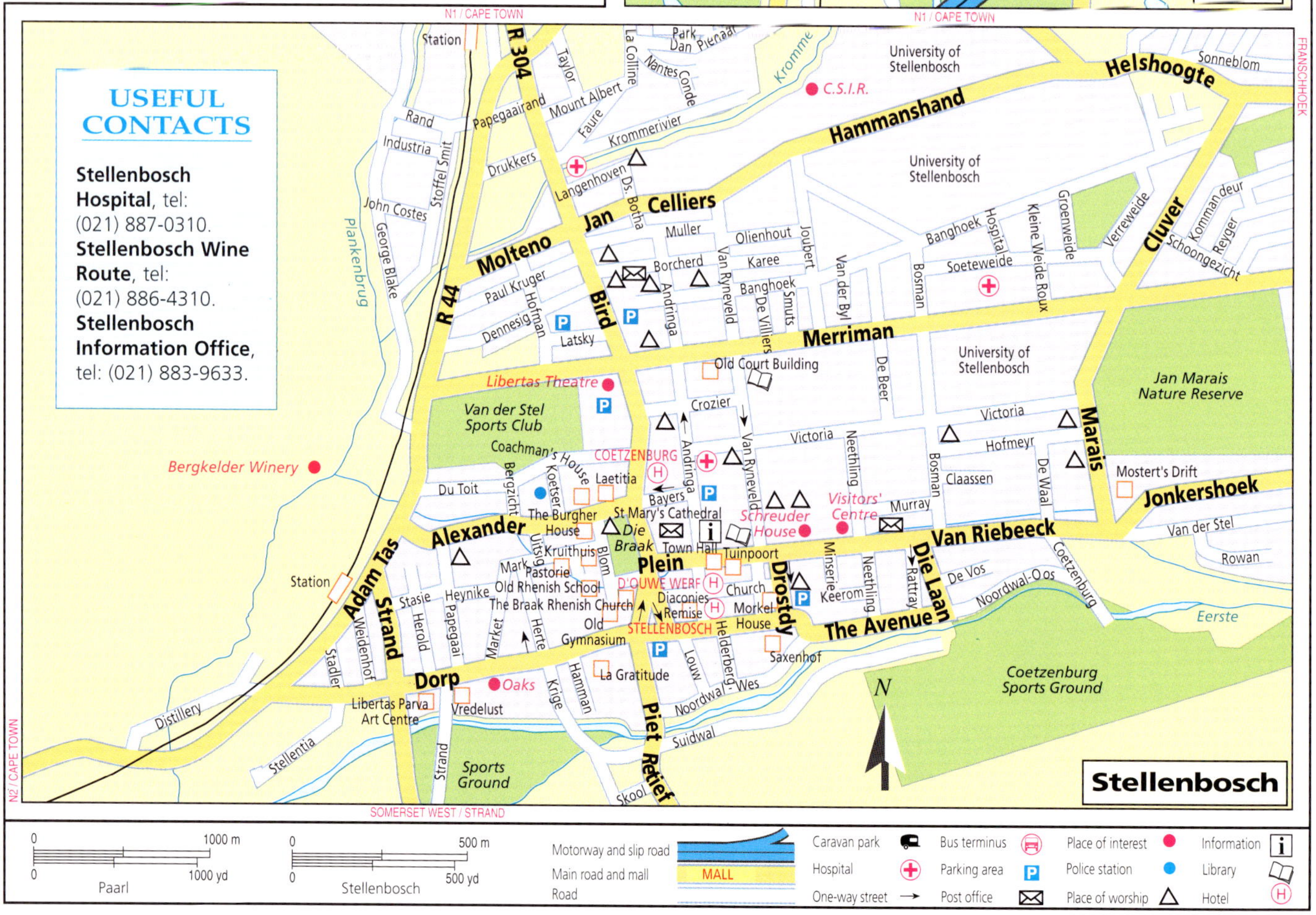

USEFUL CONTACTS

Stellenbosch Hospital, tel: (021) 887-0310.
Stellenbosch Wine Route, tel: (021) 886-4310.
Stellenbosch Information Office, tel: (021) 883-9633.

Stellenbosch

Bergkelder Winery
Libertas Theatre
Van der Stel Sports Club
University of Stellenbosch
C.S.I.R.
Jan Marais Nature Reserve
Coetzenburg Sports Ground
Old Court Building
The Burgher House
St Mary's Cathedral
Die Braak
Town Hall
Schreuder House
Visitors' Centre
Kruithuis
Old Rhenish School
The Braak Rhenish Church
Old Gymnasium
D'OUWE WERF
COETZENBURG
La Gratitude
Oaks
Libertas Parva Art Centre
Vredelust
Saxenhof
Sports Ground

Scale	
Paarl	0 – 1000 m / 1000 yd
Stellenbosch	0 – 500 m / 500 yd

Motorway and slip road · Main road and mall (MALL) · Road · Caravan park · Hospital · One-way street · Bus terminus · Parking area · Post office · Place of interest · Police station · Place of worship · Information · Library · Hotel

WEST COAST

The harsh western shores of the country, pounded by the icy Atlantic Ocean, are a rather barren region of low coastal vegetation. Sleepy fishing villages bake in the sun, while further inland little farming communities huddle together in the wide, vast emptiness. But the area is transformed after the spring rains, when a carpet of flowers erupts in a riot of colour stretching as far as the eye can see.

MAIN ATTRACTIONS

Langebaan Lagoon: a sweeping lagoon bordered by an unspoilt beach dotted with little holiday cottages. **Club Mykonos** nearby is a resort hotel for those who like to holiday in style.
West Coast National Park: beautiful natural wetland reserve with prolific **birdlife** and magnificent wildflowers each spring (August–October). The **Flowerline** provides useful information about the best displays, tel: (021) 418-3705.
Elandsbaai: buy some crayfish fresh from the factory.

Above: *After the spring rains, the parched land lies resplendent in a colourful tapestry of flowers.*

ACCOMMODATION

Protea Saldanha Bay *,** 51 Main Street, Saldanha, tel: (02281) 4-1264, fax: 4-4093.
Marine Protea Hotel *,** Lambert's Bay, tel: (027) 432-1126, fax: 432-1036; a comfortable and friendly establishment.

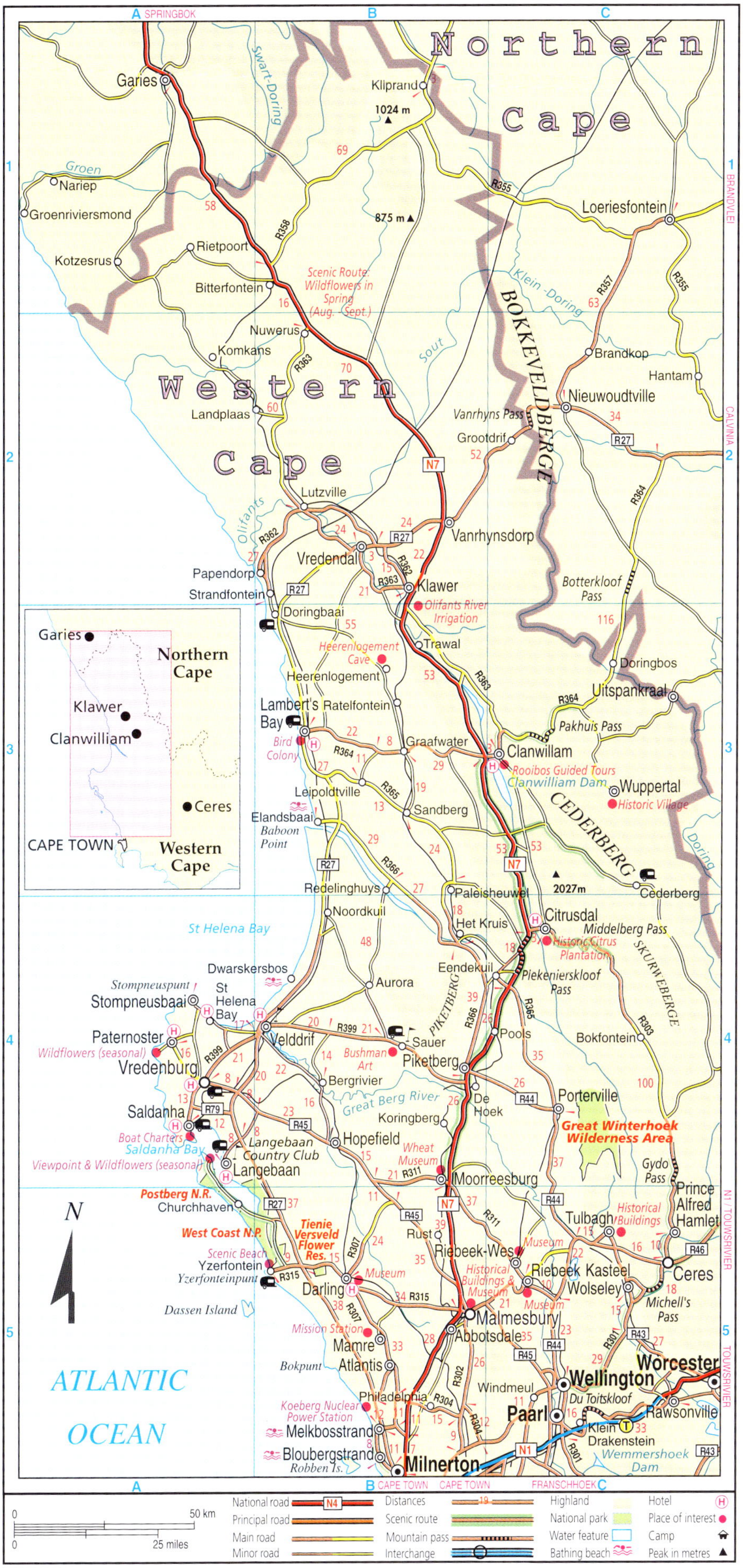

KEY TOURIST AREAS

Northern Cape
Western Cape
ATLANTIC OCEAN
Garies
Kliprand
Nariep
Groenriviersmond
Kotzesrus
Rietpoort
Bitterfontein
Nuwerus
Komkans
Landplaas
Loeriesfontein
Brandkop
Hantam
Nieuwoudtville
Vanrhyns Pass
Grootdrif
BOKKEVELDBERGE
Scenic Route: Wildflowers in Spring (Aug.–Sept.)
Lutzville
Vredendal
Papendorp
Strandfontein
Doringbaai
Vanrhynsdorp
Klawer
Olifants River Irrigation
Trawal
Botterkloof Pass
Doringbos
Heerenlogement Cave
Heerenlogement
Lambert's Bay
Ratelfontein
Bird Colony
Uitspankraal
Pakhuis Pass
Graafwater
Clanwilliam
Rooibos Guided Tours
Clanwilliam Dam
Wuppertal
Historic Village
CEDERBERG
Leipoldtville
Sandberg
Elandsbaai
Baboon Point
Redelinghuys
Paleisheuwel
Cederberg
Noordkuil
Het Kruis
Citrusdal
Middelberg Pass
Historic Citrus Plantation
SKURWEBERGE
St Helena Bay
Dwarskersbos
Eendekuil
Piekenierskloof Pass
Stompneuspunt
Stompneusbaai
St Helena Bay
Aurora
PIKETBERG
Paternoster
Wildflowers (seasonal)
Vredenburg
Velddrif
Sauer
Pools
Bokfontein
Bushman Art
Piketberg
Bergrivier
Great Berg River
De Hoek
Porterville
Saldanha
Koringberg
Great Winterhoek Wilderness Area
Boat Charters
Saldanha Bay
Langebaan Country Club
Hopefield
Wheat Museum
Viewpoint & Wildflowers (seasonal)
Langebaan
Moorreesburg
Gydo Pass
Postberg N.R.
Churchhaven
Prince Alfred Hamlet
Tulbagh
Historical Buildings
West Coast N.P.
Tienie Versveld Flower Res.
Rust
Scenic Beach
Yzerfontein
Yzerfonteinpunt
Riebeek-Wes
Museum
Riebeek Kasteel
Ceres
Darling
Historical Buildings & Museum
Wolseley
Michell's Pass
Dassen Island
Malmesbury
Mission Station
Abbotsdale
Mamre
Atlantis
Bokpunt
Worcester
Wellington
Windmeul
Philadelphia
Du Toitskloof
Koeberg Nuclear Power Station
Paarl
Rawsonville
Melkbosstrand
Klein Drakenstein
Bloubergstrand
Robben Is.
Milnerton
Wemmershoek Dam
1024 m
875 m
2027m
N
SPRINGBOK
BRANDVLEI
CALVINIA
TOUWSRIVIER
CAPE TOWN
FRANSCHHOEK

Garies
Northern Cape
Klawer
Clanwilliam
Ceres
CAPE TOWN
Western Cape

0 50 km
0 25 miles
National road
Principal road
Main road
Minor road
Distances
Scenic route
Mountain pass
Interchange
Highland
National park
Water feature
Bathing beach
Hotel
Place of interest
Camp
Peak in metres

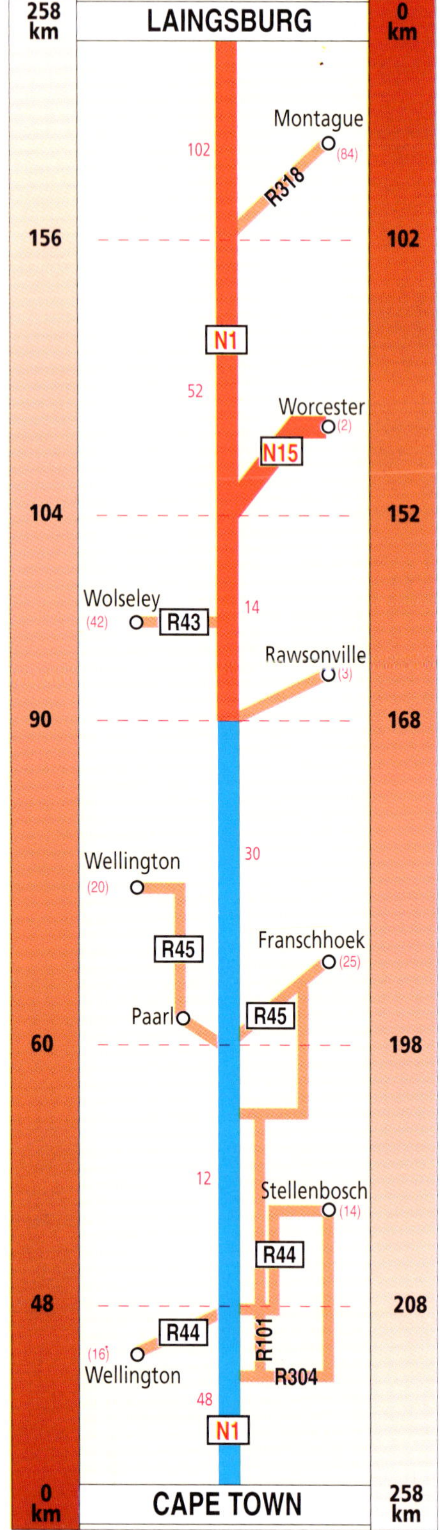

CAPE PENINSULA

The Cape Peninsula stretches from the Cape of Good Hope and Cape Point northward to Table Bay and comprises, for the most part, a strikingly beautiful plateau that achieves its loftiest and most spectacular heights in the famed Table Mountain massif overlooking Table Bay and Cape Town – a neat bustling little metropolis of handsome buildings, elegant thoroughfares and glittering shops. The western and eastern shorelines of the Peninsula are graced by superb beaches and attractive residential and resort centres that are a magnet for holiday-makers, scuba divers, boating enthusiasts, surfers and sun-worshippers.

Accommodation

Lord Charles Hotel *****, Somerset West, tel: (021) 855-1040, fax: 855-1107; gracious elegance; world-class.
Karos Arthur's Seat Hotel ****, Sea Point, tel: (021) 434-1187, fax: 434-9768; stylish accommodation.
Alphen Hotel ****, tel: (021) 794-5011, fax: 794-5710; charming wine estate in Constantia Valley.
Peninsula All-Suite Hotel ****, Sea Point, tel: (021) 439-8888, fax: 439-8886; on the promenade.
Holiday Inn Garden Court Newlands ***, tel: (021) 61-1105, fax: 64-1241; close to the cricket ground and rugby stadium.
The Lord Nelson Inn ***, Simon's Town, tel: (021) 786-1386, fax: 786-1009; colonial-style inn offering old-fashioned hospitality.
Shrimpton Manor **, Muizenberg, tel: (021) 788-5225, fax: 788-1120; whale-watching from the rooftop.
The Adams Family Guest House, Muizenberg, tel: (021) 788-9156, fax: 788-9157; overlooks False Bay.

Travel Tips

Rail, bus and taxi services are adequate. Major international car-hire companies are represented, as are local car, camper, and caravan-hire firms. Tour operators offer a wide choice of one-day and half-day scenic coach trips.
Please note: South African taxis must be booked or boarded at the designated stands, as they do not cruise for fares.

Above: *A funicular railway takes visitors up to the lookout at Cape Point for panoramic views of False Bay and the southern Atlantic Ocean.*

MAIN ATTRACTIONS

Cape Town: this charming metropolis, overshadowed by its Table Mountain, is the country's oldest urban centre.
Table Mountain: ride the cableway or climb up to the summit and marvel at the spectacular views.
Kirstenbosch: one of the world's most celebrated botanical gardens.
The V&A Waterfront: at the docks; a sophisticated complex of restaurants, shops and pubs.
Sea Point: a busy cosmopolitan seaside suburb with numerous good restaurants.
Clifton: chic suburb noted for its four magnificent beaches; popular with the trendier set.
Chapman's Peak Drive: a world-famous drive with dramatic views of the surf 600m (1980ft) below, at the foot of a sheer drop.
Hout Bay: enchanting little suburb with a quaint fishing harbour.
Cape Point: southernmost tip of the peninsula; the finest of view sites.
Simon's Town: the headquarters of the South African Navy, noted for its old-world charm and proximity to the fine beaches of Seaforth, as well as the jackass penguin colony at Boulders.
Constantia Wine Estates: four estates in the beautiful Constantia Valley: Groot and Klein Constantia, Buitenverwachting and Uitsig.

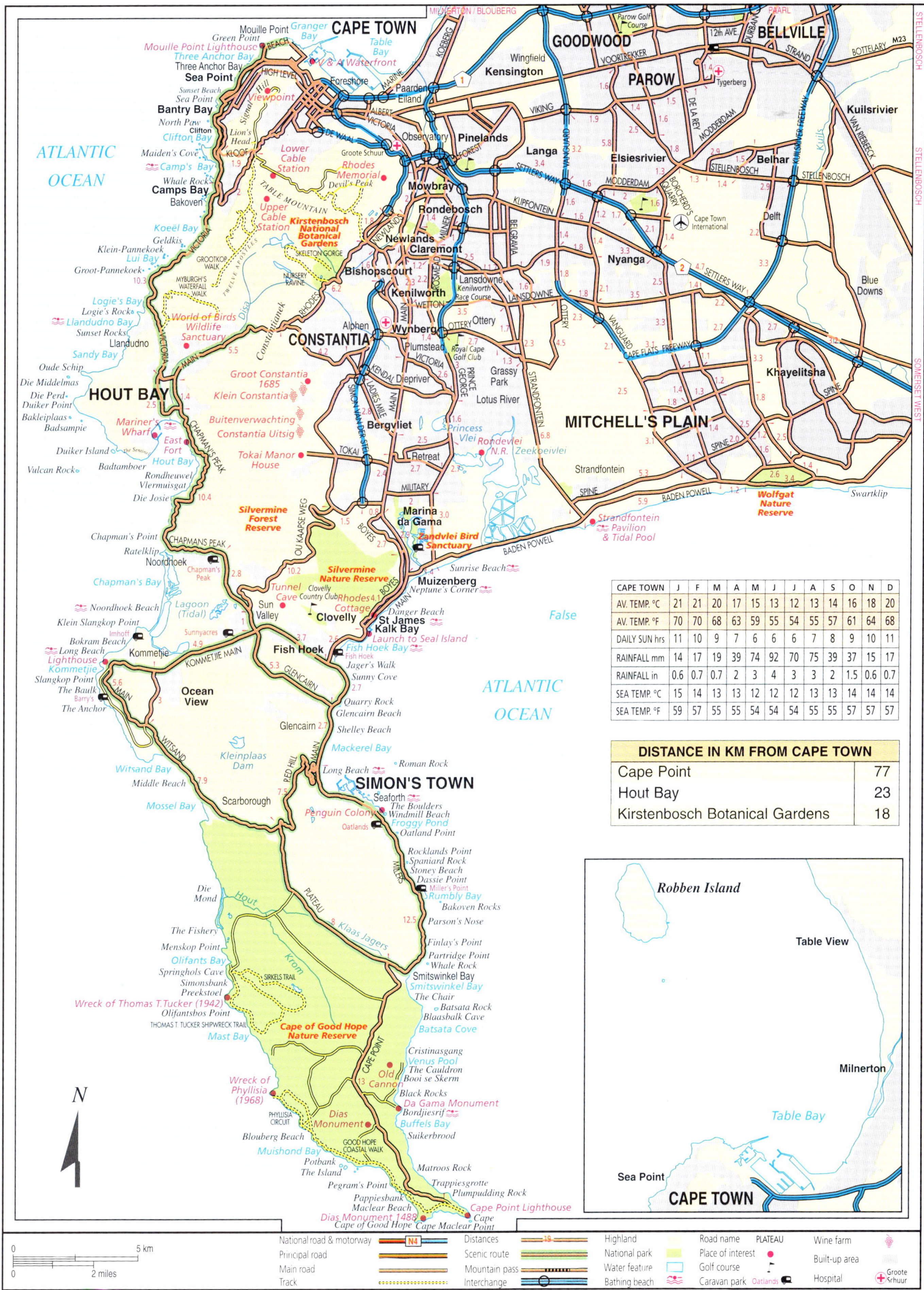

CAPE TOWN	J	F	M	A	M	J	J	A	S	O	N	D
AV. TEMP. °C	21	21	20	17	15	13	12	13	14	16	18	20
AV. TEMP. °F	70	70	68	63	59	55	54	55	57	61	64	68
DAILY SUN hrs	11	10	9	7	6	6	6	7	8	9	10	11
RAINFALL mm	14	17	19	39	74	92	70	75	39	37	15	17
RAINFALL in	0.6	0.7	0.7	2	3	4	3	3	2	1.5	0.6	0.7
SEA TEMP. °C	15	14	13	13	12	12	12	13	13	14	14	14
SEA TEMP. °F	59	57	55	55	54	54	54	55	55	57	57	57

DISTANCE IN KM FROM CAPE TOWN	
Cape Point	77
Hout Bay	23
Kirstenbosch Botanical Gardens	18

Ceres
Western Cape
Paarl
CAPE TOWN
Stellenbosch
Caledon
Kirstenbosch National Botanical Gardens

KIRSTENBOSCH

The Kirstenbosch National Botanical Garden lies on the eastern slopes of the Table Mountain range. An astonishing array of flowering plants, representative of about a quarter of South Africa's 24,000 species, are cultivated here. Delightful walks lead through herb and fragrance gardens, and through stinkwood and yellowwood groves. There is a pelargonium koppie and a cycad amphitheatre, and the birdlife, particularly the sunbirds drawn to the collection of protaceae, is enchanting.

ENCHANTED GARDEN

Braille walk/perfume garden: designed especially for blind visitors.
Restaurant: for a relaxing stop; overlooking the gardens.
Jan van Riebeeck's hedge: part of the original wild almond hedge planted by the first Dutch settlers.
Compton Herbarium: contains over 200,000 plant specimens.
Sunday concerts: spend an enchanted summer evening listening to music and picnicking, while the setting sun illuminates the magnificent mountain, creating a superb backdrop.

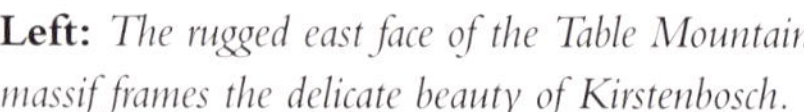

Left: *The rugged east face of the Table Mountain massif frames the delicate beauty of Kirstenbosch.*

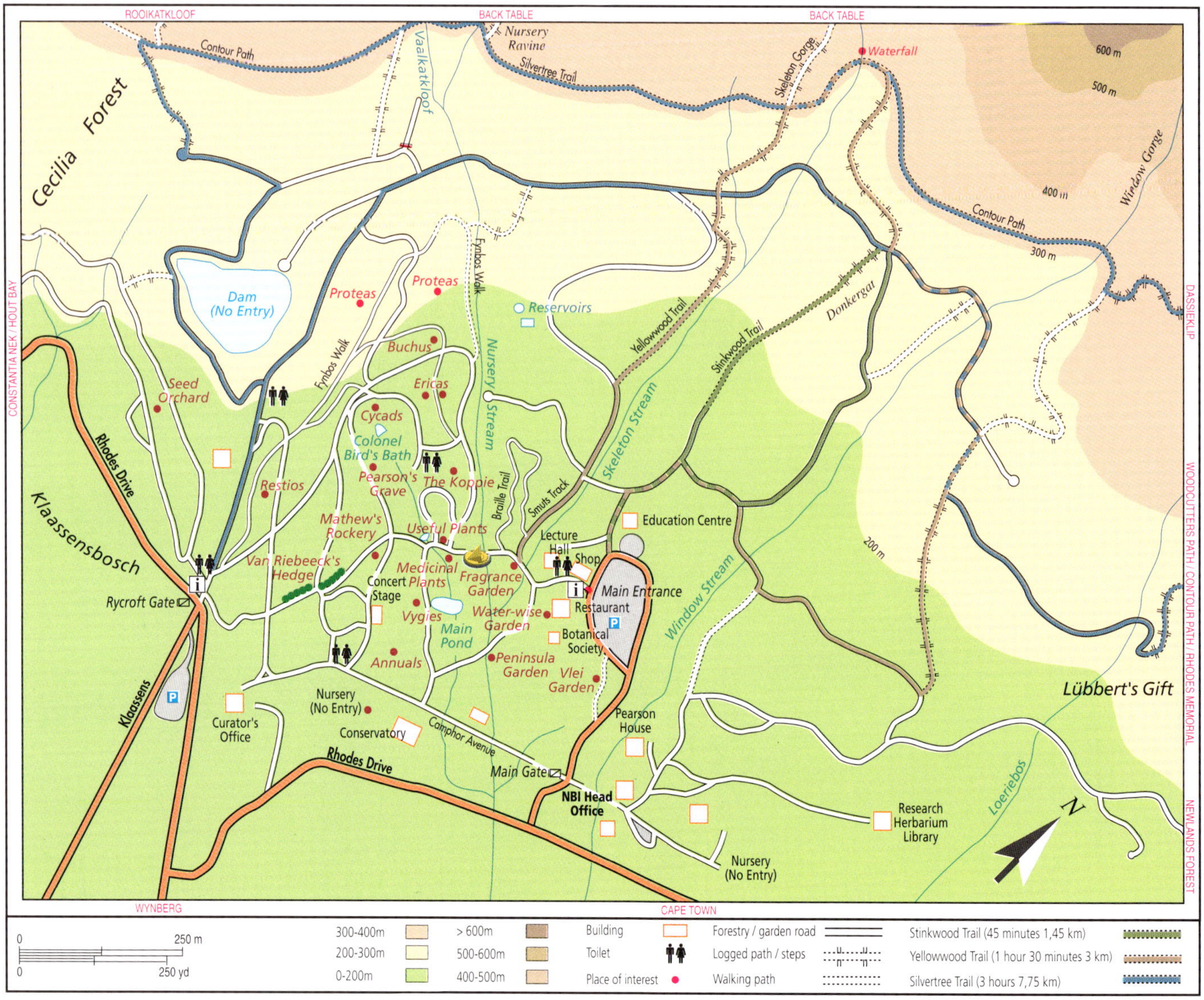

ROOIKATKLOOF
BACK TABLE
BACK TABLE
Nursery Ravine
Contour Path
Silvertree Trail
Skeleton Gorge
Waterfall
600 m
500 m
400 m
300 m
200 m
Window Gorge
Cecilia Forest
Vaalkatkloof
Dam (No Entry)
Proteas
Proteas
Reservoirs
Buchus
Ericas
Fynbos Walk
Nursery Stream
Yellowwood Trail
Stinkwood Trail
Donkergat
Skeleton Stream
Seed Orchard
Cycads
Colonel Bird's Bath
Pearson's Grave
The Koppie
Restios
Braille Trail
Smuts Track
Mathew's Rockery
Useful Plants
Education Centre
Lecture Hall
Shop
Van Riebeeck's Hedge
Medicinal Plants
Fragrance Garden
Concert Stage
Main Entrance
Restaurant
Window Stream
Rycroft Gate
Vygies
Main Pond
Water-wise Garden
Botanical Society
Annuals
Peninsula Garden
Vlei Garden
Klaassensbosch
Rhodes Drive
Klaassens
Curator's Office
Nursery (No Entry)
Conservatory
Camphor Avenue
Main Gate
Pearson House
Lübbert's Gift
NBI Head Office
Loeriebos
Research Herbarium Library
Nursery (No Entry)
Rhodes Drive
CONSTANTIA NEK / HOUT BAY
DASSIEKLIP
WOODCUTTERS PATH / CONTOUR PATH / RHODES MEMORIAL
NEWLANDS FOREST
WYNBERG
CAPE TOWN
N

0 250 m
0 250 yd

300-400m · 200-300m · 0-200m · > 600m · 500-600m · 400-500m
Building · Toilet · Place of interest
Forestry / garden road · Logged path / steps · Walking path
Stinkwood Trail (45 minutes 1,45 km)
Yellowwood Trail (1 hour 30 minutes 3 km)
Silvertree Trail (3 hours 7,75 km)

CAPE TOWN

The central metropolitan area of Cape Town huddles in a 'bowl' formed by the majestic Table Mountain, its flanking peaks and the broad sweep of Table Bay. Founded by Dutch settlers in 1652, Cape Town is the country's oldest city and fourth largest in terms of population. More than 300 years of history have created its unique character – a vibrant blend of Dutch, French, English and Malay influences. It is an attractive, colourful city that boasts excellent hotels and restaurants, open-air markets and shops catering for every pocket and taste. Fortunately for visitors, the compactness of central Cape Town makes it ideal for exploring on foot.

MAIN ATTRACTIONS

Table Mountain: ride the revamped cable car or hike to the summit, and enjoy the breathtaking views.
Castle of Good Hope: the city's most notable landmark (built between 1666 and 1679).
Victoria and Alfred Waterfront: complex of shops, restaurants and pubs in a working harbour.
Two Oceans Aquarium: at the Waterfront; unique underwater experience of kelp forests, touch pools and gigantic aquariums.
St George's Cathedral: see the famous Rose Window in this lovely church and have tea in the crypt.
Greenmarket Square: for bargain hunting in one of Africa's prettiest little plazas. Be sure not to miss the **Old Town House** (built 1761) which contains the Michaelis collection of 17-century Dutch and Flemish art.
The Company Gardens: take a walk through the lush gardens originally founded by Jan Van Riebeeck to supply fresh fruit and vegetables to the Dutch East India Company ships. While here, visit the South African Museum, the Planetarium, and the National Art Gallery.
Koopmans–De Wet House: admire the beautiful antique yellow- and stinkwood furniture.
Shopping: Cape Town's informal markets are the place to shop for contemporary African art, curios, ethnic jewellery and more. Try St George's Mall, Greenmarket Square and the Kirstenbosch Craft Market.
Rhodes Memorial: a grand monument with breathtaking views, located on the eastern slopes of Devil's Peak.
Signal Hill: have a sundowner and enjoy the panoramic view.
Bo-Kaap Museum: dedicated to the Malay culture; in one of the oldest original buildings.

ACCOMMODATION

Cape Sun Inter-Continental *****, tel: (021) 23-8844, fax: 23-8875; city centre; excellent restaurants.
Mount Nelson *****, Gardens, tel: (021) 23-1000, fax: 24-7472; one of the world's most elegant hotels.
Cellars-Hohenort Hotel *****, Constantia, tel : (021) 794-2137, fax: 794-2149; built 1693; lovely grounds; excellent restaurant.
Mijlof Manor Hotel ***, 5 Military Road, Tamboerskloof, tel: (021) 26-1476; conveniently close to town.
Holiday Inn Garden Court De Waal ***, Gardens, tel: (021) 45-1311, fax: 461-6648; close to the old Company Gardens in town.
Holiday Inn Garden Court Greenmarket Square ***, tel: (021) 23-2040, fax: 23-3664; charming position in the heart of town.
Flower Street Villa, 3 Flower Street, Gardens, tel/fax: (021) 45-7517; comfortable guest house.
The Bunkhouse, 23 Antrim Road, Three Anchor Bay, tel/fax: (021) 434-5695; budget accommodation.

Below: *To Capetonians, the arrival of the strong Southeaster gusts is heralded by the appearance of the famous 'tablecloth' over Table Mountain.*

Events and Festivals

Minstrel (Coon) Carnival: vibrant part of the **New Year** celebrations.
Metropolitan Handicap: exciting horseracing event held in **January**.
Spring Wildflower Show: held at Kirstenbosch in **September**.
Rothman's Sailing Week: colourful international regatta in **December**.
Two Oceans Marathon: this popular event takes place on **Easter Sunday**.

USEFUL CONTACTS

Groote Schuur Hospital, tel: (021) 404-9111.
Captour, tel: (021) 418-5214.
Computicket, tel: (021) 430-8080.
Table Mountain Aerial Cableway Co Ltd, tel: (021) 24-5148; information regarding weather conditions and visibility.

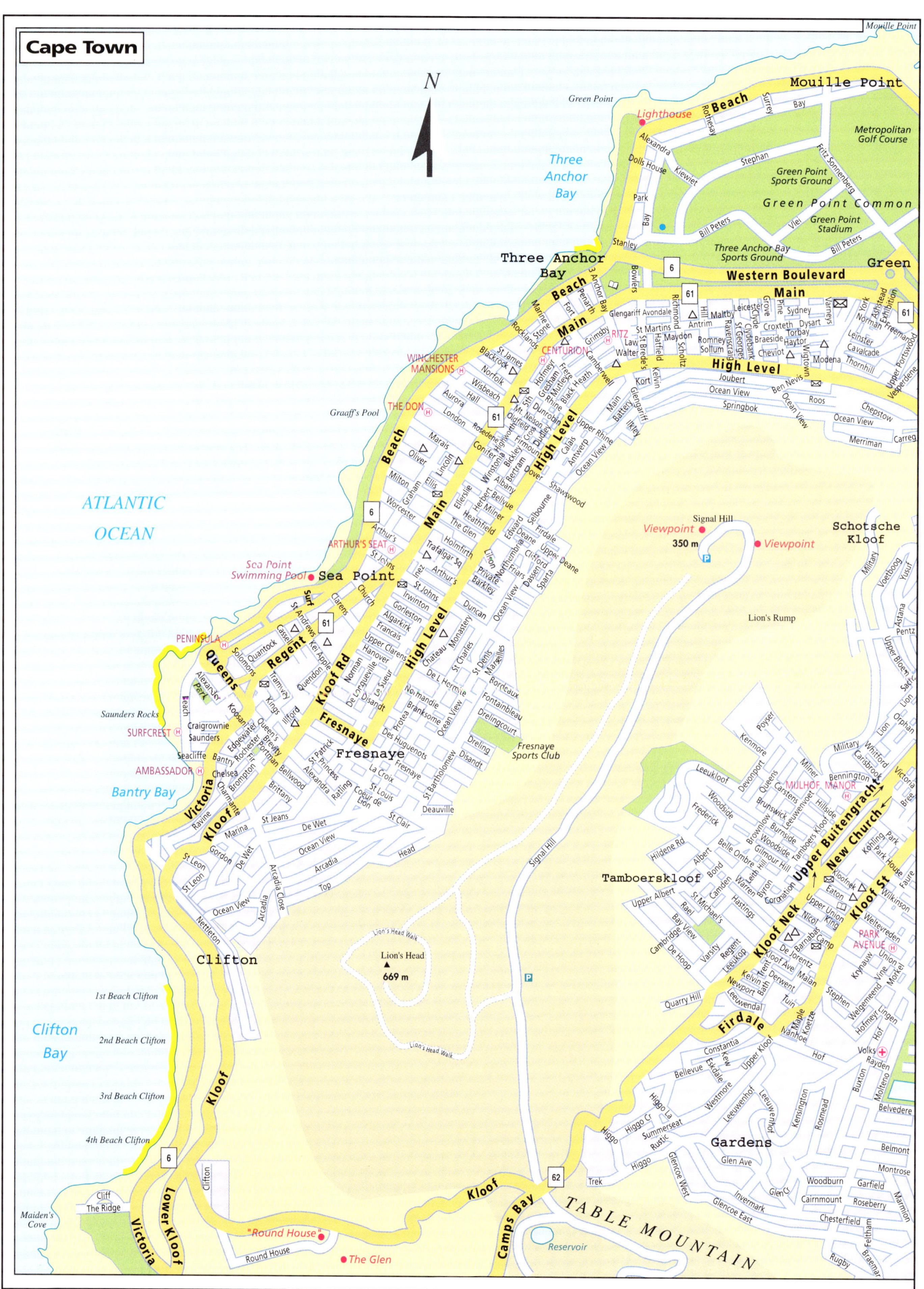
Cape Town
N
Mouille Point
Green Point
Lighthouse
Beach
Mouille Point
Metropolitan Golf Course
Three Anchor Bay
Green Point Sports Ground
Green Point Common
Green Point Stadium
Three Anchor Bay Sports Ground
Three Anchor Bay
Western Boulevard
Green
Main
High Level
Beach
Main
WINCHESTER MANSIONS
CENTURION
RITZ
THE DON
Graaff's Pool
ATLANTIC OCEAN
ARTHUR'S SEAT
Sea Point Swimming Pool
Sea Point
Signal Hill
Viewpoint
350 m
Viewpoint
Schotsche Kloof
Lion's Rump
PENINSULA
Queens
Regent
Kloof Rd
High Level
Fresnaye
Saunders Rocks
SURFCREST
AMBASSADOR
Bantry Bay
Fresnaye
Fresnaye Sports Club
Victoria
Kloof
MULHOF MANOR
Tamboerskloof
Upper Buitengracht
New Church
Kloof Nek
Kloof St
PARK AVENUE
Clifton
Lion's Head
669 m
Lion's Head Walk
Signal Hill
1st Beach Clifton
Clifton Bay
2nd Beach Clifton
3rd Beach Clifton
4th Beach Clifton
Kloof
Firdale
Gardens
Maiden's Cove
Victoria
Lower Kloof
"Round House"
The Glen
Camps Bay
Kloof
Reservoir
TABLE MOUNTAIN

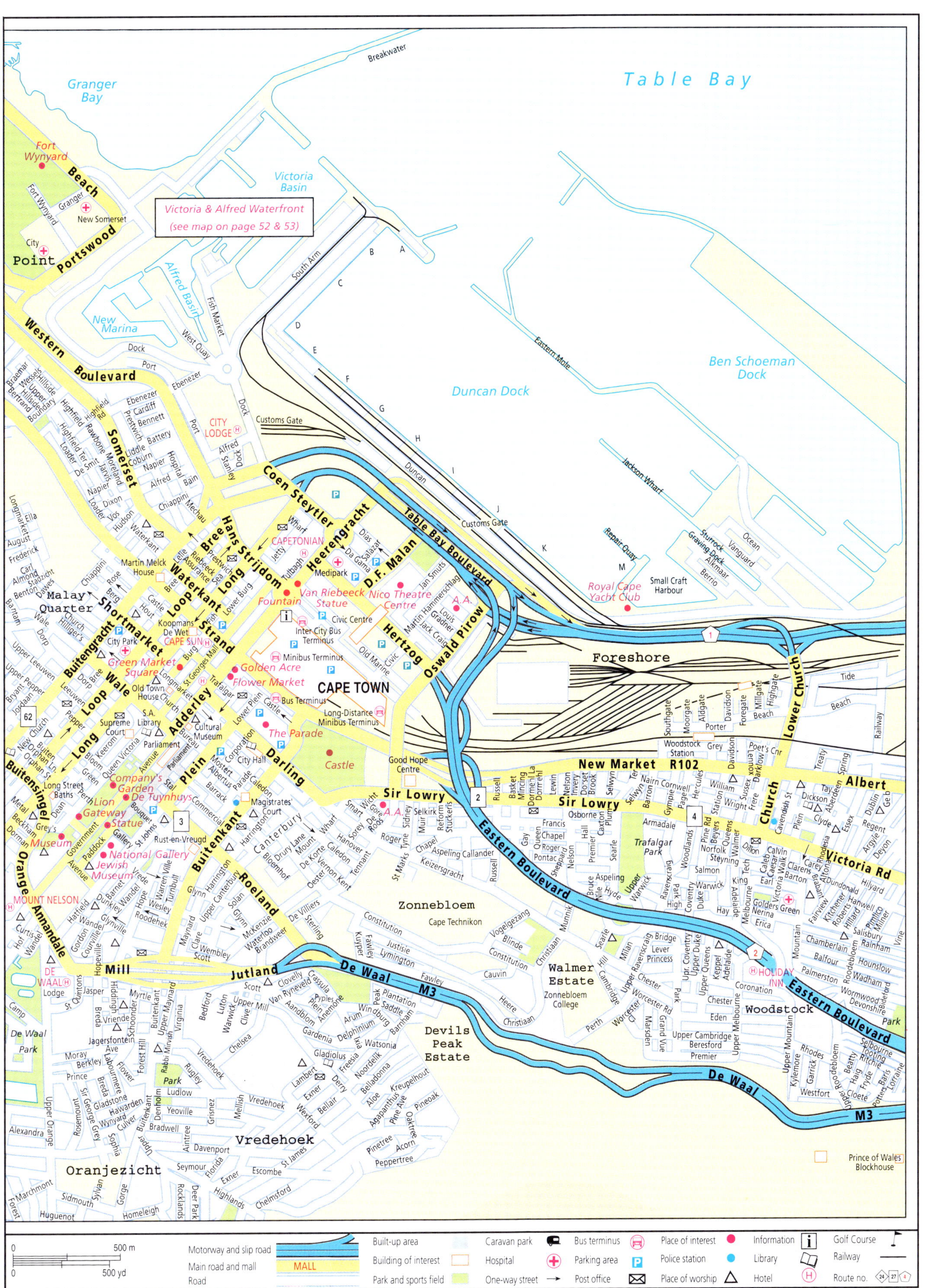
Table Bay
Granger Bay
Breakwater
Fort Wynyard
Beach
Portswood
Point
New Somerset
City
Victoria Basin
Victoria & Alfred Waterfront
(see map on page 52 & 53)
Alfred Basin
New Marina
Fish Market
West Quay
South Arm
Dock
Port
Ebenezer
Western Boulevard
Somerset
CITY LODGE
Customs Gate
Duncan Dock
Eastern Mole
Ben Schoeman Dock
Jackson Wharf
Repair Quay
Sturrock Graving Dock
Vanguard
Ocean
Small Craft Harbour
Royal Cape Yacht Club
Duncan
Coen Steytler
Heerengracht
D.F. Malan
Table Bay Boulevard
Oswald Pirow
Hertzog
Hans Strijdom
Bree
Waterkant
Long
Loop
Strand
Shortmarket
Buitengracht
Wale
Adderley
Plein
Darling
Buitenkant
Roeland
Buitensingel
Orange
Annandale
Mill
Jutland
De Waal
M3
Malay Quarter
Martin Melck House
Koopmans De Wet
CAPETONIAN
CAPE SUN
Medipark
Van Riebeeck Statue
Fountain
Nico Theatre Centre
A.A.
Civic Centre
Inter City Bus Terminus
Minibus Terminus
Golden Acre
Flower Market
Green Market Square
Old Town House
CAPE TOWN
Bus Terminus
Long-Distance Minibus Terminus
S.A. Library
Supreme Court
Cultural Museum
Parliament
The Parade
Castle
City Hall
Good Hope Centre
Company's Garden
De Tuynhuys
Lion Gateway
Statue
Long Street Baths
Magistrates' Court
Rust-en-Vreugd
National Gallery
Jewish Museum
Museum
MOUNT NELSON
DE WAAL Lodge
De Waal Park
Foreshore
Woodstock Station
New Market R102
Sir Lowry
Eastern Boulevard
Lower Church
Albert
Victoria Rd
Trafalgar Park
Zonnebloem
Cape Technikon
Walmer Estate
Zonnebloem College
Devils Peak Estate
Woodstock
HOLIDAY INN
Vredehoek
Oranjezicht
Prince of Wales Blockhouse
0 500 m
0 500 yd
Motorway and slip road
Main road and mall
MALL
Road
Built-up area
Building of interest
Park and sports field
Caravan park
Hospital
One-way street
Bus terminus
Parking area
Post office
Place of interest
Police station
Place of worship
Information
Library
Hotel
Golf Course
Railway
Route no.

Ceres
Western Cape
Victoria & Alfred Waterfront
Paarl
CAPE TOWN
Stellenbosch
Caledon

V & A WATERFRONT

After a long separation, city and harbour are once again happily reunited through the ambitious Victoria and Alfred Waterfront redevelopment scheme, a multibillion-rand private venture that borrowed ideas from the successful harbour projects of New York, Vancouver and Sydney among others, yet retains a sparkling, lively character of its own.

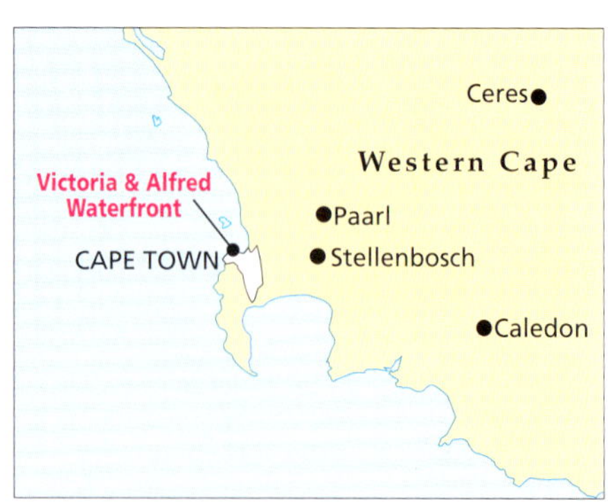

Accommodation

The Table Bay Hotel *****, tel: (021) 406-5000, fax: 406-5686; elegant luxury; modern convenience.
Cape Grace Hotel *****, tel: (021) 410-7100, fax: 419-7622; on the West Quay, spectacular views.
Victoria and Alfred Hotel ****, tel: (021) 419-6677, fax: 419-8955; alongside the Alfred Basin.
Victoria Junction Hotel ****, Ebeneezer Road, Greenpoint, tel: (021) 418-1234, fax: 418-5678; avant-garde; loft-style Art Deco.
City Lodge Waterfront **, tel: (021) 419-9450, fax: 419-0460; convenient location at main entrance to the Waterfront.

MAIN ATTRACTIONS

Two Oceans Aquarium: an imaginative 35 million-rand complex of world-class standard; watch shoals of fish swim through giant aquariums and explore the touch pools.
South African Maritime Museum: on 4000m² (13,123ft²); the largest display of model ships in South Africa. There is also a discovery cove for the children.
SAS *Somerset*: explore this interesting floating exhibit.
Art and Craft Market: filled with an enormous variety of goods that will appeal to both young and old.
Telkom Exploratorium: hands-on look at the wonders of technology.
Imax: Five-storey cinema screen and high-tech surround-sound system at the BMW Pavilion.
The *Victoria*: a floating treasure museum that exhibits artefacts salvaged from ships wrecked along the coast of the Cape of Storms.
The King's Warehouse: sample the fare of the many diverse food stalls and shop at the huge fish market.
The Red Shed: watch artists at work as they create a variety of items, from delicate glass-blown flowers to colourful ethnic oil paintings and wooden toys.
Cape fur seals: a thriving, wild community of these mammals frequents the calm harbour waters. Watch them diving, lazily floating around, or basking in the sun.
Boat trips: a number of boats and smaller vessels are available for harbour and sunset cruises, as well as longer trips to historic **Robben Island**, the former prison enclave whose most famous inmate was President Nelson Mandela.

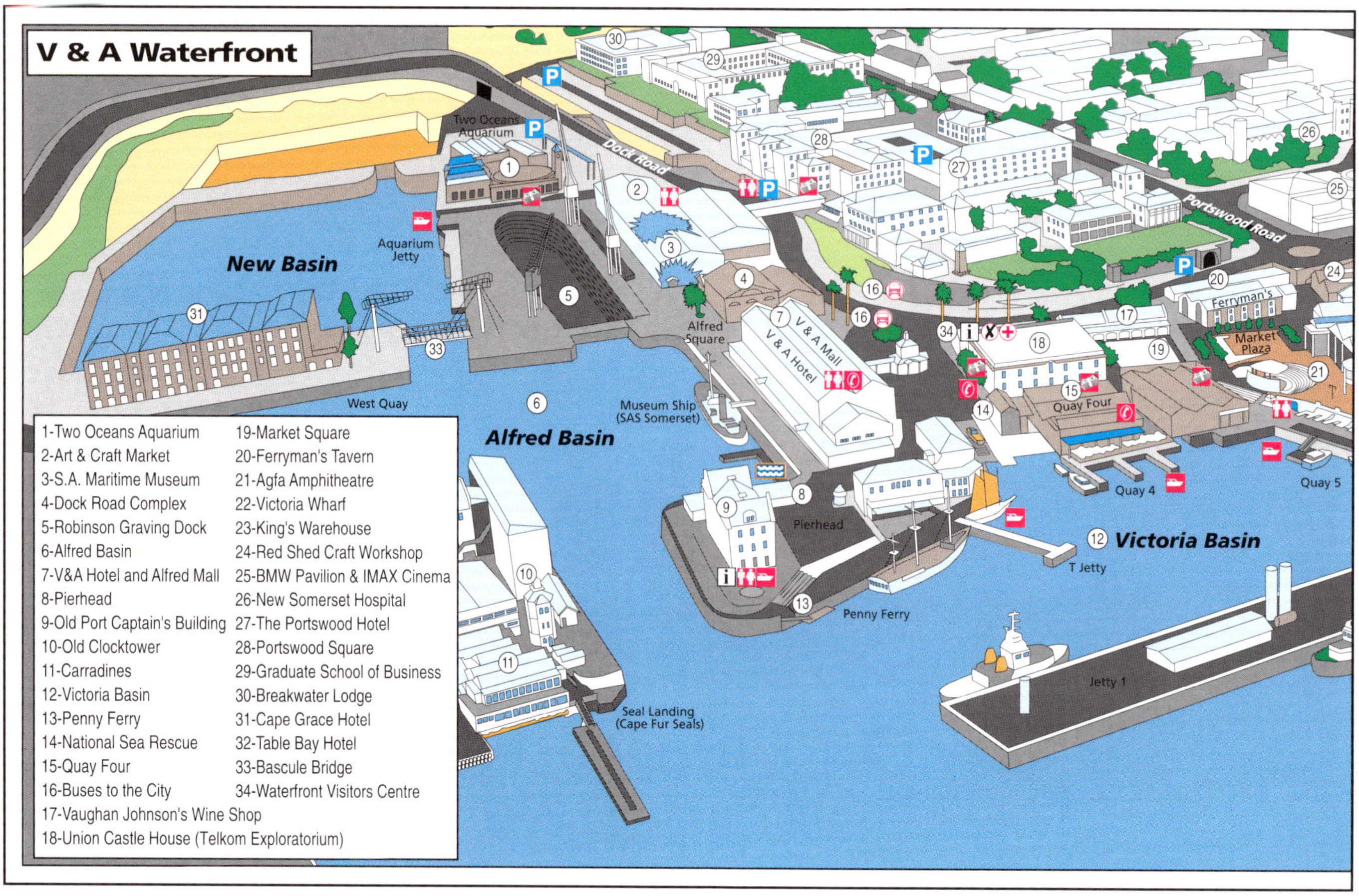

V & A Waterfront
Two Oceans Aquarium
Dock Road
Portswood Road
New Basin
Aquarium Jetty
Alfred Square
V & A Mall
V & A Hotel
West Quay
Museum Ship (SAS Somerset)
Alfred Basin
Ferryman's
Market Plaza
Quay Four
Quay 4
Quay 5
Pierhead
Victoria Basin
T Jetty
Penny Ferry
Jetty 1
Seal Landing (Cape Fur Seals)
1-Two Oceans Aquarium
2-Art & Craft Market
3-S.A. Maritime Museum
4-Dock Road Complex
5-Robinson Graving Dock
6-Alfred Basin
7-V&A Hotel and Alfred Mall
8-Pierhead
9-Old Port Captain's Building
10-Old Clocktower
11-Carradines
12-Victoria Basin
13-Penny Ferry
14-National Sea Rescue
15-Quay Four
16-Buses to the City
17-Vaughan Johnson's Wine Shop
18-Union Castle House (Telkom Exploratorium)
19-Market Square
20-Ferryman's Tavern
21-Agfa Amphitheatre
22-Victoria Wharf
23-King's Warehouse
24-Red Shed Craft Workshop
25-BMW Pavilion & IMAX Cinema
26-New Somerset Hospital
27-The Portswood Hotel
28-Portswood Square
29-Graduate School of Business
30-Breakwater Lodge
31-Cape Grace Hotel
32-Table Bay Hotel
33-Bascule Bridge
34-Waterfront Visitors Centre

Above: *The mood is always festive at the Victoria and Alfred Waterfront which has become one of Cape Town's major drawcards. The universal appeal ensures that its venues bustle with visitors both night and day.*

A DIFFICULT CHOICE

The Hildebrand: elegant, cosy dining.
Morton's on the Wharf: Cajun-Creole.
Sports Café: bistro; lots of sports action.
Den Anker: top-class Belgian cuisine.
Arlindo's: delicious seafood or venison.
Greek Fisherman: Mediterranean taverna.
The Musselcracker: traditional seafood.
Aldo's: superb, regional Italian dishes.

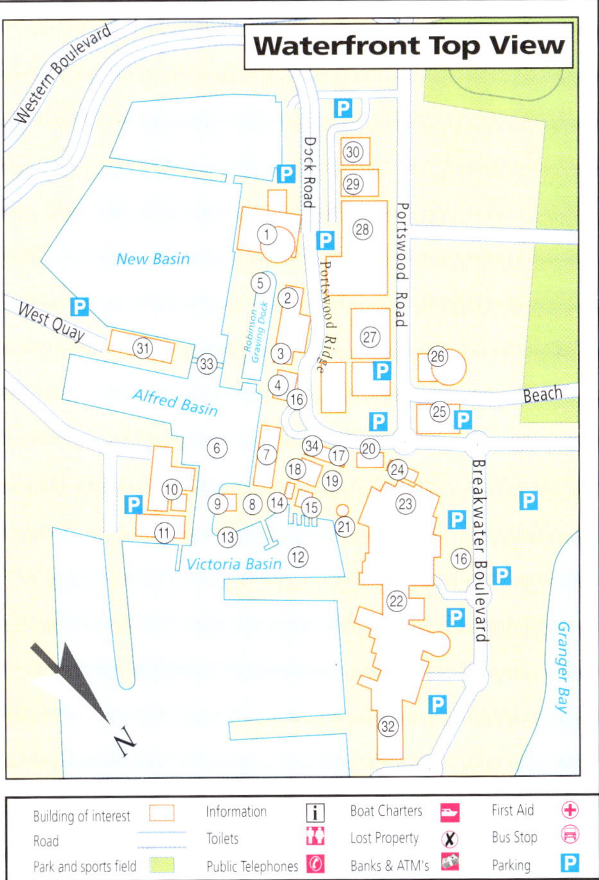

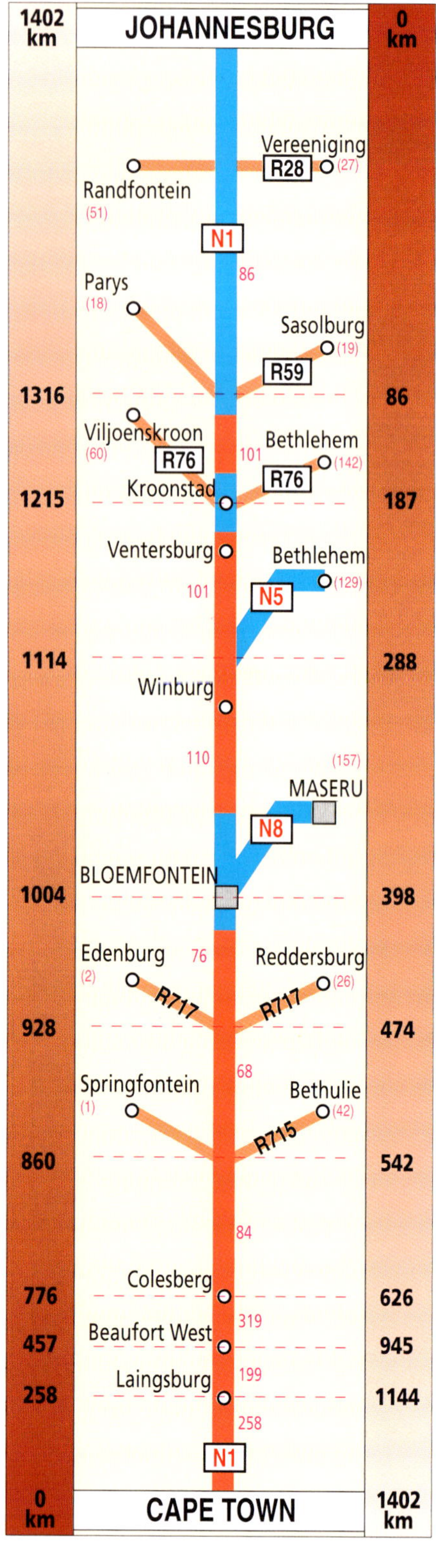

FREE STATE

This semi-arid, mostly flat and treeless central region of South Africa offers the visitor a number of interesting destinations, from game reserves teeming with a variety of wildlife to the ancient, evocative rock paintings along the eastern escarpment. Mine dumps greet your arrival at towns like Welkom, Allanridge and Virginia, all of which sprang up around the latest gold finds, during the years shortly after World War II.

MAIN ATTRACTIONS

Bloemfontein: attractive and vibrant capital of the Free State.
Thaba 'Nchu Sun: lovely hotel and casino complex in the scenic **Maria Moroka National Park** which is a sanctuary for numerous antelope and other wildlife species.
Golden Gate Highlands National Park: scenic wildlife reserve with dramatically sculpted sandstone ridges and cliffs.
The Vaal Dam: 300km² (116-sq-mile) stretch of water, popular with boating enthusiasts and fishermen.
Willem Pretorius Game Reserve: between Winburg and Ventersburg; sustains a variety of wildlife including white rhino, giraffe and buffalo.
Gariep Dam: the country's largest water reservoir; near Bethulie.
Gariep Nature Reserve: located on the vast dam's northern shore; home to a very big population of graceful springbok.

BLOEMFONTEIN	J	F	M	A	M	J	J	A	S	O	N	D
AV. TEMP. °C	23	21	19	15	11	7	7	10	14	17	19	22
AV. TEMP. °F	73	70	66	59	52	45	45	50	57	63	66	72
DAILY SUN hrs	10	9	9	9	9	9	9	9	10	10	10	10
RAINFALL mm	91	99	74	58	21	12	9	14	19	42	59	62
RAINFALL in	4	4	3	2.5	0.8	0.5	0.3	0.6	0.7	2	2.5	2.5

ACCOMMODATION

Thaba 'Nchu Sun *****, tel: (051871) 2161, fax: 2521; hotel and casino complex some 75km (47 miles) east of Bloemfontein.
Welkom Inn ***, Welkom, tel: (057) 357-3361, fax: 352-1458.
Gariep Dam Hotel, Gariep Dam, tel: (052172) ask for 60.
Toristo Hotel, Kroonstad, tel: (0562) 2-5111, fax: 3-3298.

USEFUL CONTACTS

Universitas Hospital, Bloemfontein, tel: (051) 405-3911.
Bloemfontein Publicity, tel: (051) 447-1362.
Tourism Northern Cape, Kimberley, tel: (0531) 3-1434.

DISTANCE IN KM FROM BLOEMFONTEIN	
Aliwal North	207
Bethlehem	239
Cape Town	1004
Kimberley	177
Port Elizabeth	677

TRAVEL TIPS

The Free State's main roads are in good condition, linking this central region with other major South African cities. Please note: distances between towns are vast, so be sure to fill up with petrol regularly.

Below: *This landscape, near Kroonstad, is typical of the Free State. Here, a rain-laden sky dominates the flat terrain punctuated by a solitary windpump.*

BLOEMFONTEIN

Bloemfontein is the judicial capital of South Africa and the principal city of the Free State. The most centrally situated of South Africa's major cities, it lies at the heart of an area of fertile farmland 1392m (4567ft) above sea level and owes much of its prosperity to the Free State goldfields located 160km (100 miles) to the northeast. The city is noted for its impressive old buildings, museums, monuments, memorials and public parks and gardens.

MAIN ATTRACTIONS

Franklin Nature Reserve: on Naval Hill; home to a variety of wildlife.
National Botanical Gardens: pleasant floral sanctuary dominated by impressive dolomite outcrops.
Orchid House: pools, waterfalls and over 3000 exquisite orchids at the foot of Naval Hill.
King's Park: visit Loch Logan, the zoo and the beautiful rose garden.
National Women's Memorial: in memory of the more than 27,000 Boer women and children who died in British concentration camps during the Anglo-Boer War.
The Old Raadsaal: the old town hall, housed in a lovely building.
Sand du Plessis Theatre: modern complex; the splendid works of art contribute to the decor.
Soetdoring Nature Reserve: on the R64 to Kimberley; protective habitat for antelope, as well as lion, cheetah and brown hyena.

ACCOMMODATION

Bloemfontein Hotel ★★★★, East Burger Street, tel: (051) 430-1911, fax: 47-7102; in the city centre.
President Hotel ★★★, tel: (051) 430-1111, fax: 430-4141; at the foot of Naval Hill.
Halevy House Hotel ★★, tel: (051) 448-0271, fax: 430-8749; convenient location in the centre of town, close to the museum.

TRAVEL TIPS

Bloemfontein is on the main north–south highway linking Cape Town and Gauteng. Good tarred roads connect the city with all the surrounding major centres, such as Welkom (R700 and R710); Kimberley (R64); Maseru in Lesotho (R64); and East London on the coast (R30).

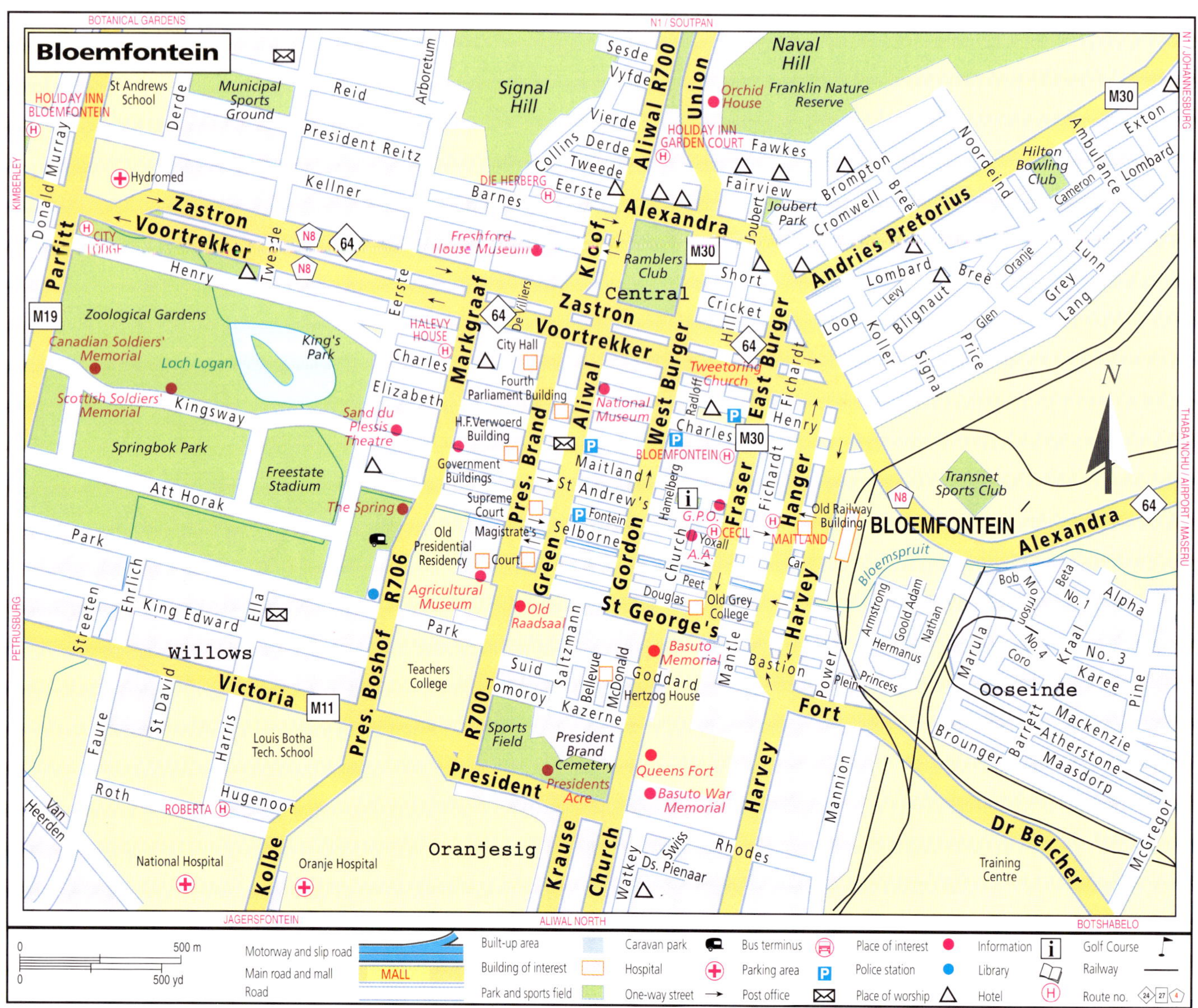

KIMBERLEY

Kimberley, the diamond town of South Africa and capital of the adjacent Northern Cape province, was born in the 1870s when tens of thousands of prospectors poured into the area to unearth the glittering gems that lay in abundance beneath the dusty ground. Kimberley still retains much of the old-world atmosphere of these heady days, when instant fortunes were made (and lost), and money and champagne flowed like water.

ACCOMMODATION

Holiday Inn Garden Court Kimberley ***, tel: (0531) 3-1751, fax: 82-1814; lovely garden setting.
Hotel Kimberlite ***, tel: (0531) 81-1966, fax: 81-1967; within easy walking distance of the Big Hole.
Horseshoe Motel, Memorial Road, tel/fax: (0531) 82 5267/8.

Right: *When diamond fever hit in 1871, no one could have guessed that just 43 years later the dig would have reached a depth of 1097m (3600ft).*

MAIN ATTRACTIONS

The Big Hole: Kimberley's historic hub. By the time it was closed in 1914 it had yielded almost three tons of diamonds.
Kimberley Mine Museum: evocative and comprehensive insight into the town's lively past.
Duggan-Cronin Gallery: an outstanding photographic display of the San-Bushman culture.
William Humphreys Gallery: an excellent collection of South African and European paintings, sculpture and furniture.
The Diggers Fountain: honours the miners who helped to build the Diamond City.
Magersfontein battlefield: call tel: (0531) 3-2645 for directions.

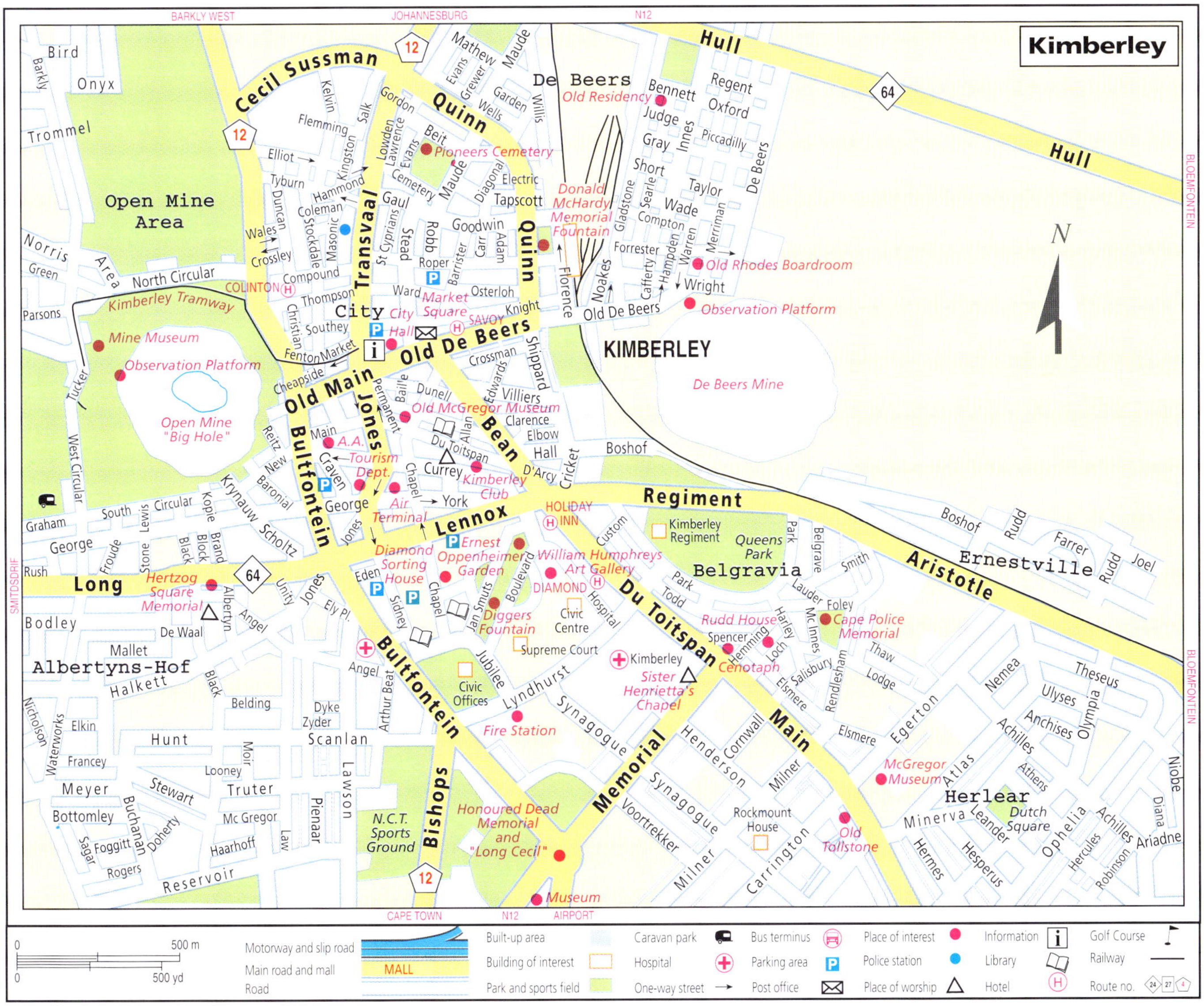

MAIN MAP SECTION KEY AND LEGEND

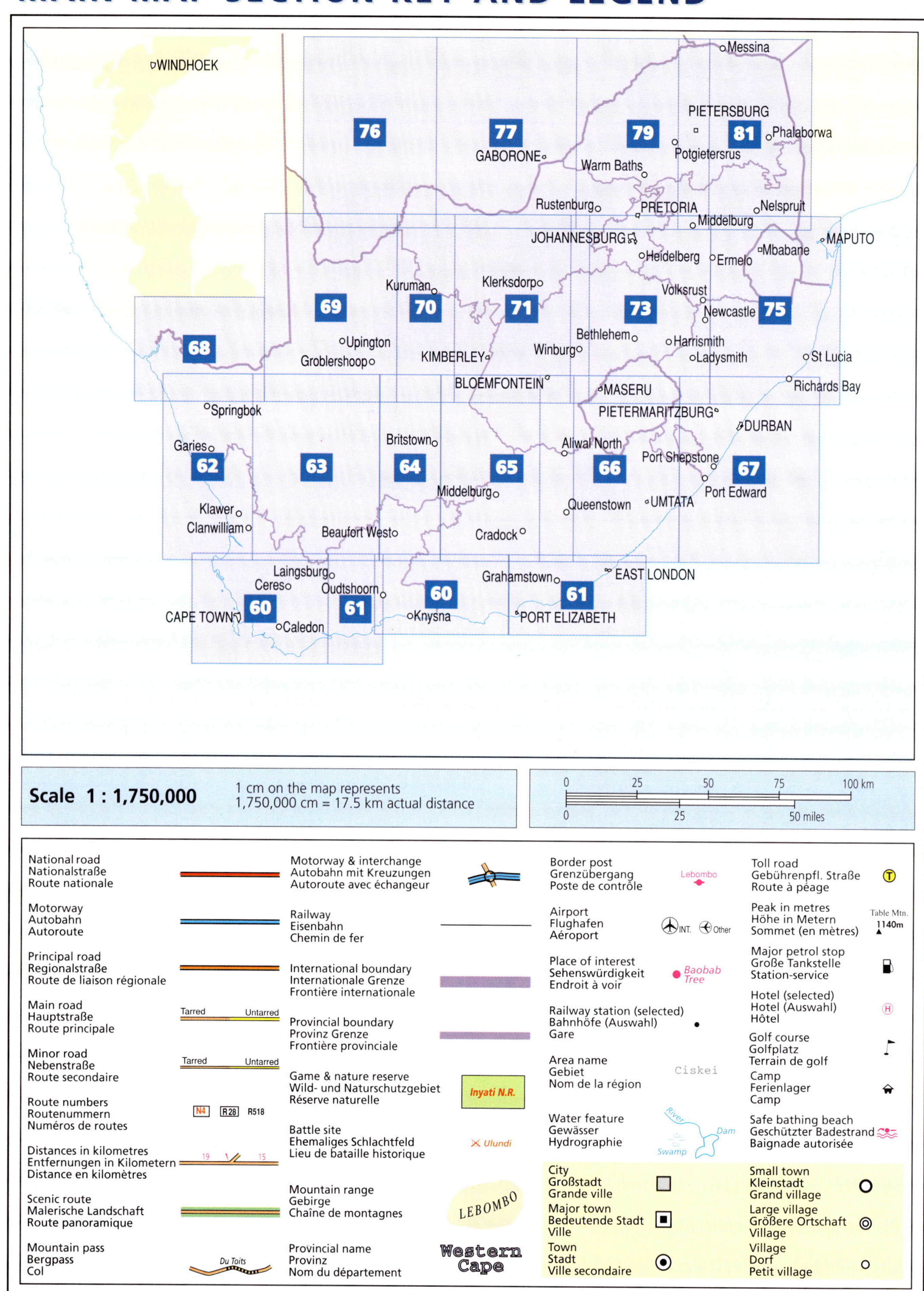

EASTERN AND WESTERN CAPE

Dominated by series after series of soaring mountain ranges, interspersed with rolling wheatfields, orchards and vineyards, the southern part of South Africa is unquestionably one of the country's most beautiful regions. Inland there are forests, deep fertile valleys and spectacular mountain passes to explore, while the rugged, rocky coastline offers the visitor countless venues for safe bathing, surfing, beachcombing and fishing, as well as a number of delightful holiday villages and towns.

MAIN ATTRACTIONS

Wineland towns: wide, tree-lined avenues and beautiful architecture.
Day drives: along the southern coastline; two are particularly recommended: from Cape Town to the little town of Hermanus, haven for southern right whales; and from Cape Town to Langebaan Lagoon on the West Coast, renowned for its birdlife.
The Garden Route: from Mossel Bay to the Storms River, scenically one of the most splendid parts of the South African coastline; visit Knysna and Plettenberg Bay.
Hex River Valley: dramatic sandstone crags dominate the green, beautiful valley, where excellent grapes are cultivated.
The Little Karoo: a beautiful and rugged region lying between the southern coastal rampart and the Swartberg uplands to the north.

EAST LONDON	J	F	M	A	M	J	J	A	S	O	N	D
AV. TEMP. °C	22	22	21	19	18	16	16	16	17	18	19	21
AV. TEMP. °F	72	72	70	66	64	61	61	61	63	64	66	70
DAILY SUN hrs	7	7	7	7	7	7	8	7	7	7	7	8
RAINFALL mm	74	95	106	80	55	40	51	75	93	95	90	74
RAINFALL in	3	4	4.5	3.5	2.5	2	2.5	3	4	4	4	3.5
SEA TEMP. °C	19	19	19	18	18	17	17	17	17	18	18	18
SEA TEMP. °F	66	66	66	64	64	63	63	63	63	64	64	64

TRAVEL TIPS

The N2 national route leads eastward along the southern coastline from Cape Town to East London, and is the best way to see the beautiful South African countryside. The road is wide and in excellent condition and petrol stations are frequent in the towns it traverses.

LANGEBAAN	J	F	M	A	M	J	J	A	S	O	N	D
AV. TEMP. °C	17	17	17	16	15	14	13	13	14	15	16	17
AV. TEMP. °F	63	63	63	61	59	57	55	55	57	59	61	63
DAILY SUN hrs	7	6	7	7	8	8	8	7	6	7	7	7
RAINFALL mm	3	2	6	15	20	21	22	18	11	8	4	5
RAINFALL in	0.1	0	0.2	0.6	0.8	0.8	0.9	0.7	0.4	0.3	0.1	0.2
SEA TEMP. °C	15	14	13	13	12	12	12	13	13	14	14	14
SEA TEMP. °F	59	57	55	55	54	54	54	55	55	57	57	57

Below: *Countless vineyards were established in the fertile soil of the beautiful Hex River Valley.*

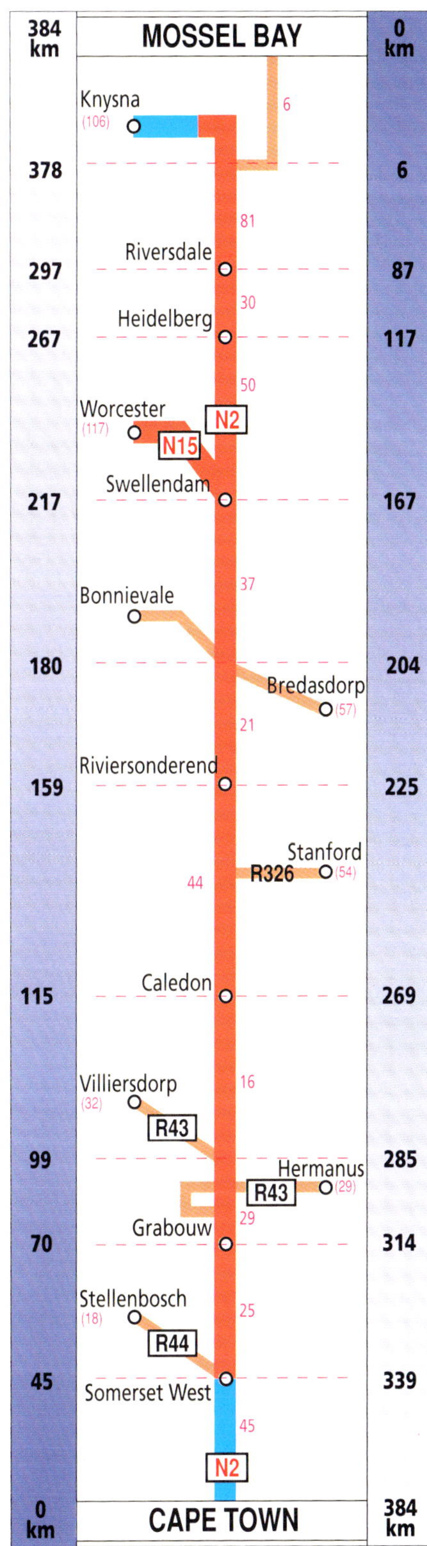

CITRUSDAL 63

A B C D

1 2 3

Stompneusbaai
Paterntoster
Laaiplek
Velddrif
Sauer
Piketberg
Pools
Bokfontein
Swartruggens
Koringplaas
Vredenburg
Bergrivier
Great Berg
De Hoek
Porterville
Western
Saldanha
Hopefield
Koringberg
Gt. Winterhoek Wilderness Area
1666 m
Hillandale
Laingsburg
Saldanha Bay
Langebaan
Moorreesburg
Gydo Pass
Pieter Meintjies
Postberg N.R.
Churchhaven
Historical Buildings
Prince Alfred Hamlet
Hottentotskloof
Die Venster
Matjiesfontein
Rooinek
West Coast National Park
Tienie Versveld Flower Res.
Riebeek-Wes
Gouda
Riebeek Kasteel
Tulbagh
2251 m
Bushman's Cave
Touwsriver
Witberge
1382 m
Yzerfontein
Yzerfonteinpunt
Darling
Malmesbury
Wolseley
Ceres
Verkeerdevlei
Hex River
De Doorns
Tunnel
Matroosberg
Avondrust
Anysberg
Touwsberg
Dassen Island
Mission Station
Abbotsdale
Kalbaskraal
Michells
Hex River Mtns
Mamre
Atlantis
Drostdy
Touws
Plathuis
Bokpunt
Philadelphia
Windmeul
Wellington
Du Toitskloof
Worcester
Rooihoogte
Boerboonfontein
Hot Springs
Melkbosstrand
Bloubergstrand
Paarl
Rawsonville
Brandvlei Dam
Nuy
Burgers
Montagu
Warmwaterberg
Robben Island
Milnerton
Durbanville
Klein Drakenstein
Moordkuil
Kogmanskloof
Lemoenshoek
Table Bay
Bellville
Kraaifontein
Wemmershoek Dam
Doorn
Robertson
Ashton
Barrydale
Lighthouse
Parow
Helshoogte
Pniel
Vrolijkheid N.R.
Bonnievale
Marloth N.R.
Langeberge
Cape Town
Castle
Kuilsriver
Hist. Sq.
Kylemore
Franschhoek
McGregor
Riviersonderendberge
Tradouws
Table Mtn
Llandudno
Stellenbosch
Villiersdorp
Drostdy
Suurbraak
Hout Bay
Faure
Hottentots-Holland N.R.
Genadendal
Swellendam
Heidelberg
Firgrove
Bereaville
Greyton
Stormsvlei
Bontebok National Park
Noordhoek
Kommetjie
Muizenberg
Strand
Somerset West
Theewaterskloof Dam
Lindeshof
Fish Hoek
Grabouw
Elgin
Dwarskloof
Askraal
Scarborough
Simon's Town
Gordon's Bay
Sir Lowry's Pass
Houhoek
Botrivier
Caledon
Rietpoel
Riviersonderend
Protem
Breede
Cape of Good Hope Nature Reserve
False Bay
Kleinmond
Oukraal
Klipdale
N.G. Church
Malgas
Port Beaufort
Ouplaas
Botriviervlei
Shaw's
Barry Church
Witsand
Cape of Good Hope
Cape Point
Pringle Bay
Betty's Bay
Hawston
Akkedisberg
Fairfield
De Hoop N.R.
Infanta
Hermanus
Stanford
Salmonsdam N.R.
Napier
Cape Infanta
Atlantic Ocean
Walker Bay
Papiesvlei
Maritime Museum
Bredasdorp
Skipskop
Gansbaai
Elim
Fishermen's Cottages
Pearly Beach
Viljoenshof
Soetendalsvlei
Waenhuiskrans (Arniston)
Struisbaai
Quoin Point
Hotagterklip
Fishermen's Cottages
Struisbaai
L'Agulhas
Cape Agulhas

50 km
25 miles

National road & motorway	N4
Main road [tarred & untarred]	R28
Minor road [tarred & untarred]	R318
Distances in kilometres	19

N1 / BEAUFORT WEST 65 BEAUFORT WEST

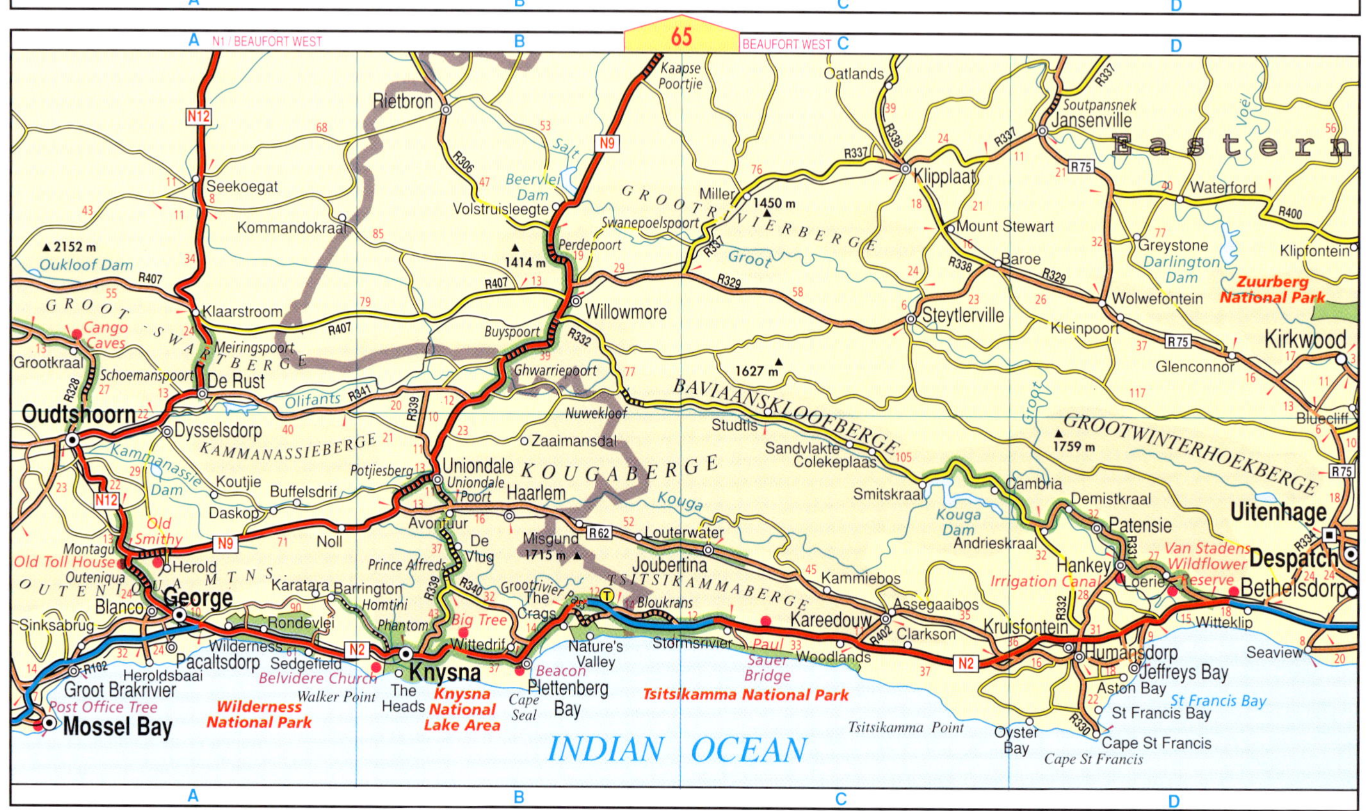

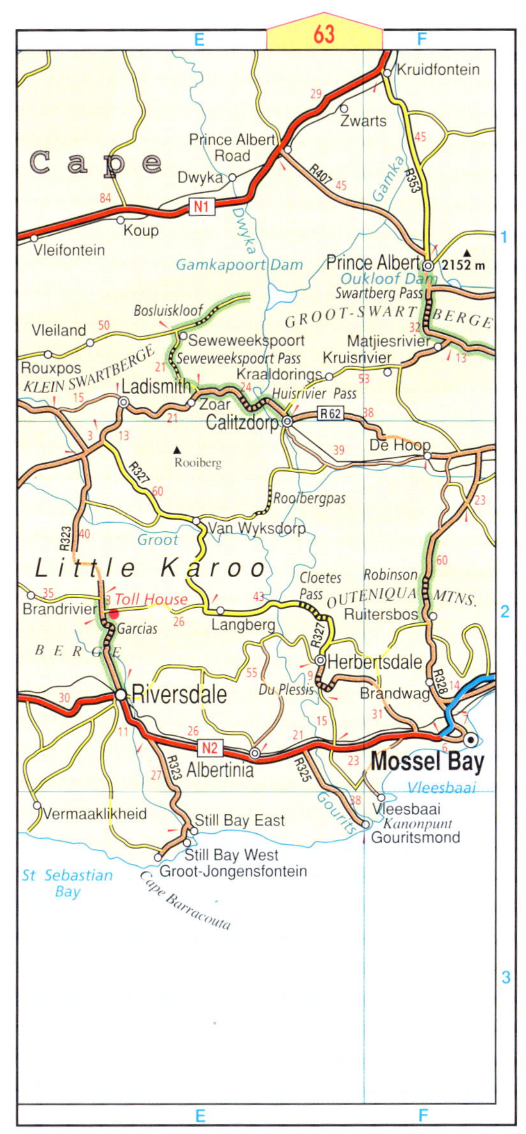

Above: *The scenic splendour of Knysna Lagoon ensured the resort town's popularity and the lagoon is lined with many attractive homes and holiday retreats in garden settings.*

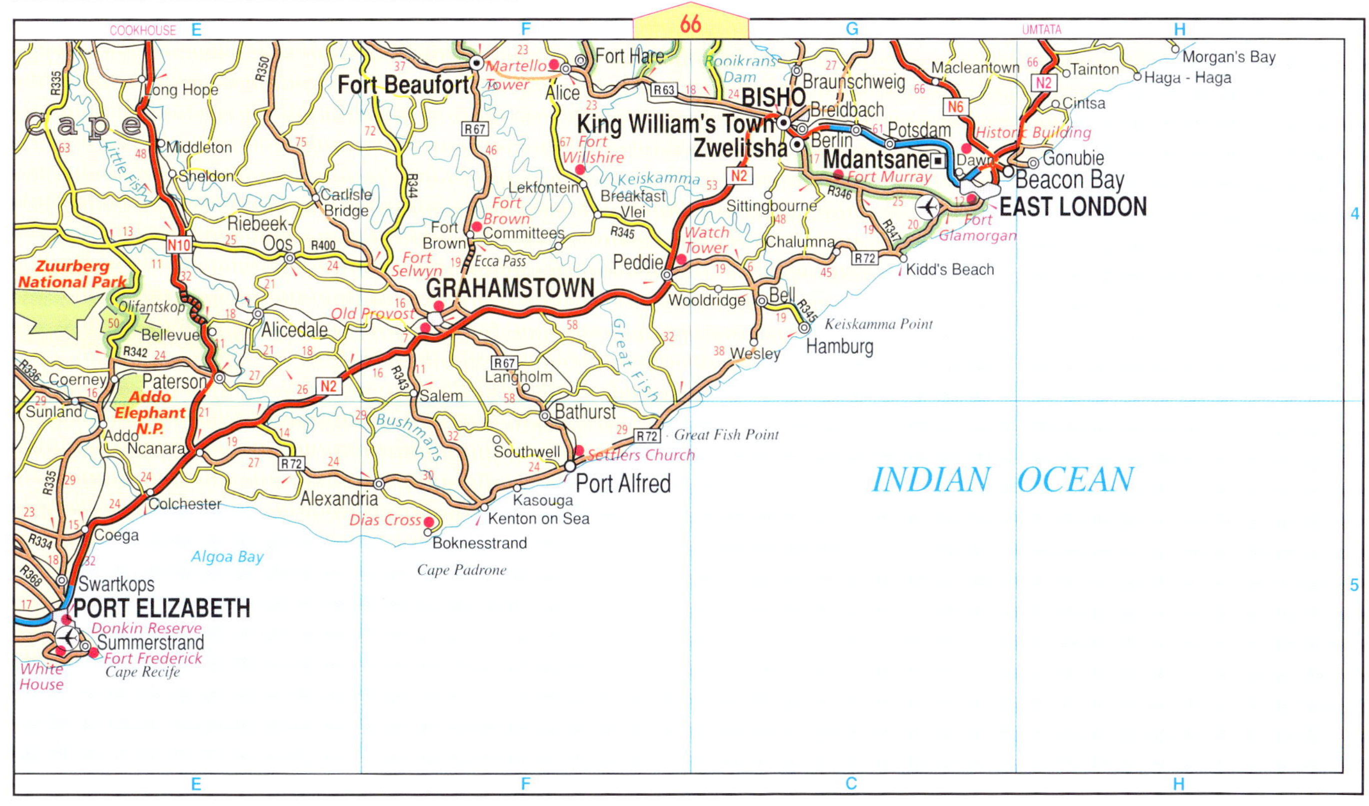

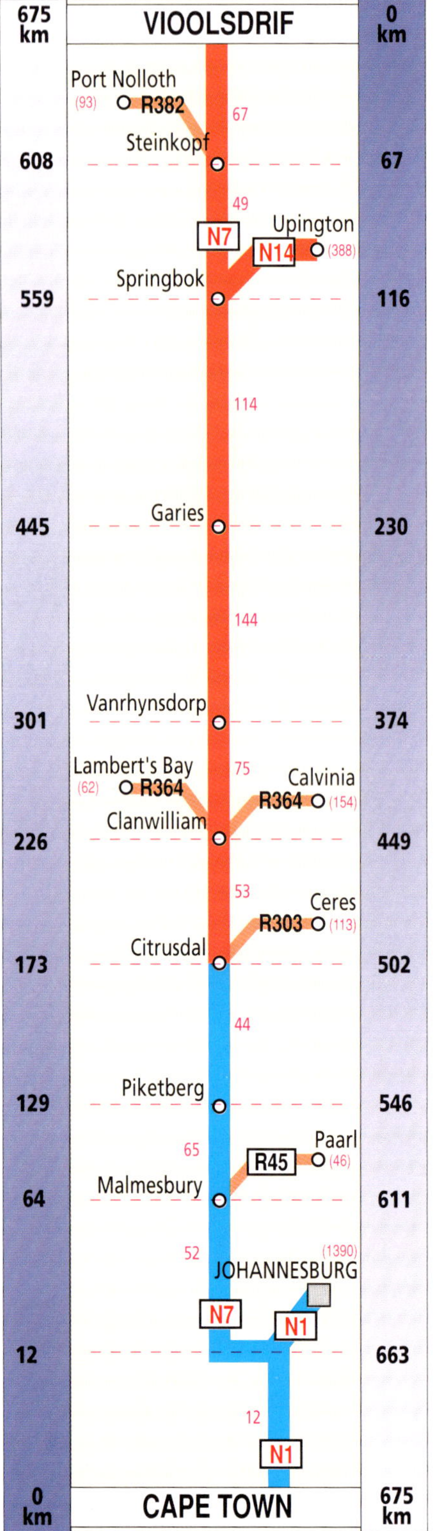

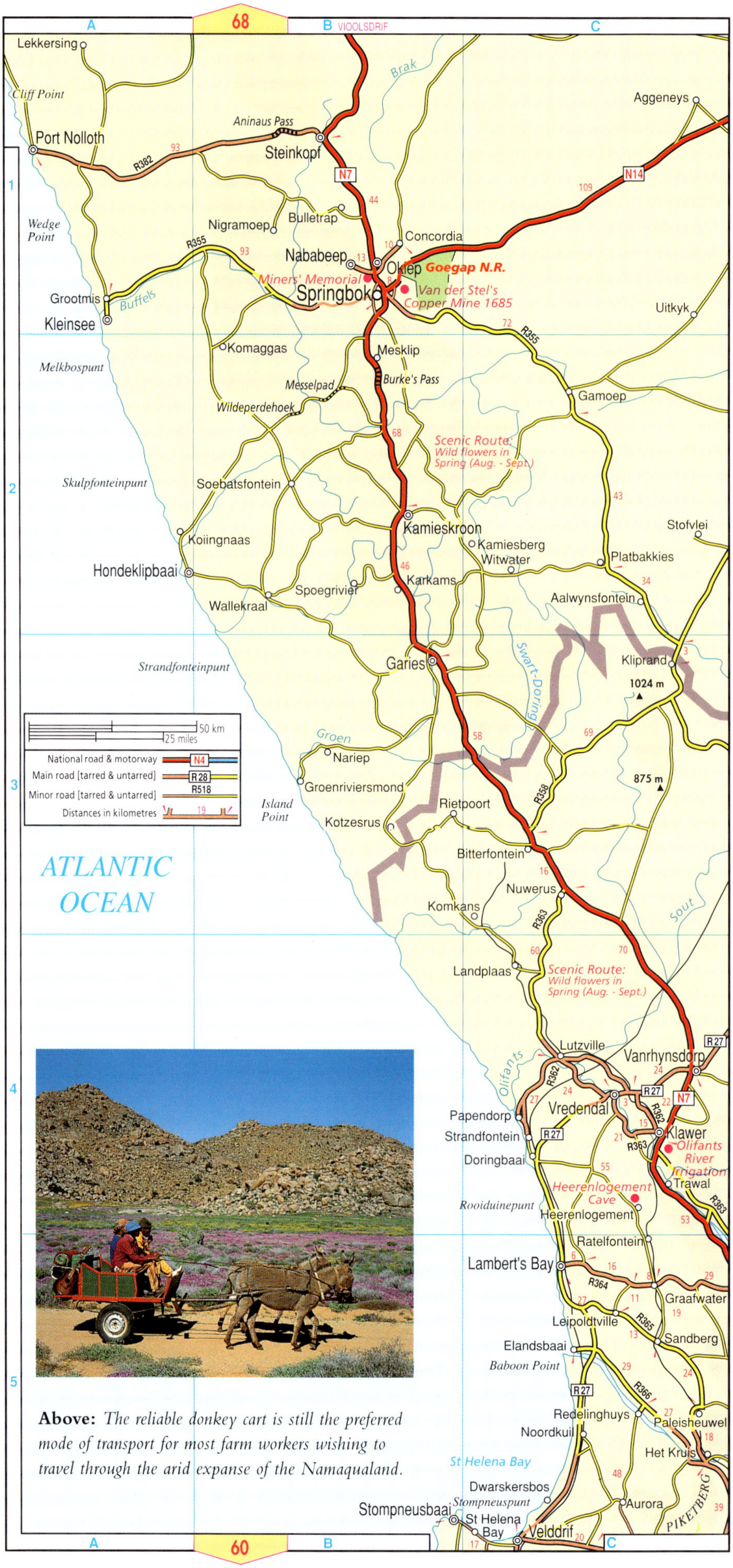

68

A B VIOOLSDRIF C

Lekkersing, Cliff Point, Port Nolloth, Aninaus Pass, Steinkopf, Aggeneys, Wedge Point, Nigramoep, Bulletrap, Concordia, Nababeep, Okiep, Goegap N.R., Miners' Memorial, Springbok, Van der Stel's Copper Mine 1685, Grootmis, Kleinsee, Buffels, Komaggas, Mesklip, Uitkyk, Melkbospunt, Messelpad, Burke's Pass, Gamoep, Wildeperdehoek, Scenic Route: Wild flowers in Spring (Aug. - Sept.), Skulpfonteinpunt, Soebatsfontein, Kamieskroon, Stofvlei, Koiingnaas, Kamiesberg, Witwater, Platbakkies, Hondeklipbaai, Karkams, Spoegrivier, Wallekraal, Aalwynsfontein, Strandfonteinpunt, Garies, Kliprand, 1024 m, Swart-Doring, Groen, Nariep, 875 m, Groenriviersmond, Island Point, Kotzesrus, Rietpoort, Bitterfontein, Nuwerus, Komkans, Sout, Landplaas, Scenic Route: Wild flowers in Spring (Aug. - Sept.), Lutzville, Vanrhynsdorp, Olifants, Vredendal, Papendorp, Strandfontein, Klawer, Olifants River Irrigation, Doringbaai, Trawal, Heerenlogement Cave, Rooiduinepunt, Heerenlogement, Ratelfontein, Lambert's Bay, Graafwater, Leipoldtville, Sandberg, Elandsbaai, Baboon Point, Redelinghuys, Paleisheuwel, Noordkuil, Het Kruis, St Helena Bay, Dwarskersbos, Aurora, Stompneuspunt, Stompneusbaai, St Helena Bay, Velddrif, Piketberg, Brak

ATLANTIC OCEAN

50 km
25 miles
National road & motorway N4
Main road [tarred & untarred] R28
Minor road [tarred & untarred] R518
Distances in kilometres 19

A B C

60

Above: *The reliable donkey cart is still the preferred mode of transport for most farm workers wishing to travel through the arid expanse of the Namaqualand.*

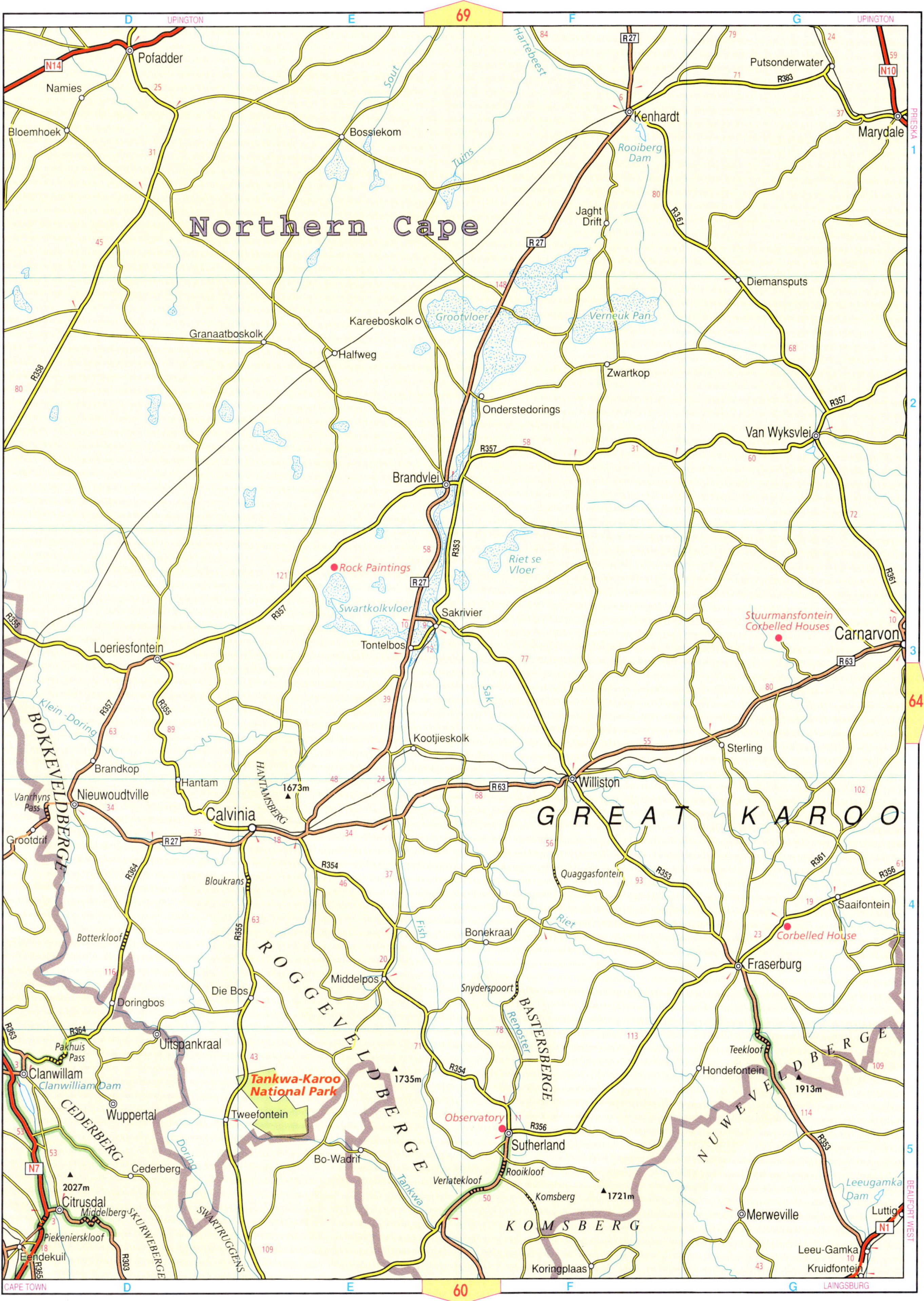

Northern Cape
GREAT KAROO
Pofadder
Namies
Bloemhoek
Bossiekom
Kenhardt
Putsonderwater
Marydale
Rooiberg Dam
Jaght Drift
Diemansputs
Kareeboskolk
Grootvloer
Verneuk Pan
Granaatboskolk
Halfweg
Zwartkop
Onderstedorings
Van Wyksvlei
Brandvlei
Rock Paintings
Riet se Vloer
Swartkolkvloer
Sakrivier
Tontelbos
Loeriesfontein
Stuurmansfontein Corbelled Houses
Carnarvon
Kootjieskolk
Sterling
Brandkop
Hantam
Williston
Nieuwoudtville
Vanrhyns Pass
Grootdrif
Calvinia
Hantamsberg
1673m
Bokkeveldberge
Klein-Doring
Bloukrans
Quaggasfontein
Saaifontein
Corbelled House
Botterkloof
Bonekraal
Roggeveldberge
Fraserburg
Middelpos
Snyderspoort
Die Bos
Doringbos
Basterberge
Renoster
Uitspankraal
Pakhuis Pass
Teekloof
Clanwilliam
Clanwilliam Dam
Hondefontein
1913m
1735m
Tankwa-Karoo National Park
Wuppertal
Tweefontein
Observatory
Sutherland
Nuweveldberge
Cederberg
Bo-Wadrif
Verlatekloof
Rooikloof
2027m
Citrusdal
Middelberg
Piekenierskloof
Eendekuil
Skurweberge
Swartruggens
Komsberg
1721m
KOMSBERG
Merweville
Leeugamka Dam
Lutti
Leeu-Gamka
Kruidfontein
Koringplaas
Doring
Tankwa
Sout
Hartebeest
Tuins
Sak
Fish
Riet
UPINGTON
PRIESKA
BEAUFORT WEST
CAPE TOWN
LAINGSBURG
69
64
60

GREAT KAROO

This hauntingly beautiful, semi-arid region of bone-dry air, minimal rainfall and intense sunshine dominates the Cape interior. The landscape consists of largely featureless countryside stretching endlessly to the distant horizons, lonely windmills, a few isolated farmsteads, and flocks of sheep sustained by underground water.

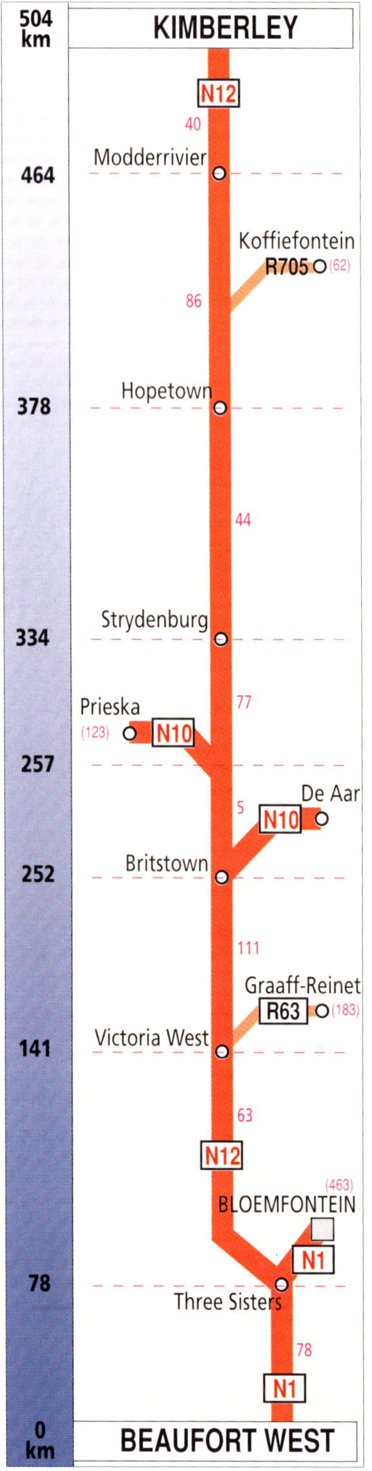

MAIN ATTRACTIONS

Beaufort West: birthplace of the famed heart surgeon Chris Barnard, this little town is also noted for its lovely, pear-tree-lined streets.
Karoo National Park: north of Beaufort West; wildlife includes Cape mountain zebra, shy leopard and a variety of antelope.
Graaff-Reinet: third-oldest town in the Cape, with some fine old architecture.
Valley of Desolation: near Graaff-Reinet; a fantasia of wind-eroded, strangely shaped dolerite peaks, pillars and balancing rocks.
Nieu-Bethesda: tiny hamlet, 50km (31 miles) north of Graaff-Reinet; home to the Owl House museum's bizarre sculptures, many of which are decorated with ground glass.
Cradock: in the vicinity are the Mountain Zebra National Park and well-known author Olive Schreiner's grave.
Aliwal North: this pleasant town to the far east of the Great Karoo has hot sulphur springs and an excellent spa.

TRAVEL TIPS

The main highways that traverse the vast Karoo region, and those servicing the northern and north-western Cape are generally in good condition. Note: be sure to stop for petrol and refreshments in good time, as the towns (and the service stations) tend to lie rather far apart in this area.

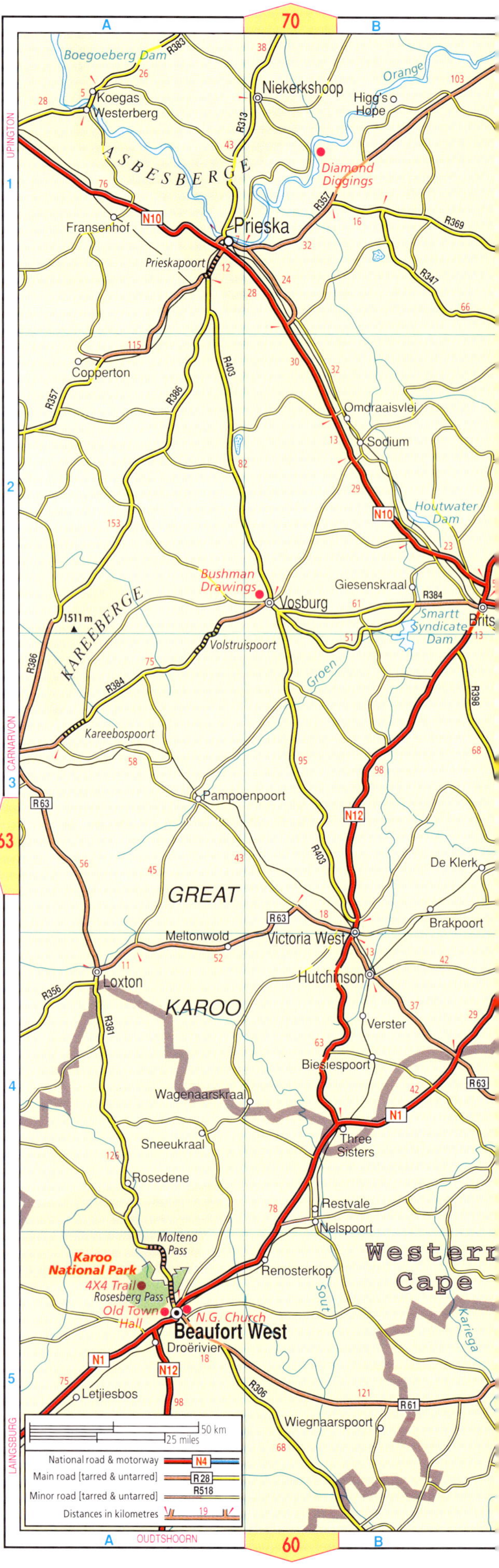

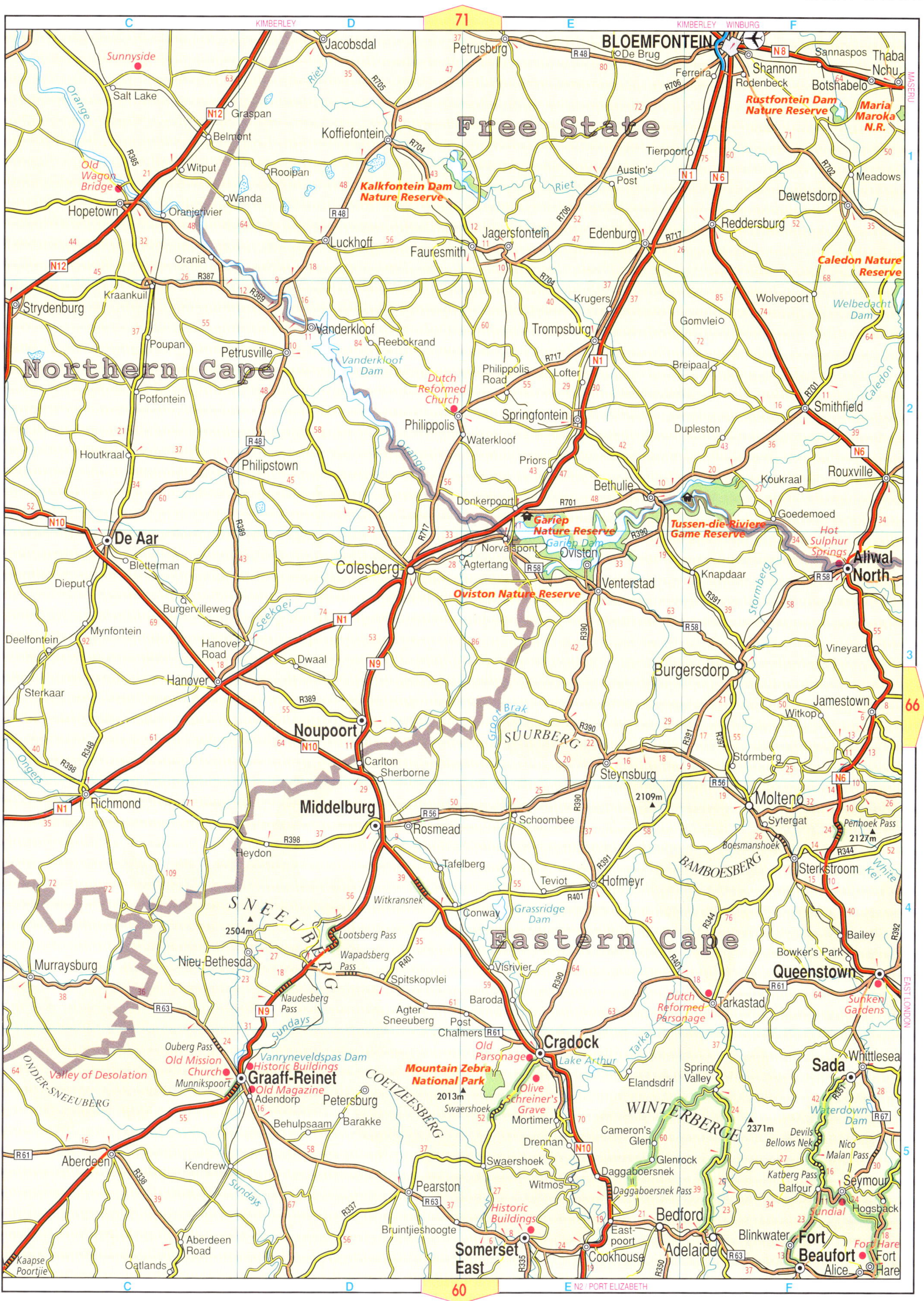

71
66
60
KIMBERLEY
KIMBERLEY WINBURG
MASERU
EAST LONDON
N2 / PORT ELIZABETH
Free State
Northern Cape
Eastern Cape
BLOEMFONTEIN
Jacobsdal
Petrusburg
De Brug
Sannaspos
Thaba Nchu
Shannon
Ferreira
Rodenbeck
Botshabelo
Rustfontein Dam Nature Reserve
Maria Maroka N.R.
Sunnyside
Salt Lake
Graspan
Belmont
Koffiefontein
Tierpoort
Austin's Post
Meadows
Witput
Rooipan
Old Wagon Bridge
Wanda
Kalkfontein Dam Nature Reserve
Dewetsdorp
Hopetown
Oranjerivier
Reddersburg
Jagersfontein
Edenburg
Luckhoff
Fauresmith
Orania
Caledon Nature Reserve
Strydenburg
Kraankuil
Krugers
Wolvepoort
Welbedacht Dam
Vanderkloof
Reebokrand
Gomvlei
Trompsburg
Poupan
Petrusville
Vanderkloof Dam
Philippolis Road
Lofter
Breipaal
Potfontein
Dutch Reformed Church
Springfontein
Smithfield
Philippolis
Waterkloof
Dupleston
Houtkraal
Philipstown
Priors
Rouxville
Bethulie
Koukraal
Donkerpoort
Goedemoed
Gariep Nature Reserve
Tussen-die-Riviere Game Reserve
De Aar
Gariep Dam
Norvalspont
Oviston
Hot Sulphur Springs
Aliwal North
Bletterman
Colesberg
Agtertang
Knapdaar
Dieput
Venterstad
Oviston Nature Reserve
Burgervilleweg
Deelfontein
Mynfontein
Hanover Road
Dwaal
Vineyard
Burgersdorp
Sterkaar
Hanover
Jamestown
Witkop
Noupoort
SUURBERG
Stormberg
Carlton
Sherborne
Steynsburg
2109m
Richmond
Middelburg
Molteno
Schoombee
Rosmead
Sytergat
Penhoek Pass
2127m
Heydon
Boesmanshoek
BAMBOESBERG
Tafelberg
Sterkstroom
Teviot
Hofmeyr
Witkransnek
Conway
Grassridge Dam
SNEEUBERG
2504m
Lootsberg Pass
Wapadsberg Pass
Bailey
Bowker's Park
Murraysburg
Nieu-Bethesda
Vlakrivier
Spitskopvlei
Queenstown
Baroda
Naudesberg Pass
Agter Sneeuberg
Post Chalmers
Dutch Reformed Parsonage
Tarkastad
Sunken Gardens
Cradock
Oubergs Pass
Old Mission Church
Vanryneveldspas Dam
Historic Buildings
Old Parsonage
Lake Arthur
Valley of Desolation
Munnikspoort
Graaff-Reinet
Old Magazine
Adendorp
Mountain Zebra National Park
Olive Schreiner's Grave
Elandsdrif
Spring Valley
Sada
Whittlesea
ONDER-SNEEUBERG
COETZEESBERG
2013m
Swaershoek
Petersburg
Barakke
Mortimer
WINTERBERGE
2371m
Waterdown Dam
Behulpsaam
Cameron's Glen
Devils Bellows Nek
Nico Malan Pass
Aberdeen
Drennan
Glenrock
Kendrew
Swaershoek
Daggaboersnek
Daggaboersnek Pass
Katberg Pass
Balfour
Seymour
Pearston
Witmos
Historic Buildings
Bedford
Sundial
Hogsback
Bruintjieshoogte
East-poort
Blinkwater
Fort Beaufort
Fort Hare
Aberdeen Road
Somerset East
Cookhouse
Adelaide
Alice
Fort Hare
Kaapse Poortjie
Oatlands
Orange
Riet
Seekoei
Ongers
Sundays
Groot Brak
Tarka
Stormberg
Caledon
White Kei
N1
N6
N8
N9
N10
N12
R48
R56
R58
R61
R63

73
BLOEM-FONTEIN
MASERU
LESOTHO
Free State
Eastern Cape
Aliwal North
Queenstown
UMTATA
Ladybrand
Mohales Hoek
Qacha's Nek
Burgersdorp
Molteno
Sterkstroom
Dordrecht
Elliot
Maclear
Ugie
Mount Frere
Butterworth
Idutywa
Stutterheim
Kei Road
Fort Beaufort
Adelaide
Bedford
Cathcart
Komga
Wild
65
61

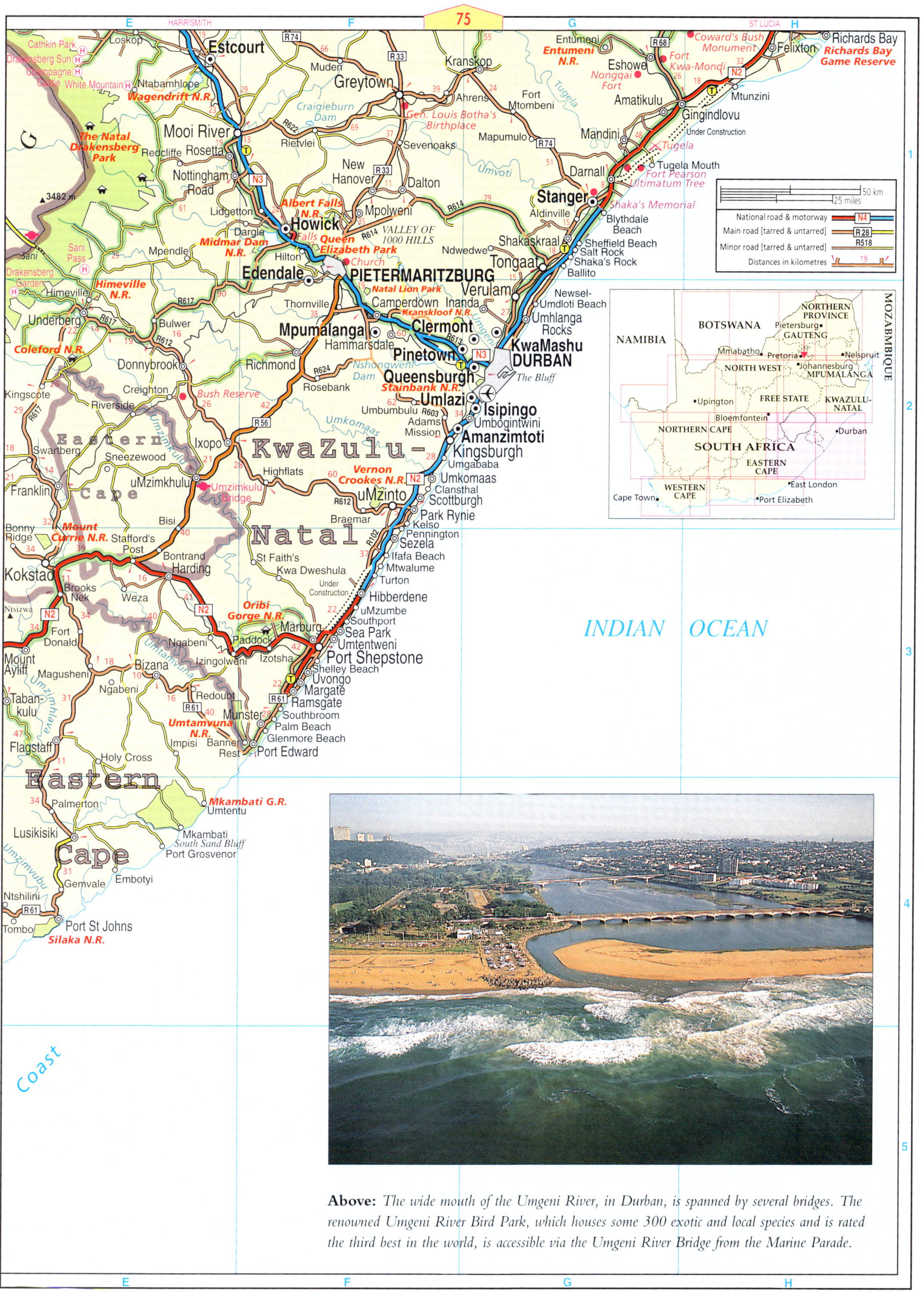

Above: *The wide mouth of the Umgeni River, in Durban, is spanned by several bridges. The renowned Umgeni River Bird Park, which houses some 300 exotic and local species and is rated the third best in the world, is accessible via the Umgeni River Bridge from the Marine Parade.*

MAIN MAP SECTION

NORTHERN CAPE

This is a dry, rather forbidding moonscape of low mountains and strange plants like the kokerboom. After the rainy season, however, the arid veld is transformed into a riot of colour as wildflowers bloom in abundance. Towns are few and small, with the exception of Upington, which is beautifully situated along the banks of the Orange River.

DISTANCE IN KM FROM UPINGTON	
Bloemfontein	588
Cape Town	894
Kimberley	411
Windhoek (Namibia)	1005

TRAVEL TIPS

Remember: towns (and service stations) are set rather far apart. Beware of wild animals crossing the road, especially at dawn, dusk and through the night.

MAIN ATTRACTIONS

Upington: visit one of the dried fruit co-ops around the town.
Augrabies Falls National Park: marvel at the lovely waterfall (one of the five biggest in the world) in this otherwise harsh area, and take a drive through the reserve to spot the bird- and wildlife.
Kalahari Gemsbok National Park: located on the Botswana border, 280km (108 miles) north of Upington. Red sand dunes, oryx (gemsbok), shy Kalahari lion, an abundance of raptor species, and magnificent sunsets attract nature lovers to this unique desert park.
Goegap Nature Reserve: east of Springbok; spot eland, springbok and mountain zebra along hiking trails and game drives.
Richtersveld National Park: in the far northwestern corner of the province; excellent game-viewing.
Vioolsdrif/Noordoewer: South Africa/Namibia border post, for travellers heading to Namibia.

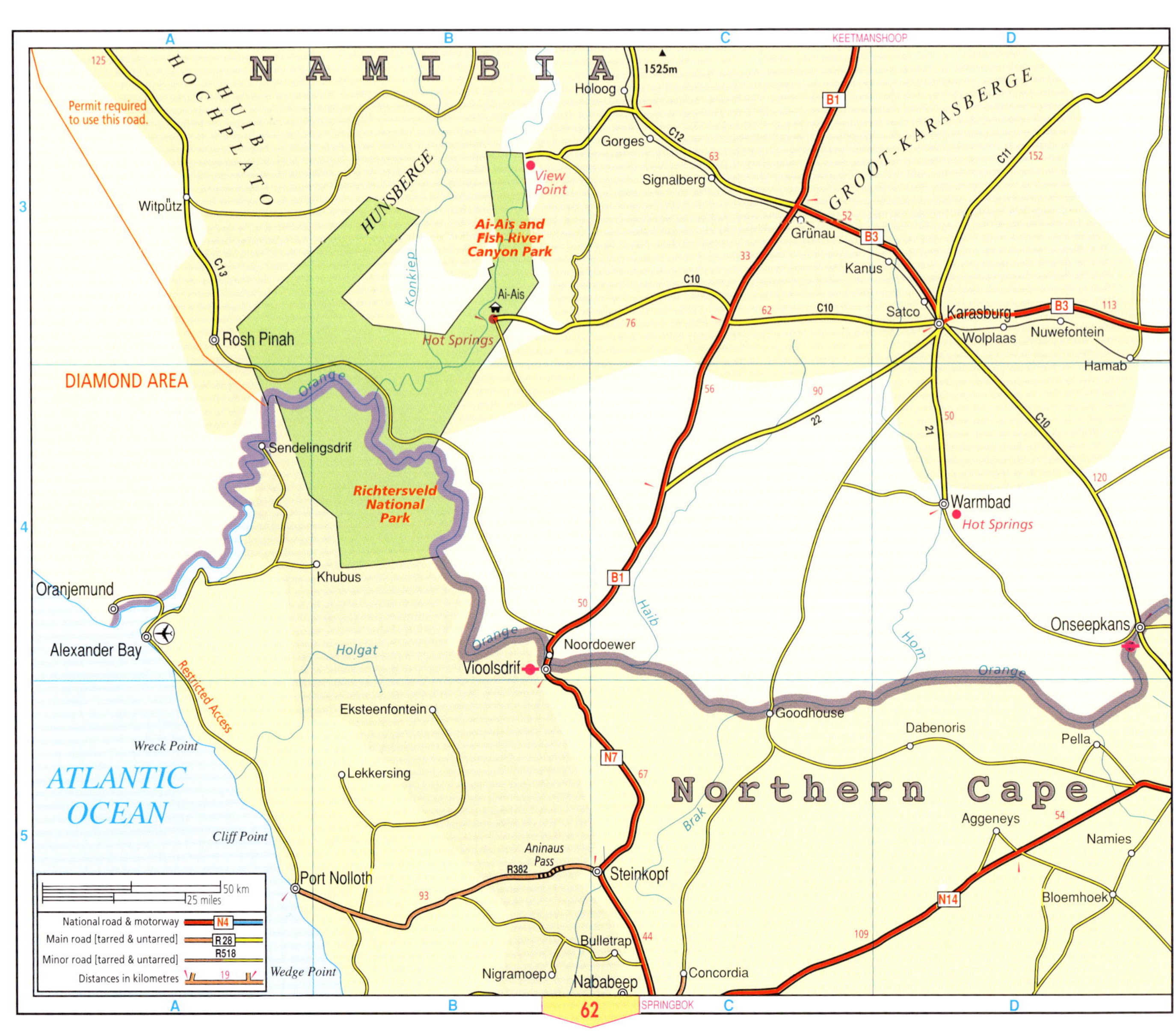

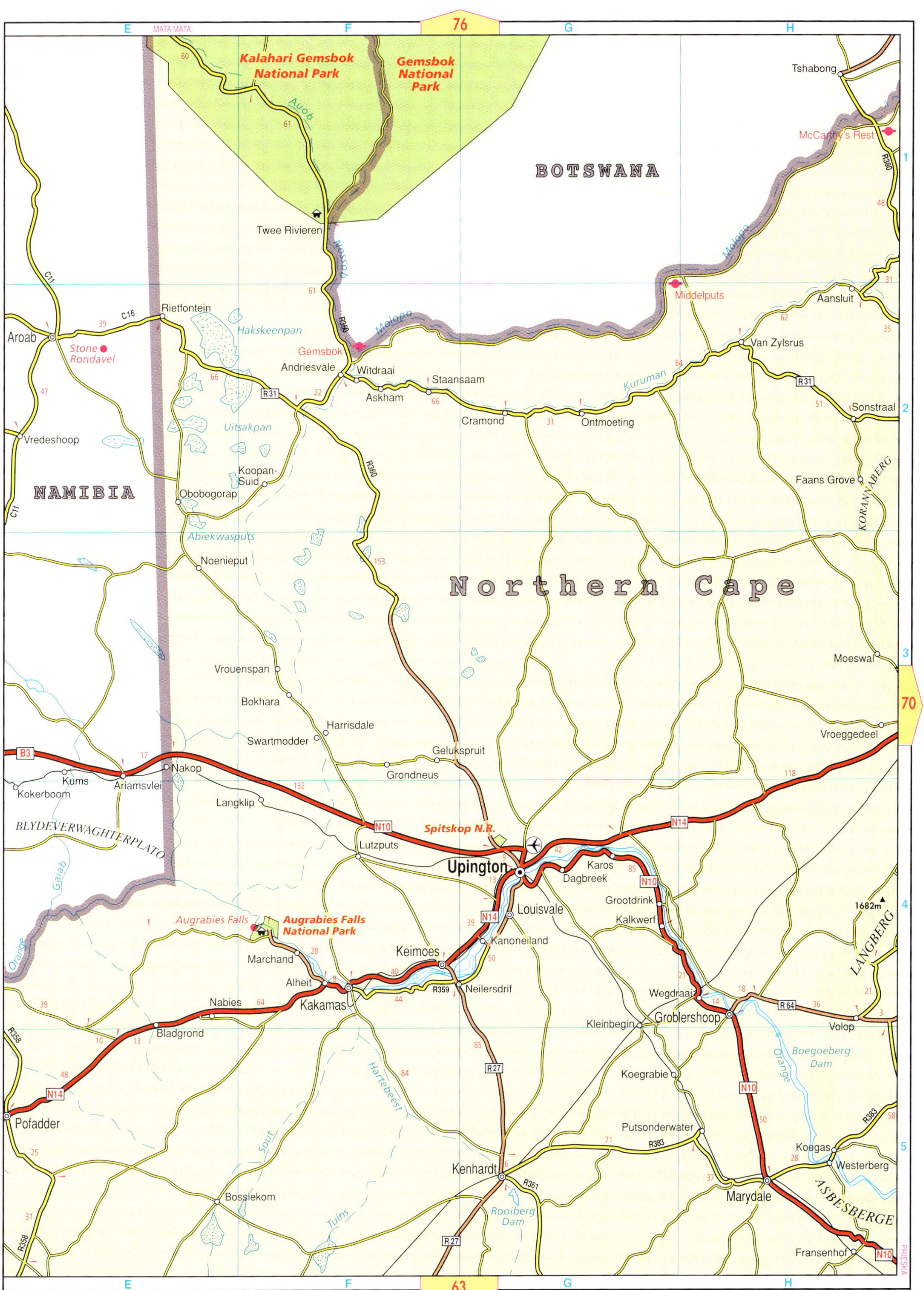
Kalahari Gemsbok National Park
Gemsbok National Park
BOTSWANA
NAMIBIA
Northern Cape
Tshabong
McCarthy's Rest
Twee Rivieren
Middelputs
Aansluit
Rietfontein
Aroab
Stone Rondavel
Hakskeenpan
Gemsbok
Andriesvale
Witdraai
Staansaam
Askham
Van Zylsrus
Kuruman
Molopo
Nossob
Auob
Cramond
Ontmoeting
Sonstraal
Vredeshoop
Uitsakpan
Koopan-Suid
Obobogorap
Abiekwasputs
Faans Grove
KORANNABERG
Noenieput
Moeswal
Vrouenspan
Bokhara
Harrisdale
Swartmodder
Gelukspruit
Vroeggedeel
Kums
Kokerboom
Ariamsvlei
Nakop
Grondneus
Langklip
BLYDEVERWAGHTERPLATO
Spitskop N.R.
Lutzputs
Upington
Karos
Dagbreek
Grootdrink
Louisvale
Kalkwerf
Augrabies Falls
Augrabies Falls National Park
Kanoneiland
1682m
LANGBERG
Marchand
Keimoes
Alheit
Neilersdrif
Nabies
Kakamas
Wegdraai
Groblershoop
Kleinbegin
Volop
Bladgrond
Boegoeberg Dam
Hartebeest
Koegrabie
Pofadder
Putsonderwater
Koegas
Westerberg
Kenhardt
Marydale
ASBESBERGE
Sout
Bossiekom
Rooiberg Dam
Tuins
Fransenhof
Gaiab
Orange
MATA MATA
PRIESKA
N10
N14
R31
R360
R380
R64
R27
R359
R361
R383
R358
B3
C11
C16
76
70
63

KIMBERLEY AND BLOEMFONTEIN

km		km
576 km	MASERU	0 km
557	19	19
	Ladybrand (16) — 74	
483	Thaba 'Nchu — N8	93
	JOHANNESBURG (398) — 64 — N1	
419	BLOEMFONTEIN	157
	N1 — CAPE TOWN (1004) — 177	
	R64 — Klerksdorp — N12 (308)	
242	KIMBERLEY	334
	N12 — Britstown (253) — 32	
210	Barkly West	366
	113 — R31	
	Postmasburg (49) — R385	
97		479
	97 — R31	
0 km	KURUMAN	576 km

These neighbouring towns, the capitals of the Northern Cape and Free State provinces respectively, are situated on the high interior plateau. Both towns offer many interesting museums and lovely sandstone buildings of historical interest and are surrounded by nature reserves and dams.

Above: *The statue of Christiaan Rudolph De Wet stands in front of the classic sandstone structure of the Fourth Raadsaal, the last government seat of the old Republic.* ***Below:*** *The Kimberley Diamond Mine Museum portrays life on the diamond fields 100 years ago.*

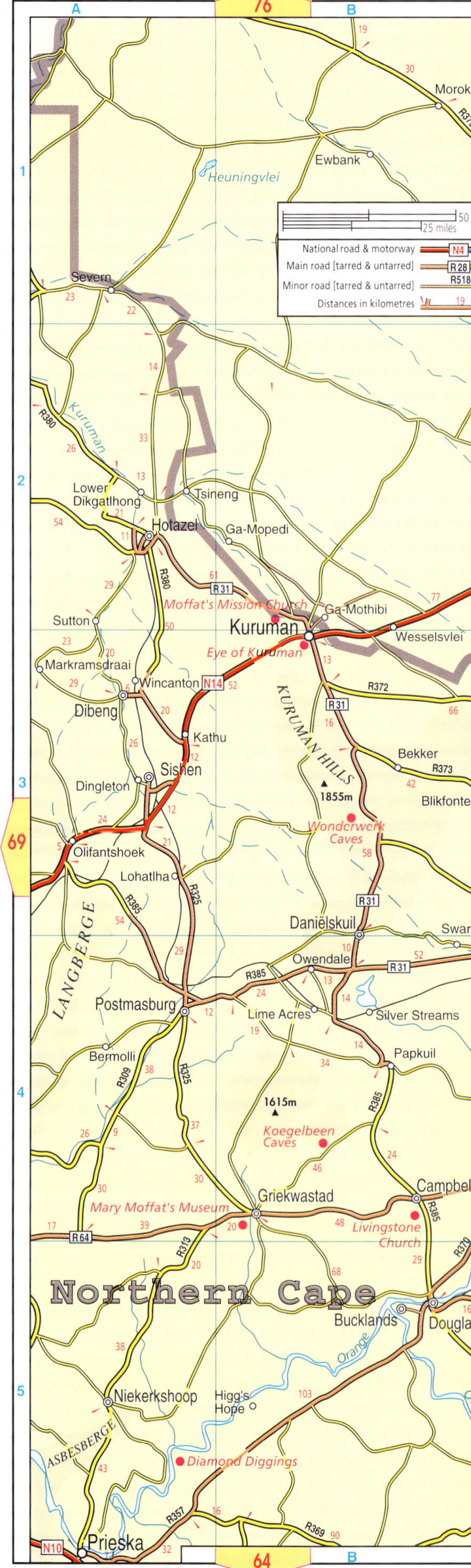

77
MMABATHO
N4 / PRETORIA
C
D
E
F
North West
Free State
Tosca
Gemsbokvlakte
Logageng
Mafikeng
Rooigrond
Elandsputte
Carlsonia
Grootpan
Koster
Derby
Grasfontein
Bakerville
Itsoseng
Lichtenburg
Swartplaas
Piet Plessis
Mosita
Madiakgama
Setlagole
Mooifontein
Langehorn
Deelpan
Biesiesvlei
Bodenstein
Ventersdorp
Coligny
Madibogo
Tlhakgameng
Geysdorp
Sannieshof
Gerdau
Vermaas
Dovesdale
Mesa
Ganyesa
Stella
Kameel
Barberspan
Hauptsrus
Alettasrus
Devonlea
Delareyville
Bospoort
Potchefstroom
Setuat
Coetzersdam
Broederstput
Rostrataville
Hartbeesfontein
Braksprui
Ottosdal
Stilfontein
New Machavie
Louwna
Klein Tswaing
Vryburg
Migdol
Klerksdorp
Renostersprui
Sendelingsfontein
Orkney
Geluk
Strydpoort
Schweizer-Reneke
Wentzel Dam
Wolmaransstad
Broadbent's Mission
Witpoort
Harrisburg
Leeudoringstad
Vierfontein
Spes Bona
Lykso
Amalia
Mirage
Viljoenskroon
Steekdorings
Salpeterpan
Dry Harts
Makwassie
Koosfontein
Pudimoe
Avondster
Boskuil
Bothaville
Kingswood
Taung
Manthestad
Reivilo
Bloemhof Dam Nature Reserve
Vals
Winkelpos
Bloemhof
Bloemhof Dam
Blesmanspos
Hartswater
Pampierstad
Sandveld Nature Reserve
Allanridge
Prospectors Borehole Monument
Hoopstad
Geneva
Mineral Springs
Rock Engravings
Odendaalsrus
Egspagsdrif
Madipelesa
Ganspan
Jan Kempdorp
Christiana
Wesselsbron
Riebeeckstad
Hennenman
Boetsap
Tierfontein
Whites
Vaalharts Dam
Mount Rupert
Warrenton
Hertzogville
WELKOM
Bloudrif
Virginia
Ventersburg
Koopmansfontein
Content
Welgeleë
Windsorton
Bultfontein
Ulco
Delportshoop
Windsorton Road
Theron
Allemanskraal Dam
Theunissen
St. Mary's Church
Volkspele Monument
Barkly West
Erfenis Dam
Winburg
Vaalbos National Park
Boshof
Archaeological Reserve
Schmidtsdrif
Kenilworth
Dealesville
Soutpan
Brandfort
KIMBERLEY
Big Hole Old Mine
Paardeberg
Florisbad
Verkeerdevlei
Wolwespruit
Krugerdrif Dam
Soetdoring Nature Reserve
Spytfontein
Karee
Allandale
Koedoesberg
Magersfontein
Modder
Riet
Plooysburg
Modderrivier
Excelsior
Glaciated Rocks & Engravings
Ritchie
Mazelspoort
Jacobsdal
Petrusburg
BLOEMFONTEIN
De Brug
Sannaspos
Tweespruit
Sunnyside
Shannon
Ferreira
Rodenbeck
Botshabelo
Thaba 'Nchu
Salt Lake
Rustfontein Dam Nature Reserve
Maria Moroka N.R
Graspan
Leeurivier Dam
Belmont
Koffiefontein
Glenrock
Tierpoort
Old Wagon Bridge
Witput
Rooipan
Austin's Post
Meadows
Hopetown
Wanda
Kalkfontein Dam Nature Reserve
Dewetsdorp
Hobhouse
73
65
N1 / BEAUFORT WEST
COLESBERG
ALIWAL NORTH
JOHANNESBURG
HARRISMITH
MASERU

NORTHEASTERN FREE STATE

Though much of the Free State consists of flat, treeless grassland plain, the eastern and southern parts are scenically very appealing, rising in a series of picturesquely weathered sandstone hills, and culminating in the Maluti Mountains in the southeastern corner. The northeastern part of the province is blessed with rich farmland, making the Free State one of the most important agricultural areas of the country. The province is also rich in deposits of gold ore estimated to be worth in the region of 8,5 billion rand.

MAIN ATTRACTIONS

Golden Gate Highlands National Park: south of Bethlehem; sandstone ridges sculpted by the elements; see antelope and over 160 bird species.
Vaal River: border between Free State and Gauteng; good boating and fishing, especially on the dam.
Willem Pretorius Game Reserve: good game-viewing, including white rhino and buffalo, near Ventersburg.
Pretoriuskloof Bird Park: located near the little town of Bethlehem.
Bushman paintings: in the Phuthaditjhaba area, close to Lesotho.

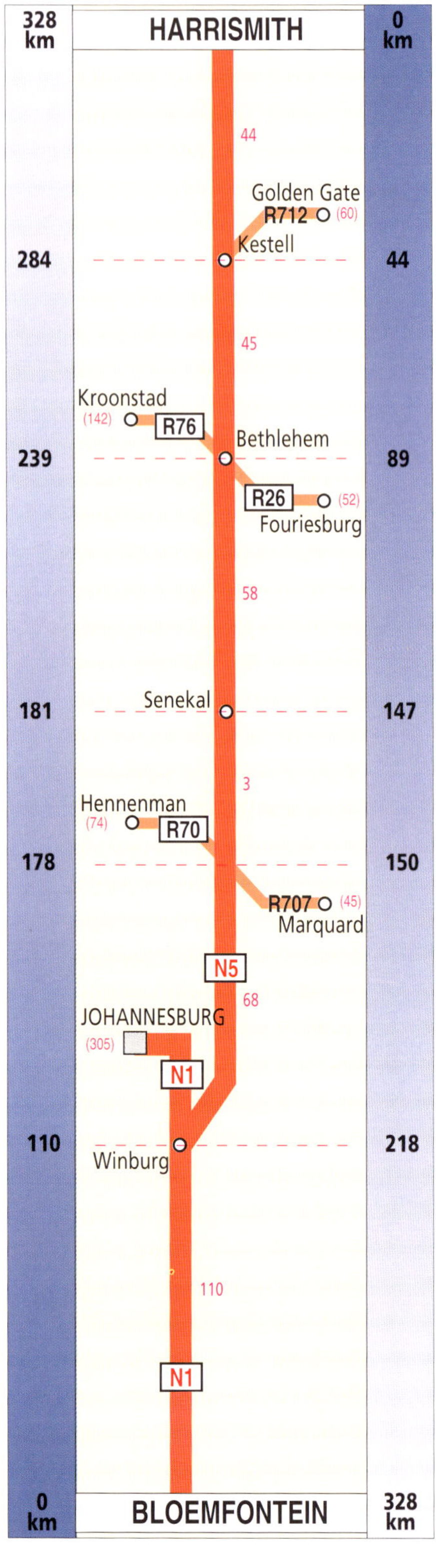

BETHLEHEM	J	F	M	A	M	J	J	A	S	O	N	D
AV. TEMP. °C	19	19	18	14	10	6	7	9	13	16	18	19
AV. TEMP. °F	66	66	64	57	50	43	45	48	55	61	64	66
DAILY SUN hrs	9	8	8	8	9	8	9	9	9	8	9	9
RAINFALL mm	120	89	71	50	28	10	11	14	33	67	85	97
RAINFALL in	5	4	3	2	1	0.4	0.4	0.6	1	3	3.5	4

Below: *Along the Free State roads, travellers are often greeted by large fields of glorious golden-yellow sunflowers. These constitute a major crop in the region which has rich soil, despite relatively poor rainfall and very little surface water.*

79
PRETORIA
66
71
75
NELSPRUIT
ERMELO
UPINGTON
KLERKSDORP
BLOEMFONTEIN
PIETERMARITZBURG
North West
Gauteng
Mpumalanga
Free State
KwaZulu-Natal
LESOTHO
MALUTI
DRAKENSBERG
WITTEBERGE
ROOIBERG
BIGGARSBERG
MAGALIESBERG
Koster
Derby
Heldina
Boons
Magaliesburg
Blockhouse
Hekpoort
Erasmia
Centurion
Van Riebeeck N.R.
Bronkhorstspruit
Kromdraai
Witbank
Middelburg
Midrand
Snake Park
Lion Park
Tembisa
Bapsfontein
Balmoral
Clewer
Klipfontein
Merindol
Krugersdorp
Krugersdorp Game Park
Randburg
Sandton
Kempton Park
Daveyton
Kendal
Ogies
Coalville
Gloria
Roodepoort
Randfontein
Edenvale
Benoni
Vandyksdrif
Hendrina
Klerkskraal
JOHANNESBURG
Soweto
Boksburg
Brakpan
Springs
Ventersdorp
Westonaria
Alberton
GERMISTON
Katlehong
Devon
Leandra
Kriel
Welverdiend
Bank
Carletonville
Walkerville
Nigel
Kinross
Dovesdale
Mesa
Fochville
Grasmere
Blockhouse
Daleside
N.G. Church
Jameson Park
Evander
Bethal
Davel
Danie Theron Monument
Evaton
Heidelberg
Transport Museum
Trichardt
Secunda
Potchefstroom
N.H.Church
Vanderbijlpark
Meyerton
Vereeniging
Balfour
Roodebank
Greylingstad
Charl Cilliers
Maizefield
New Machavie
Sasolburg
Vaal
Viljoensdrif
Dasville
Grootvlei
Holmedene
Morgenzon
Venterskroon
Parys
Deneysville
Vaal Dam N.R.
Standerton
Bettiesdam
Grootdraai Dam
Reitzburg
Vredefort
Wolwehoek
Oranjeville
Villiers
Waterval
Robert's Drift
Meyerville
Amersfoort
Dover
Platrand
Spes Bona
Koppies Dam N.R.
Viljoenskroon
Koppies
Heilbron
Frankfort
Cornelia
Perdekop
Rooiwal
Klip
Rustig
Volksrust
Charlestown
Convention Bridge
Amajuba Mtn
O'Neill's Cottage
Laings-nek
Vals
Heuningspruit
Vegkop
Free State
Vrede
Westleigh
Edenville
Renoster
Tweeling
Wilge
Kroonstad
Prehistoric Stone Huts
Petrus Steyn
Seekoeivlei N.R.
Ingogo
Memel
Botha's Pass
Geneva
Reitz
Warden
Newcastle
Mullers Pass
Wonderkop
Lindley
Hennenman
Whites
Steynsrus
Arlington
Verkykerskop
Mont Pelaan
Normandien
Danielsrus
Liebenbergs Vlei
Molen
Ventersburg
Kransfontein
Chelmsford Public Resort N.R.
Fort Mistake
Libertas
Valsrivier
Willem Pretorius G.R.
Aberfeldy
Blockhouse
Bethlehem
Pretoriuskloof Bird Park
Bushman Paintings
Harrismith
Senekal
Paul Roux
Kestell
Allemanskraal Dam
Swinburne
De Beers Pass
Van Reenen
Wyford
Driefontein
Elands-laagte
Winburg
Noupoortsnek
Golden Gate Highlands National Park
Phuthaditjhaba
Van Reenen's Pass
Sterkfontein Dam N.R.
Rosendal
Clarens
2477 m
2408 m
Geluksburg
Sand River Valley
Ladysmith
Fouriesburg
Monontsa Pass
Sefako
Bushman Paintings
The Cavern
Olivershoek Pass
Marquard
Hendrick's Drift
Rugged Glen N.R.
Hotel
Mont-Aux Sources
Roosboom
Wagon Hill
Joel's Drift
Caledonspoort
Moteng Pass
Witsieshoek Mountain Resort
Spioenkop Dam N.R.
Battle of Colenso
Butha-Buthe
Oxbow
Royal Natal National Park
Bergville
Colenso
Allandale
Clocolan
Gumtree
Ficksburg
Prehistoric Footprints
3282 m
Woodstock Dam
Winterton
Weenen G.R.
Excelsior
Hlotse
Fort
Khabo
Zunckels
Chieveley
Cathedral Peak
Blaauwkrans Monument
Pekabrug
Peka
Corn Exchange
Matlameng
3277 m
Malibamatso
Mothae
Frere
Kolonyama
Pitseng
Loskop
Koenong
Kao
Letseng-la-Terae
Cathkin Park
Drakensberg Sun
Champagne Castle Hotel
Estcourt
Tweespruit
Westminster
Rock Paintings
Mamates
Rock Paintings
Ntabamhlope
Teyateyaneng
White Mountain
Wagendrift N.R.
Ladybrand
Mateka
Moletsane
Motsitseng
Sefikeng
Maserubrug
St Martin
Mooi River
Kommissiepoort
MASERU
Methalaneng
Tlokoeng
Leeurivier Dam
Moshoeshoe's Fortress
Katse Dam
Mokhotlong
Rosetta
Redcliffe
The Natal Drakensberg Park
Glenrock
Thaba Bosiu
Bokong
Bushman's Pass
Molimo Nthuse Pass
Blue Mountain Pass
Highlands Water Scheme
Nottingham Road
Mazenodo
Roma
Cheche Pass
Mokhoabong Pass
Hobhouse
Caledon
Makhaleng
Thaba Tseka
3482 m
Marakabei
Mantsonyane
Linakeng
Lidgetton
Tlali
National road & motorway
Main road [tarred & untarred]
Minor road [tarred & untarred]
Distances in kilometres
50 km
25 miles

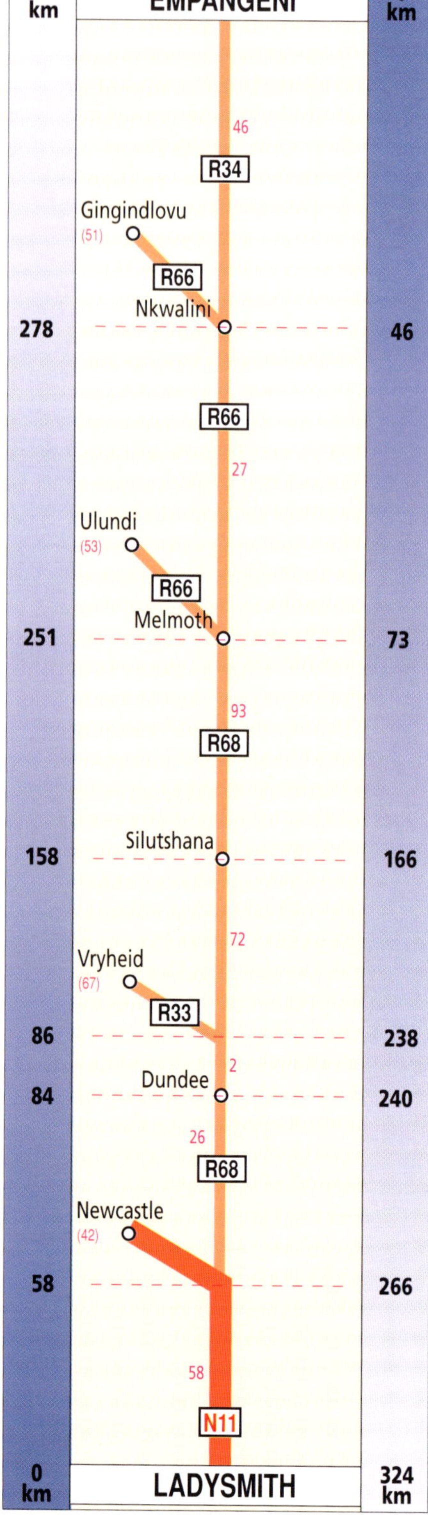

NORTHERN KWAZULU-NATAL

The midlands and northern parts of KwaZulu-Natal, overlooked by the Drakensberg massif to the west, are noted for their rolling green hills, rich farmlands, charming country towns – and for their place in the military annals. For much of the 1800s this region served as an immense battleground as three nations fought bitterly for mastery of the land. Closer to the coast lie the splendours of the Greater St Lucia Wetland Park and some of Africa's very finest wildlife reserves. The seaboard offers superb angling and boating, while offshore the world's southernmost coral reefs are guaranteed to delight scuba divers.

Above: *The Itala Game Reserve, a 30,000ha (74,000-acre) wildlife sanctuary located along the lush banks of the Pongola River, is a haven for the white, or square-lipped, rhino, a highly endangered species. The term 'white' derives from the Afrikaans word 'wyd' (wide) describing the broad, squarish mouth of this mammal.*

RICHARDS BAY	J	F	M	A	M	J	J	A	S	O	N	D
AV. TEMP. °C	25	25	25	23	20	18	17	19	20	21	23	25
AV. TEMP. °F	77	77	77	73	68	64	63	66	68	70	73	77
DAILY SUN hrs	7	7	7	8	8	7	8	8	7	6	7	7
RAINFALL mm	144	138	110	111	126	31	47	59	84	97	97	83
RAINFALL in	6	5.5	4.5	4.5	5	1	2	2.5	3.5	4	4	3.5
SEA TEMP. °C	24	24	24	23	22	21	20	20	20	21	21	23
SEA TEMP. °F	75	75	75	73	72	70	68	68	68	70	70	73

MAIN ATTRACTIONS

Howick Falls: outside of Howick, the Umgeni River plunges some 100m (328ft) into a rock pool.
Hluhluwe/Umfolozi Park: the oldest of South Africa's wildlife sanctuaries, this park sustains a great number of animals and some 400 species of bird.
Itala Game Reserve: home to some 70 species of mammal, among them both white and black rhino, zebra, giraffe, elephant, brown hyena, cheetah and various antelope. Beautiful Ntshondwe rest camp is just one accommodation alternative that is available here.
Phinda Resource Reserve: an upmarket ecotourist venture that shares its resources with the local communities, while providing the visitor with an exhilarating wilderness experience.

81
73
67
MOZAMBIQUE
SWAZILAND
Mpumalanga
KwaZulu-Natal
INDIAN OCEAN
MAPUTO
MBABANE
Manzini
Piet Retief
Vryheid
Ermelo
Barberton
Dundee
Glencoe
Greytown
Stanger
Empangeni
Richards Bay
Melmoth
Ulundi
Nongoma
Mkuze
Pongola
Paulpietersburg
Utrecht
Madadeni
Howick
Hluhluwe-Umfolozi Park
Greater St Lucia Wetland Park
Maputo Elephant Reserve
Tembe Elephant Park
Mkuzi Game Reserve
Itala N.R.
Kosi Bay Nature Reserve
Sodwana Bay N.P.
Maputaland Marine Reserve
St Lucia Marine Reserve
Lake St Lucia
Lake Sibaya
Pongolapoort Dam
NELSPRUIT
KOMATIPOORT
JOHANNESBURG
N11 LADYSMITH
ESTCOURT
DURBAN
50 km
25 miles
National road & motorway
Main road [tarred & untarred]
Minor road [tarred & untarred]
Distances in kilometres

NAMIBIA
BOTSWANA
NORTHERN PROVINCE
Pietersburg
GAUTENG
Mmabatho
Pretoria
Nelspruit
NORTH WEST
Johannesburg
MPUMALANGA
MOZAMBIQUE
Upington
FREE STATE
KWAZULU-NATAL
Bloemfontein
NORTHERN CAPE
SOUTH AFRICA
Durban
EASTERN CAPE
WESTERN CAPE
East London
Cape Town
Port Elizabeth
Okwa
Takatshwaane Pan
B O T S
Ghanzi
Lone Tree Borehole
K A L A H A R I
Ukwi Pan
Tsetseng
Boritse Pan
Kang
Phuduhudu Borehole
Lehututu
Hukuntsi
Tshane
Morwamosu
Motokwe
Lokgwabe
Kokong
Kgalagadi
Khakhea
Mpaathutlwa Pan
Mabuasehube Area
Gemsbok National Park
Makopong
Werda
R375
R378
Nossob
Nossob Camp
Terra Firma
Molopo
Vorstershoop
Kalahari Gemsbok National Park
Tshabong
North West
50 km
25 miles
National road & motorway
N4
Main road [tarred & untarred]
R28
Minor road [tarred & untarred]
R518
Distances in kilometres
KURUMAN
69

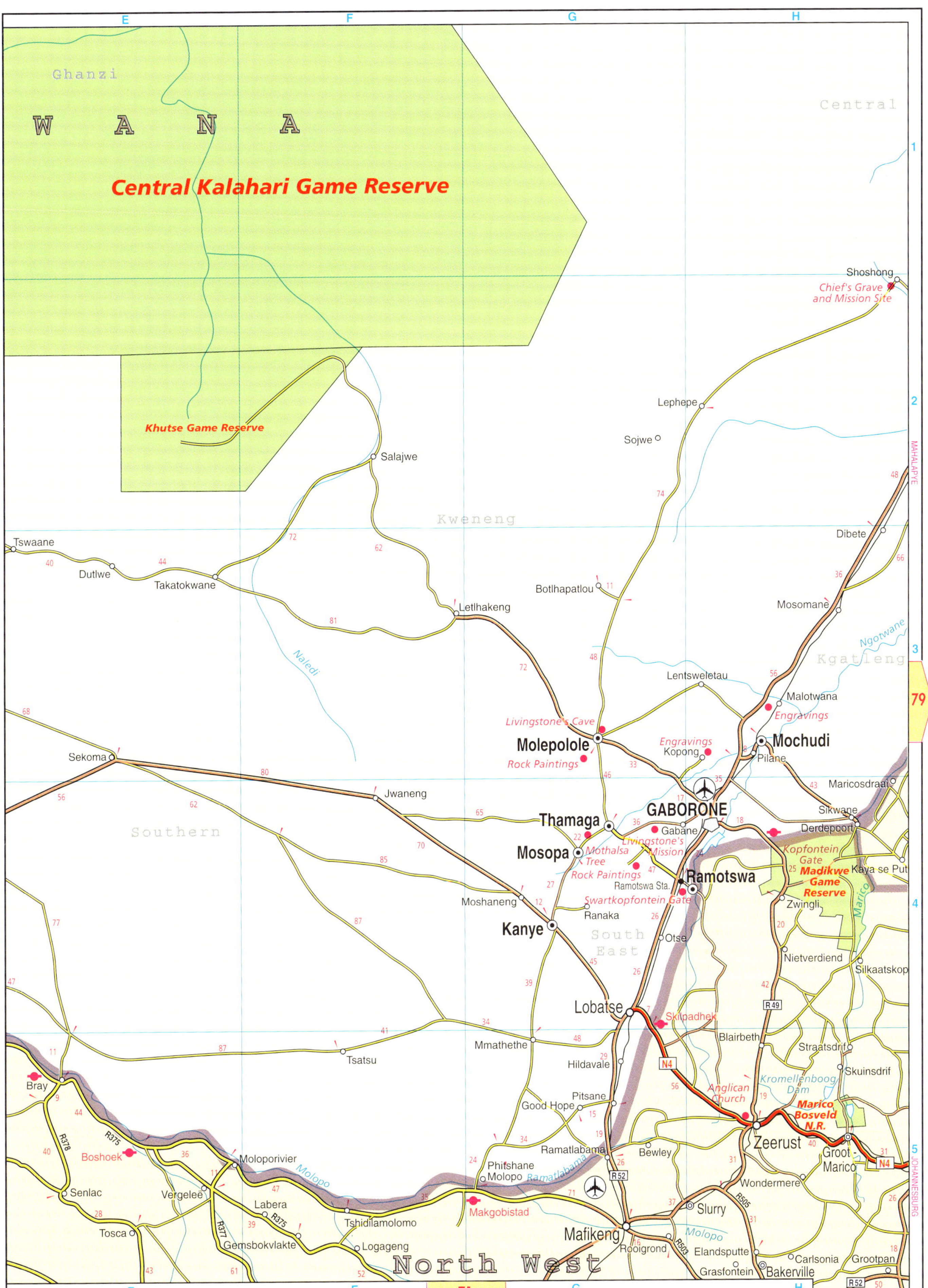
Central Kalahari Game Reserve
Khutse Game Reserve
Ghanzi
W A N A
Central
Kweneng
Kgatleng
Southern
South East
North West
Shoshong
Chief's Grave and Mission Site
Lephepe
Sojwe
Salajwe
Tswaane
Dutlwe
Takatokwane
Letlhakeng
Botlhapatlou
Dibete
Mosomane
Lentsweletau
Malotwana
Engravings
Mochudi
Pilane
Livingstone's Cave
Molepolole
Rock Paintings
Engravings
Kopong
Sekoma
Jwaneng
GABORONE
Gabane
Thamaga
Livingstone's Mission
Mosopa
Mothalsa Tree
Rock Paintings
Ramotswa
Ramotswa Sta.
Swartkopfontein Gate
Ranaka
Moshaneng
Kanye
Otse
Maricosdraai
Sikwane
Derdepoort
Kopfontein Gate
Madikwe Game Reserve
Kaya se Put
Zwingli
Nietverdiend
Silkaatskop
Lobatse
Skilpadhek
Blairbeth
Straatsdrif
Skuinsdrif
Kromellenboog Dam
Anglican Church
Marico Bosveld N.R.
Zeerust
Groot-Marico
Mmathethe
Hildavale
Tsatsu
Pitsane
Good Hope
Ramatlabama
Bewley
Phitshane Molopo
Bray
Boshoek
Moloporivier
Senlac
Vergelee
Labera
Tosca
Gemsbokvlakte
Tshidilamolomo
Logageng
Makgobistad
Mafikeng
Rooigrond
Slurry
Wondermere
Elandsputte
Grasfontein
Bakerville
Carlsonia
Grootpan
Naledi
Ngotwane
Marico
Molopo
Ramatlabama
N4
R49
R52
R375
R378
R377
R503
R505
MAHALAPYE
JOHANNESBURG
E
F
G
H
1
2
3
4
5
79
71

NORTH WEST AND NORTHERN PROVINCE

The North West is a vast, hot, flattish country of bushveld and thorn, of lonely farmsteads, of fields of sunflowers, groundnuts, tobacco, and citrus, and of villages that sleep soundly in the sun. This is one of the great granaries of southern Africa, with endless fields of maize stretching out to the far horizon. Scattered over this region and across the more densely populated Northern Province to the northeast is an impressive number of natural and man-made attractions well worth travelling to from the main centres of Pretoria and Johannesburg.

km	BEIT BRIDGE	km
492 km	BEIT BRIDGE	0 km
	16	
476	Messina	16
	92	
384	Louis Trichardt	108
	N1	
	117	
	Tzaneen (95) via R71	
267	Pietersburg	225
	57	
	Zebediela (42) via R518	
210	Potgietersrus	282
	51	
	Roedtan (39) via N11	
159	Naboomspruit	333
	58	
	Warm Baths (3) via R516	
101		391
	101	
	N1	
0 km	PRETORIA	492 km

TRAVEL TIPS

All national roads in this area are tarred and generally in excellent condition; most of the secondary roads are gravelled and reasonably well maintained.
Please note: The stretch of road between Warm Baths and Pietersburg can get very busy over the Easter weekend. Holiday-makers travelling to the towns and game reserves of the Lowveld join a cavalcade of minibus taxis and public buses ferrying worshippers of the ZCC (Zionist Christian Church) to their destination on the outskirts of Pietersburg. Traffic is congested and extreme caution is advised.

DISTANCE IN KM FROM PRETORIA	
Klerksdorp	164
Messina	530
Pietersburg	319
Rustenburg	125
Witbank	92

MAIN ATTRACTIONS

Sun City and Palace of the Lost City: luxury hotel-casino complex of pure innovation and fantasy.
Pilanesberg National Park: great expanse of wildlife-rich habitat.
Warm Baths: renowned for its curative springs; the Hydro Spa is of world standard.
Pietersburg: principal town of the Northern Province; nearby are the **Percy Fyfe Nature Reserve**, where several antelope species may be seen, and the interesting **Bakone Malapa Open-air Museum**, with traditional *kraal* and handicrafts.

Below: *The natural springs at Warm Baths are not the only attraction at this world-class spa resort.*

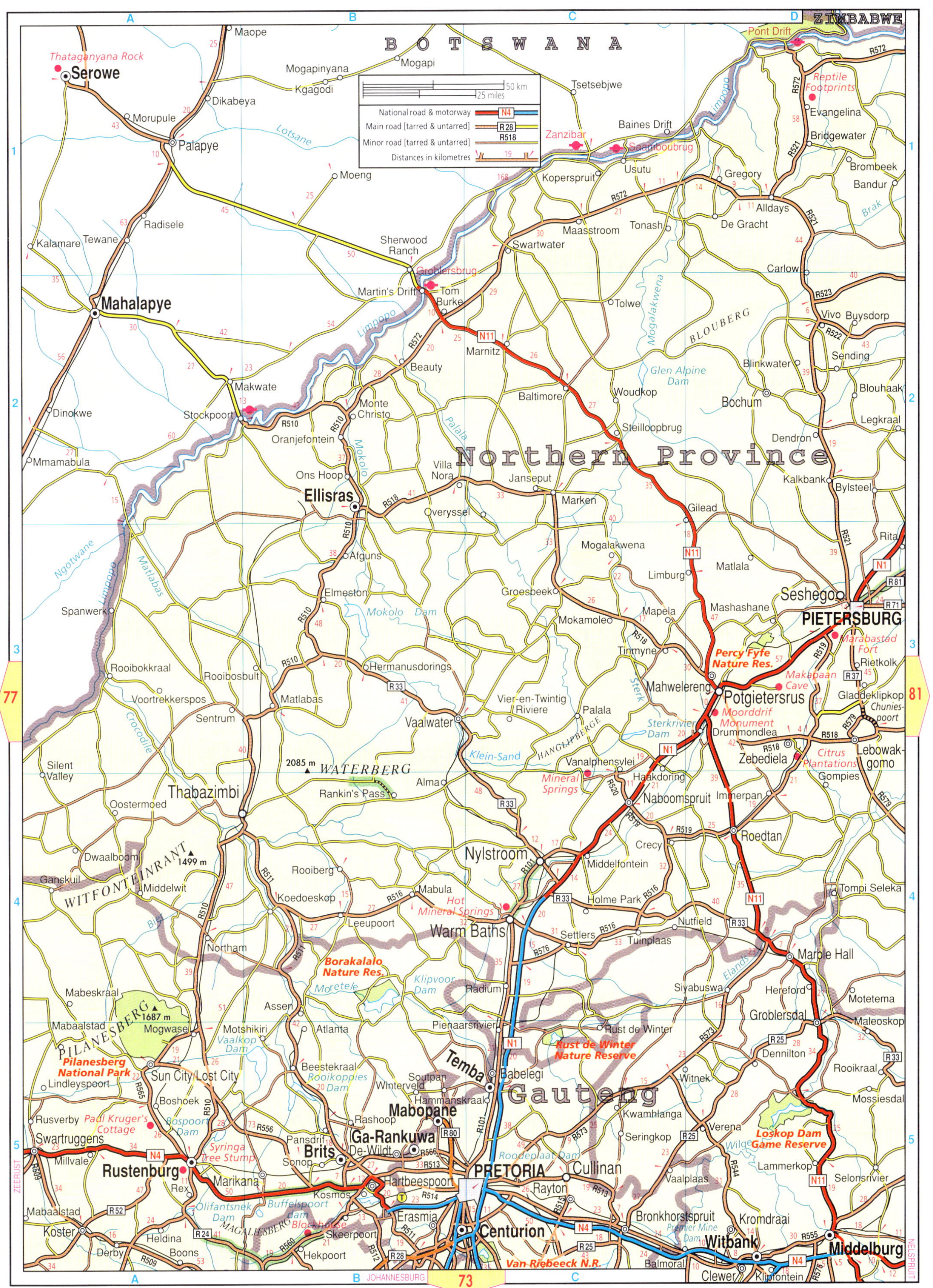

BOTSWANA
ZIMBABWE
Northern Province
Gauteng
National road & motorway
Main road [tarred & untarred]
Minor road [tarred & untarred]
Distances in kilometres
50 km
25 miles
Serowe
Palapye
Mahalapye
Ellisras
Thabazimbi
Nylstroom
Warm Baths
Potgietersrus
PIETERSBURG
Seshego
PRETORIA
Centurion
Rustenburg
Brits
Ga-Rankuwa
Mabopane
Temba
Cullinan
Witbank
Middelburg
Marble Hall
Groblersdal
WATERBERG
PILANESBERG
WITFONTEINRANT
BLOUBERG
Pilanesberg National Park
Borakalalo Nature Res.
Rust de Winter Nature Reserve
Loskop Dam Game Reserve
Percy Fyfe Nature Res.
Van Riebeeck N.R.
77
81
73

NORTHERN PROVINCE AND MPUMALANGA

Much of this region is dominated by the Great Escarpment, a spectacular compound of forest-mantled mountains, deep ravines, crystal-clear streams and delicate waterfalls. For sheer scenic beauty, few other parts of the country can compare with this imposing range, which rises near Nelspruit and runs to the northeast for some 300km (186 miles). To the east of the escarpment lies the wildlife-rich Louveld, where the vast Kruger National Park and a host of beautiful private reserves are situated.

436 km — **PIETERSBURG** — 0 km
N1
57
Tom Burke (178) N11
Potgietersrus
379 — 57
PRETORIA (216) N1
74
N11
305 — 131
16
289 — Marble Hall — 147
21
268 — Groblersdal — 168
78
190 — Middelburg — 246
5
N11
PRETORIA (140) N4
185 — 251
N12 JOHANNESBURG (170)
55
Belfast (2) R33
130 — 306
37
93 — Waterval-Boven — 343
93
N4
0 km — **NELSPRUIT** — 436 km

MAIN ATTRACTIONS

Pilgrim's Rest: a living showcase of the early gold-mining days.
Zebediela: South Africa's largest citrus estates are located here.
Pietersburg: this is the principle town of the Northern Province.
Tzaneen: little town surrounded by lovely waterfalls and forests. Visit nearby **Duiwelskloof** and **Magoebaskloof** and see the realm of the mysterious **Modjadji Rain Queen** (the source for Sir Rider Haggard's classic novel *She*) and the impressive cycad forest.
Loskop Dam Game Reserve: a wildlife sanctuary around a large dam; accommodation is offered in several air-conditioned chalets.

PIETERSBURG	J	F	M	A	M	J	J	A	S	O	N	D
AV. TEMP. °C	22	22	20	18	15	12	12	14	17	20	21	22
AV. TEMP. °F	72	72	68	64	59	54	54	57	63	68	70	72
DAILY SUN hrs	8	8	8	8	9	9	9	9	9	9	8	8
RAINFALL mm	91	72	61	31	11	4	5	4	14	41	80	91
RAINFALL in	4	3	2.5	1	0.4	0.1	0.2	0.1	0.6	2	3.5	4

TRAVEL TIPS

Most of the roads are tarred and generally in excellent condition and well signposted. The climate is equable, though rainfall during the summer months, from November to February, often occurs in the form of sudden torrential downpours which are accompanied by thunder and lightning. The storms tend to be brief, however, and there are very few days without long hours of sunshine.
A common feature of the escarpment is the occurrence of dense fog patches, and caution is therefore advised.
During the previous century, malaria claimed the lives of many pioneers in this area. While the disease is under control today thanks to insecticides, it is essential to take precautionary measures before travelling into the region.

Below: *The Blyde River winds its way through the magnificent canyon of the same name.*

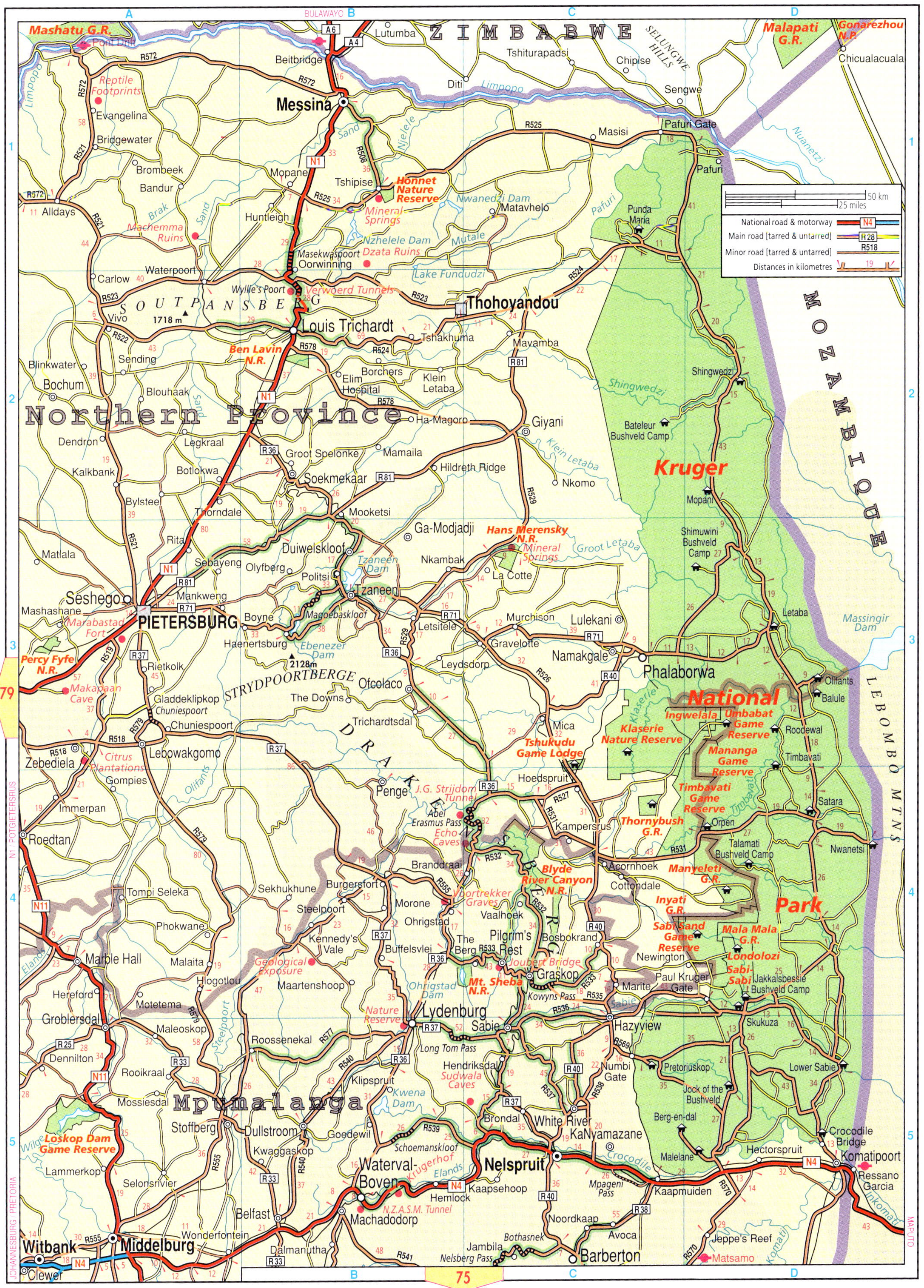

ZIMBABWE
MOZAMBIQUE
Northern Province
Mpumalanga
Kruger National Park
SOUTPANSBERG
STRYDPOORTBERGE
DRAKENSBERG
LEBOMBO MTNS
SELUNGWE HILLS
Messina
Beitbridge
Lutumba
Tshiturapadsi
Chipise
Sengwe
Chicualacuala
Malapati G.R.
Gonarezhou N.P.
Mashatu G.R.
Pont Drift
Reptile Footprints
Evangelina
Bridgewater
Brombeek
Bandur
Alldays
Machemma Ruins
Mopane
Tshipise
Honnet Nature Reserve
Mineral Springs
Nwanedzi Dam
Matavhelo
Huntleigh
Nzhelele Dam
Dzata Ruins
Masekwaspoort
Oorwinning
Lake Fundudzi
Waterpoort
Carlow
Wyllie's Poort
Verwoerd Tunnels
Thohoyandou
Vivo
1718 m
Louis Trichardt
Tshakhuma
Mavamba
Sending
Blinkwater
Ben Lavin N.R.
Borchers
Elim Hospital
Klein Letaba
Bochum
Blouhaak
Ha-Magoro
Giyani
Dendron
Legkraal
Groot Spelonke
Mamaila
Kalkbank
Botlokwa
Soekmekaar
Hildreth Ridge
Nkomo
Bylstee
Thorndale
Mooketsi
Ga-Modjadji
Hans Merensky N.R.
Rita
Duiwelskloof
Nkambak
Matlala
Sebayeng
Olyfberg
Politsi
Tzaneen Dam
La Cotte
Seshego
Mankweng
Tzaneen
Mashashane
PIETERSBURG
Boyne
Magoebaskloof
Letsitele
Murchison
Lulekani
Marabastad Fort
Haenertsburg
Ebenezer Dam
Gravelotte
Namakgale
Phalaborwa
Percy Fyfe N.R.
Rietkolk
2128m
Leydsdorp
Makapaan Cave
Gladdeklipkop
Chuniespoort
Ofcolaco
The Downs
Mica
Trichardtsdal
Zebediela
Lebowakgomo
Citrus Plantations
Gompies
Tshukudu Game Lodge
Hoedspruit
Immerpan
Penge
J.G. Strijdom Tunnel
Abel Erasmus Pass
Echo Caves
Kampersrus
Roedtan
Branddraai
Blyde River Canyon N.R.
Acornhoek
Cottondale
Tompi Seleka
Sekhukhune
Burgersfort
Steelpoort
Morone
Voortrekker Graves
Ohrigstad
Vaalhoek
Phokwane
Kennedy's Vale
Buffelsvlei
The Berg
Pilgrim's Rest
Bosbokrand
Marble Hall
Malaita
Geological Exposure
Joubert Bridge
Graskop
Newington
Hogotlou
Maartenshoop
Ohrigstad Dam
Mt. Sheba N.R.
Kowyns Pass
Marite
Hereford
Motetema
Nature Reserve
Lydenburg
Sabie
Hazyview
Groblersdal
Maleoskop
Roossenekal
Long Tom Pass
Dennilton
Hendriksdal
Sudwala Caves
Numbi Gate
Rooikraal
Klipspruit
Kwena Dam
Mossiesdal
Brondal
White River
KaNyamazane
Stoffberg
Dullstroom
Goedewil
Schoemanskloof
Loskop Dam Game Reserve
Kwaggaskop
Waterval-Boven
Krugerhof
Elands
Nelspruit
Mpageni Pass
Kaapmuiden
Lammerkop
Selonsrivier
Hemlock
Kaapsehoop
N.Z.A.S.M. Tunnel
Belfast
Machadodorp
Noordkaap
Avoca
Wonderfontein
Witbank
Middelburg
Clewer
Dalmanutha
Jambila
Bothasnek
Nelsberg Pass
Barberton
Jeppe's Reef
Matsamo
Masisi
Pafuri Gate
Pafuri
Punda Maria
Shingwedzi
Bateleur Bushveld Camp
Mopani
Shimuwini Bushveld Camp
Letaba
Massingir Dam
Olifants
Balule
Ingwelala
Umbabat Game Reserve
Klaserie Nature Reserve
Roodewal
Manyeleti Manganga Game Reserve
Timbavati
Timbavati Game Reserve
Satara
Thornybush G.R.
Orpen
Talamati Bushveld Camp
Nwanetsi
Manyeleti G.R.
Inyati G.R.
Sabi Sand Game Reserve
Mala Mala G.R.
Londolozi
Sabi-Sabi
Paul Kruger Gate
Jakkalsbessie Bushveld Camp
Skukuza
Pretoriuskop
Lower Sabie
Jock of the Bushveld
Berg-en-dal
Malelane
Hectorspruit
Crocodile Bridge
Komatipoort
Ressano Garcia
Limpopo
Sand
Njelele
Mutale
Pafuri
Nuanetzi
Shingwedzi
Klein Letaba
Groot Letaba
Klaserie
Olifants
Steelpoort
Elands
Wilge
Crocodile
Komati
Inkomati
Brak
BULAWAYO
MAPUTO
N1 POTGIETERSRUS
JOHANNESBURG PRETORIA
79
75
50 km
25 miles
National road & motorway
Main road [tarred & untarred]
Minor road [tarred & untarred]
Distances in kilometres
N4
R28
R518

KEY TOURIST AREA AND TEXT INDEX

Note: Numbers in **bold** denote photographs

	Grid Ref	Page No.
Abbotsdale	B5	45
Aberfeldy	C2	55
accommodation		
Bloemfontein		56
Cape Peninsula		46
Cape Town		49
Waterfront		52
Drakensberg		30
Durban		28
East London		37
Eastern Cape		34
Free State		54
Garden Route		38
George		40
Johannesburg		12
Kimberley		57
Knysna		41
Kruger Park		20
Mpumalanga		22
Nelspruit		23
Paarl		44
Pilanesberg		
National Park		18
Port Elizabeth		36
Pretoria		16
Stellenbosch		44
Sun City		18
West Coast		45
Wild Coast		33
Acornhoek	B4	21
Adams Mission	C2	27
Addo	C3	34
Adelaide	D1	35
Agtertang	C5	55
Ahrens	B3	32
Alberton	A1	55
Alderley	B2	33
Alexandria	D3	35
Alice	E1	35
Alicedale	C2	34
Aliwal North	D5	55
		64
All Saints Nek	B1	33
Allandale	C3	55
Allanridge	A3	55
Amanzimtoti	C2	27
Amatikulu	A5	25
	C3	32
ambulance		
(national number)		10
Amherst	E1	35
Amsterdamhoek	C4	34
Anerley	B4	27
Arlington	B2	55
Arnoldton	G2	35
Askeaton	A1	33
Aston Bay	A4	34
Atlantis	B5	45
Aurora	B4	45
Avoca	D2	22
Babanango	C2	32
Balfour	B1	55
Banner Rest	A5	27
	D2	33
Barberton	D2	22
Barkly East	D4	55
Barkly Pass	B1	33
Barkly West	A5	55
Barrington	D2	39
Bashee Bridge	B1	33
Bathurst	E3	35
Baven-on-Sea	B5	27
Baynesfield	A1	27
Beacon Bay	G2	35
Beaufort West		64
Bedford	D1	35
Belfast	B2	22
Bell	F2	35
Bellevue	C2	34
Belmont	A5	55
Bendigo	B4	27
Berbice	C1	32
Bergplaas	C2	38
Bergrivier	B4	45
Bergville	B2	31
	D2	55
Berlin	F1	35
Bethel	F1	35
Bethelsdorp	B4	34
Bethlehem	C2	55
Bethulie	C5	55
Big Hole		**57**
Biggarsberg	D1	31
Bisho	F1	35
Bisi	D1	33
Bitterfontein	B1	45
Bityi	B1	33
Bivane	C1	32
Bizana	D2	33
Blanco	B2	38
Bloedrivier	B1	32
Bloemfontein	B4	55
		70
Bloemhof	A3	55
Bloubergstrand	B5	45
Bloudrif	B3	55
Bluecliff	B3	34
Bluegums	D4	55
Blyde River Canyon		**80**
Bodiam	F2	35
Boesmanskop	C4	55
Boesmanspoort	C3	34
Bokfontein	C4	45
Boknesstrand	D3	35
Bokong	D3	55
Boksburg	A1	55
Bolo	A1	33
Bolotwa	A1	33
Bongolethu	A1	38
Bongonoma	B1	25
Bonny Ridge	D1	33
Bontrand	D1	33
Bonza Bay	G2	35
Bosbokrand	B4	21
	D1	22
Boshof	A4	55
Boskuil	A3	55
botanic gardens		
Bloemfontein		56
Cape Town		48
Durban		28
East London		37
Nelspruit		23
Port Elizabeth		36
Bothaville	A2	55
Botshabelo	C4	55
Bourke's Luck		
Potholes		22
Braemar	B3	27
Branddraai	B4	21
	C1	22
Brandfort	B3	55
Brandkop	C2	45
Braunschweig	F1	35
Breakfast Vlei	E2	35
Breidbach	F1	35
Breipaal	C4	55
Brenton-on-Sea	D3	39
Brondal	C2	22
Brooks Nest	D1	33
Bruintjieshoogte	B1	34
Bucklands	A5	55
Buffelsbaai	D3	39
Buffelsdrif	C1	38
Buffelsvlei	C1	22
Bultfontein	B3	55
Bulwer	B5	31
Buntingville	B2	33
Burgersdorp	D5	55
Burgersfort	A4	21
	C1	22
Bushmans River		
Mouth	E3	35
Butha-Buthe	C2	55
Butterworth	A2	33
Cala	A1	33
Calvert	B2	32
Campbell	A5	55
Camperdown	B1	27
Candover	D1	32
Cape fur seals		52
Cape Point		**46**
Cape Town		**49**
Carletonville	A1	55
Carlisle Bridge	D2	35
Castle of Good		
Hope (Cape Town)		49
Cato Ridge	B1	27
caves		
Cango		39
Echo		22
Sterkfontein		10
Sudwala		22
Cedarville	D1	33
Cederberg	C3	45
Ceres	C5	45
Chalumna	F2	35
Chapman's Peak		46
Charlestown	A1	32
Christiana	A4	55
Churchhaven	A5	45
Cintsa	G1	35
Citrusdal	C4	45
Clanville	D4	55
Clanwilliam	C3	45
Clarens	C2	55
Clarkebury	B1	33
Clermont	C1	27
Clewer	A2	22
Clifford	D4	55
Clocolan	C3	55
Coega	C3	34
Coerney	C3	34
Coffee Bay	B2	33
Cofimvaba	A1	33
Coghlan	B1	33

Colchester C3 34
Coldstream G2 39
Colenso C2 31
A3 32
Colenso D1 55
Committees E2 35
Commondale C1 32
Constantia 46
Content A4 55
Cookhouse C1 34
Coombs E2 35
Cornelia B1 55
Cottondale C4 21
D1 22
Cradock 64
Craigsforth D1 31
Crossroads F2 35
Curry's Post D4 31

Dalmanutha B2 22
Dalton B3 32
Damwal A2 22
Danielsrus C2 55
Dannhauser A2 32
Dargle C5 31
Darling B5 45
Darnall A5 25
C3 32
Daskop C1 38
De Brug B4 55
De Hoek B4 45
De Vlug E2 39
Dealesville B4 55
Deepdale C5 31
Delportshoop A5 55
Demistkraal A3 34
Deneysville A1 55
Dennitlon A2 22
Despatch B4 34
Dewetsdorp C4 55
Die Hoek D2 39
Dimbaza F1 35
Diphuti B3 21
Dlolwana B3 32
Dlomodlomo A1 25
Donkerpoort C5 55
Dordrecht D5 55
Doringbaai B3 45
Doringbos C3 45
Douglas A5 55
Dover B1 55
Drakensberg **30**
Driefontein A2 32
Dublin B3 21
Dududu B3 27
Dullstroom B2 22
Dundee B2 32
D1 55
Dupelston C5 55
Durban **67**
Golden Mile **28**
Dwarskersbos B4 45
Dwarsrand A1 25
Dysselsdorp B1 38

East London G2 35
East Poort C1 34
Edenburg C4 55
Edendale A1 27
Edendale D5 31
Edenville B2 55
Edinglassie B1 27
Eendekuil C4 45
Ekuseni C1 25
Ekutuleni A4 25
Elandsbaai 45
B3 45
Elandshoek B5 21
Elandskraal B2 32
Elandslaagte A2 32
elephant **20**
Elliot B1 33
Elliotdale B2 33
embassies (international) 16
Embotyi C2 33
Empangeni B4 25
D3 32
Enon B3 34
Entumeni A4 25
C3 32
eNyamazaneni D2 22
Escombe C1 27
Eshowe A4 25
C3 32
Esikhawini B4 25
Esperanza B3 27
Estcourt C3 31
A3 32
D1 55
Eston B1 27
Evaton A1 55
Excelsior C3 55

Fallodon F3 35
Fauresmith B5 55
Felixton B4 25
D3 32
Ferreira B4 55
Ficksburg C3 55
Fitzsimon's Snake Park 28
Flagstaff C2 33
Florisbad B4 55
Forestry Station B3 34
Fort Beaufort E1 35
Fort Brown E2 35
Fort Donald D1 33
Fort Frederick 36
Fort Hare E1 35
Fort Mtombeni C3 32
Fouriesburg C2 55
Frankfort F1 35
B1 55
Franklin D1 33
Frasers Camp E2 35
FREE STATE **54**, **72**
Frere A3 32

Garies A1 45
Garryowen A1 33
Geluksburg B1 31
Gemvale C2 33
Geneva B2 55
George B2 38
40
Gingindlovu A5 25
C3 32
Gladstone F1 35
Glen Beulah A3 27
Glen Echo B3 27
Glenashley D1 27
Glencoe A2 32
D1 55
Glenconnor B3 34
Glenmore Beach A5 27
D2 33
Glenrock C3 55
Glentana B3 38
Gluckstadt C2 32
God's Window 22
Goedemoed C5 55
Goedewil B2 22
Gold Reef City 12
Golden Valley C1 34
Gompies A1 22
Gonubie G2 35
Gonzana E1 35
Gqweta B4 21
Graaff-Reinet 64
Graafwater B3 45
Grahamstown **35**
D2 35
Graskop B4 21
C1 22
Graspan A5 55
Greystone A2 34
Greytown B3 32
Groblersdal A1 22
Groenriviersmond A1 45
Groenvlei B1 32
Groot-Brakrivier A3 38
Grootdrif C2 45
Grootspruit B1 32
Grootvlei B1 55
Gumtree C3 55

Haarlem E1 39
Haga-Haga A2 33
Halcyon Drift C1 33
Hamburg F2 35
Hankey A4 34
Hantam C2 45
Harding D1 33
Harper E2 35
Harrisburg A2 55
Harrismith B1 31
C1 55
Hartebeespoort Dam 10
Hartenbos A3 38
Hattingspruit A2 32
Hazyview C4 21
D1 22
Hectorspruit D5 21
D2 22
Heerenlogement B3 45
Heidelberg B1 55
Heilbron B1 55
Helpmekaar B2 32
Hemlock C2 22
Hendriksdal B5 21
C2 22
Hennenman B3 55
Hereford A1 22
Hermanus 59
Herold B2 38
Heroldsbaai B3 38
Herschel D4 55
Hertzogville A4 55
Het Kruis B4 45
Heuningspruit B2 55
Hex River Valley **42**
Hibberdene B4 27
Hibberds B4 25
high commissions (international) 16
Highflats A3 27
Highveld 10
Hillcrest C1 27
Himeville B5 31
Hlabisa B2 25
D2 32
Hlobane C1 32
Hlogotlou B1 22
Hlomela B1 21
Hlotse C2 55
Hluhluwe C2 25
D2 32
Hlutankungu A3 27
Hobeni B2 33
Hobhouse C3 55
Hoedspruit B3 21
Hoekwil C2 38
Hogsback 35
E1 35
Hole-in-the-Wall 33
Holy Cross C2 33
Hoopstad A3 55
Hopefield B4 45
Hopewell B2 34
Hornlee D3 39
hospitals
Bloemfontein 54
Cape Town 49
Durban 28
Johannesburg 10
Knysna 41
Nelspruit 23

hospitals cont.
Port Elizabeth 36
Pretoria 16
Scottburgh 26
Stellenbosch 44
Hout Bay 46
Howick D5 31
Humansdorp A4 34

Idutywa A2 33
Ifafa B3 27
Illovo C2 27
Immerpan A1 22
Impisi D2 33
Inanda C1 27
Ingwavuma D1 32
Isipingo Beach C2 27
Isipingo C2 27
Isithebe A5 25
Ixopo A2 27

Jacobsdal A5 55
Jagersfontein B5 55
Jambila C2 22
Jamestown D5 55
Jammerdrif C4 55
Jan Kempdorp A4 55
Jeffreys Bay A4 34
Jeppe's Reef D2 22
Jock of the Bushveld 22
Joel's Drift C2 55
Johannesburg A1 55
Jolivet A3 27
Joubertina G2 39
Jozini D1 32

Kaapmuiden C5 21
D2 22
Kaapsehoop C2 22
Kaffir Drift E3 35
Kampersrus B3 21
D1 22
Karatara C2 38
Karee B4 55
Kariega E3 35
Kasouga E3 35
Keate's Drift B3 32
Kei Mouth A2 33
Kei Road F1 35
Keiskammahoek F1 35
Kenilworth A4 55
Kennedy's Vale B1 22
Kentani A2 33
Kenterton B3 27
Kenton on Sea E3 35
Kestell C2 55
Keurboomsrivier F3 39
Keurboomstrand F3 39
Kidds Beach G2 35
Kiepersol B4 21
Kimberley A4 55
57, **70**

King William's
Town F1 35
Kingsburgh C2 27
Kingscote D1 33
Kingsley B1 32
Kingswood A3 55
Kirkwood B3 34
Kirstenbosch **48**
Klaserie B3 21
Klawer B2 45
Klein Brakrivier A3 38
Klein Drakenstein C5 45
Kleinplaat C2 38
Kleinpoort A2 34
Kleinrivier A4 34
Klerksdorp A2 55
Klerkskraal A1 55
Klipfontein B2 34
Kliprand B1 45
Klipspruit C2 22
Kloof C1 27
Knapdaar C5 55
Knysna D3 39
61
Koffiefontein B5 55
Kokstad D1 33
Komatipoort D5 21
Komga A2 33
G1 35
Komkans A2 45
Kommissiepoort C3 55
Koonap E2 35
Koppies B2 55
Koringberg B4 45
Kotzesrus A1 45
Koukraal C4 55
Koutjie C1 38
Krakeelrivier G2 39
Kransfontein C2 55
Kranskop B3 32
Kromdraai A2 22
Kromellenboog A3 21
Kroonstad B2 55
Kruger Park camps
Balule D2 21
Bateleur C1 21
Berg-en-Dal C5 21
Biyamiti D5 21
Boulders C1 21
Crocodile Bridge D5 21
Jakkalsbessie D4 21
Jock of the
Bushveld C5 21
Letaba C2 21
Lower Sabie D5 21
Malelane C5 21
Maroela C3 21
Mopani C1 21
Nwanetsi D3 21
Olifants D2 21
Orpen C3 21
Pafuri B1 21

Kruger Park camps cont.
Pretoriuskop C5 21
Punda Maria A1 21
Roodewal D3 21
Satara D3 21
Shimuwini C2 21
Shingwedzi B2 21
Sirheni A2 21
Skukuza C4 21
Talamati C3 21
Krugers C5 55
Krugerspos A4 21
Kruisvallei E2 39
Ku-Mayima B1 33
Kwa Magwaza A4 25
Kwa-Makhuta C2 27
Kwa Mnyaise D1 25
Kwa Pita E1 35
Kwaggaskop B2 22
KwaMashu C1 27
KwaMbonambi C4 25
D3 32
Kwanyana A5 27

La Mercy D1 27
Lady Grey D4 55
Ladybrand C3 55
Ladysmith C2 31
A2 32
D1 55
Lambert's Bay B3 45
Lammerkop A2 22
Landplaas A2 45
Langdon B1 33
Langebaan A4 45
Lagoon 45
Langholm E3 35
Lavumisa D1 32
Leeudoringstad A3 55
Leipoldtville B3 45
Leisure Bay A5 27
Leisure Crest A5 27
Lekfontein E2 35
Lewuswood E2 35
Libertas B2 55
Libode C2 33
Liddleton D1 35
Lidgetton C4 31
Lindley B2 55
Little Karoo 59
Loch Vaal A1 55
Loeriesfontein C1 45
Lofter C5 55
Long Hope C1 34
Loskop A3 32
Louwsburg A1 25
Lower Loteni B4 31
Lower Pitseng C1 33
Luckhof B5 55
Lundin's Nek D4 55
Luneberg B1 32
Lupatana C2 33

Lusikisiki C2 33
Lutzville B2 45
Lydenburg A5 21
C1 22
Maartenshoop B1 22
Machadodorp B2 22
Macleantown G1 35
Maclear B1 33
Madadeni A1 32
Mafeteng C4 55
Magudu B1 25
D1 32
Magusheni D1 33
Mahlabatini A3 25
C2 32
Mahlangasi B1 25
D1 32
Makowe C2 25
Makwassie A3 55
Malaita B1 22
Maleoskop A1 22
Malmaison B3 34
Malmesbury B5 45
Mamre B5 45
Manaba Beach B5 27
Mandini A5 25
C3 32
Mangeni B2 32
Mapumulo C3 32
Marble Hall A1 22
Marburg B4 27
D2 33
Margate B5 27
D2 33
Mariannhill C1 27
Marina Beach A5 27
Marite D1 22
Marquard C3 55
Masenkeng A4 31
Maseru C3 55
Matatiele D1 33
Mauchsberg B4 21
Mazeppa Bay A2 33
Mdantsane G2 35
Meadows C4 55
Mehlomnyama A4 27
Melkbosstrand B5 45
Melkhoutboom A3 34
Melmoth A4 25
C2 32
Memel A1 32
Methalaneng D2 55
Meyerton A1 55
Meyerville B1 55
Mica B3 21
Mid Illovo B2 27
Middelburg A2 22
Middelrus D3 31
Middleton C1 34
Middlewater B2 34
Milnerton B5 45
Mirage A2 55

Mkambati C2 33
Mkuze C1 25
D1 32
Modderrivier A5 55
Modjadji Rain Queen 80
Mogaba B3 21
Mohales Hoek D4 55
Mokhotlong A3 31
D2 55
Molteno D5 55
Mont-Aux-Sources 30
Mont Pelaan A1 32
C1 55
Monzi C3 25
Mooiplaats A4 21
Mooi River C4 31
A3 32
Moorreesburg B4 45
Morgan's Bay A2 33
Morone C1 22
Moshesh's Ford D4 55
Mossel Bay A3 38
39
Mossiesdal A2 22
Motetema A1 22
Motsitseng A3 31
Mount Edgecombe C1 27
Mount Fletcher C1 33
Mount Frere C1 33
Moyeni D4 55
Mpemvana B1 32
Mpendle C5 31
Mpetu A2 33
G1 35
Mpumalanga B1 27
Mpunzi Drift A5 27
Msinsini B4 27
Mtonjaneni A3 25
C2 32
Mtubatuba C3 25
D2 32
Mtunzini B5 25
D3 32
Mtwalume B3 27
Muden B3 32
Munster A5 27
D2 33
Munyu B1 33
museums
Bakone Malapa 78
Bartolomeu Dias 39
Bo-Kaap Malay 49
Cape Town 49
East London 37
George 40
Kimberley Mine 57, **70**
Knysna 41
Letaba Elephant 20
Mahatma Gandhi 28
MuseumAfrica 12
Pilgrim's Rest 22
Port Elizabeth 36
Port Natal Maritime 28
SA Maritime 52
Stephenson-Hamilton 20
Talana 32
Transvaal Museum
of Natural History 16
Mutale Graphite A1 21

Nagana C3 25
Nahoon G2 35
Namakgale B2 21
Namaqualand **45**, **62**
Nariep A1 45
national parks
Addo Elephant 36
Augrabies Falls 68
Golden Gate 54, 72
Kalahari Gemsbok 68
Karoo 64
Kruger 20
Maria Moroka 54
Mountain Zebra 64
Pilanesberg 18
Richtersveld 68
Royal Natal 30
Tsitsikamma 39
West Coast 45
nature/game reserves
Dwesa 33
Franklin 56
Gariep 54
Giant's Castle 30
Goegap 68
Goukamma 39
Great Fish River 35
Greater St Lucia
Wetland Park 24
Himeville 30
Hluhluwe/Umfolozi 24, 74
Itala **74**
Loskop Dam 80
Maputaland 24
Oribi Gorge 26
Percy Fyfe 78
Phinda Resource 24, 74
Soetdoring 56
Tsolwana 35
Vernon Crookes 26
Willem Pretorius 54, 72
Nature's Valley F3 39
Nbandane A5 27
Ncanara C3 34
Ndaleni A2 27
Ndundulu A4 25
C3 32
Nelspruit B5 21
C2 22
New Amalfi D1 33
New England D4 55
New Germany C1 27
New Hanover B3 32
Newcastle A1 32
Newcastle C1 55
Newington D1 22
Newsel-Umdloti D1 27
Ngobeni C1 32
Ngome A1 25
C1 32
Ngqeleni B2 33
Ngqungu B2 33
Ngwelezana B4 25
Nhlavini A2 27
Nhlazatshe C2 32
Nieu-Bethesda 64
Nieuwoudtville C2 45
Nigel B1 55
Nkandla C2 32
Nkwalini C3 32
Nobantu B1 33
Nobokwe A1 33
Noetzie E3 39
41
Noll D1 39
Nondweni B2 32
Nongoma B2 25
Noordkaap D2 22
Noordkuil B4 45
Normandien A2 32
Norvalspont C5 55
Nottingham C4 31
Nottingham Road C4 31
A3 32
Nqabara B2 33
Nqamakwe A1 33
Nqutu B2 32
Ntabamhlope A3 32
Ntambanana B4 25
Ntibane B1 33
Ntseshe A1 33
Ntshilini C2 33
Ntywenke C1 33
Nuwerus B2 45
Nyaliza A1 25
Nyokana A2 33
Nyoni A5 25

Oak Valley E2 35
Odendaalsrus B3 55
Ofcolaco A3 21
Ohrigstad A4 21
C1 22
Old Bunting C2 33
Old Morley B2 33
Orania B5 55
Oranjerivier B5 55
Oranjeville B1 55
Oribi Flats A4 27
Orkney A2 55
Osborn A4 25
Osizweni A1 32
Otter Trail 39
Oudtshoorn A1 38
39
Outeniqua Choo-Tjoe 40
Oviston C5 55
Oxbow C2 55

Paarl C5 45
Pacaltsdorp B3 38
Paddock D2 33
Paleisheuwel B3 45
Palm Beach A5 27
D2 33
Palmerton C2 33
Palmietfontein D4 55
Papendorp B2 45
Paradysstrand A4 34
Park Rynie C3 27
Parys A2 55
Patensie A3 34
Paternoster A4 45
Paul Roux C2 55
Paulpietersburg B1 32
Peddie F2 35
Peka C3 55
Penge A3 21
penguin colony 46
Petrus Steyn B2 55
Petrusburg B4 55
Petrusville B5 55
Phalaborwa C2 21
Philadelphia B5 45
Phillipolis C5 55
Phillipolis Road C5 55
Phokwane B1 22
Phuthaditjhaba A1 31
C2 55
72
Pietermaritzburg B1 27
D5 31
Pietersburg 78
Piketberg B4 45
Pilgrim's Rest B4 21
C1 22
Pinetown C1 27
Plaston B5 21
Pleasant View E1 35
Plettenberg Bay 39
E3 39
Plooysburg A5 55
police
(national number) 10
Pomeroy B2 32
Pongola D1 32
Pools C4 45
Port Alfred E3 35
Port Edward A5 27
D2 33
Port Elizabeth C4 34
Port Grosvenor C2 33
Port Shepstone B4 27
D2 33
Port St Johns C2 33
Porterville C4 45
Portobello Beach A5 27
Potchefstroom A2 55

Potsdam G1 35
Prince Alfred
Hamlet C5 45
Pretoria **16**
Pretoriuskloof Bird Park 72
Priors C5 55
Prudhou F3 35
Punzana F2 35

Qamata A1 33
Qiba B1 33
Qoboqobo A2 33
Qolora Mouth A2 33
Qora Mouth A2 33
Qudeni B2 32
Queensburgh C1 27
Quko A2 33
Qumbu C1 33

Raisethorpe D5 31
Ramsgate A5 27
D2 33
Randalhurst C2 32
Ratelfontein B3 45
Rawsonville C5 45
Redcliffe C4 31
A3 32
Reddersdorp C4 55
Redelinghuys B3 45
Redoubt D2 33
Reebokrand B5 55
Reitz C2 55
Reitzburg A2 55
Renosterspruit A2 55
Ressano Garcia D5 21
rhino (white) **74**
Rhodes Memorial 49
Richards Bay C4 25
D3 32
Richmond A1 27
Riebeeckstad B3 55
Riebeek Kasteel C5 45
Riebeek Oos D2 35
Riebeek-Wes C5 45
Rietkuil C1 55
Rietpoort A1 45
Rietvlei D4 31
B3 32
Ritchie A5 55
River View C3 25
D2 32
Robben Island 52
Rockmount C3 31
Rode C1 33
Roedtan A1 22
Roma C3 55
Rooikraal A2 22
Rooipan B5 55
Rooiwal B2 55
Roosboom C2 31
A2 32
Roossenekal B2 22
Rorke's Drift B2 32
Rosebank B2 27
Rosemoor B3 38
Rosendal C2 55
Rosetta C4 31
A3 32
Rossouw D4 55
Rouxville D4 55
Rust B5 45
Rustig B2 55

Saasveld B2 38
Sabie B5 21
C1 22
Saldanha A4 45
Salem D3 35
Salt Lake A5 55
Sand River Valley C1 31
Sandberg B3 45
Sandton 12
Sannaspos B4 55
Sasolburg B1 55
SATOUR offices
Durban 28
Pretoria 10
Sauer B4 45
Sawoti B3 27
Schmidtsdrif A5 55
Scottburgh C3 27
26
Sea Park B4 27
Sea View B4 34
Sea World 28
Sebapala D4 55
Sedgefield C3 38
Sefako C2 55
Sekhukhune B1 22
Selonsrivier A2 22
Senekal B2 55
Seven Fountains D3 35
Sevenoaks B3 32
Sezela B3 27
Shakaland 24
Shallcross C2 27
Shannon B4 55
Sheldon C2 34
Sidbury D3 35
Sidwadweni C1 33
Sihlengeni A1 25
Silutshana B2 32
Simon's Town 46
Sinksabrug A1 38
Sittingbourne F2 35
Siyabuswa A1 22
Skoenmakerskop B4 34
Smithfield C4 55
Sneezewood D1 33
Sodwana Bay 24
Somerset East C1 34
Somkele C3 25
D2 32
South Downs C3 31
Southbroom A5 27
D2 33
Southeyville A1 33
Southwell E3 35
Soutpan B4 55
Soweto 10, 12
A1 55
Spes Bona A2 55
Springfontein C5 55
Spytfontein A5 55
St Faith's A4 27
St Francis Bay A4 34
St Helena Bay A4 45
St Lucia **24**
D3 25
St Matthew's F1 35
St Michaels on Sea B5 27
Stafford's Post D1 33
Stanger C3 32
Steelpoort A4 21
B1 22
Steilrand C1 32
Sterkspruit D4 55
Sterkstroom D5 55
Steynsburg D5 55
Steynsrus B2 55
Stilfontein A2 55
Stoffberg B2 22
Stompneusbaai A4 45
Stoneyridge C1 33
Stormberg D5 55
Stormsrivier G2 39
Strandfontein B2 45
Summerstrand C4 34
Sun City – Palace
of the Lost City **18**
Sundumbili A5 25
Sunland C3 34
Swart Umfolozi C2 32
Swartkops C4 34
Swempoort D5 55
Swinburne D1 55
Syfergat D5 55

Tabankulu C1 33
Table Mountain **49**, **52**
Tainton G1 35
Taleni A2 33
Tanga G1 35
Tatafalaza A4 25
Tergniet A3 38
Teyateyaneng C3 55
Teza D2 32
Thaba 'Nchu C3 55
The Berg C1 22
The Crags F2 39
The Downs A3 21
The Grove D4 31
The Haven B2 33
The Heads D3 39
The Ranch B3 32
Theron B3 55
Theunissen B3 55
Tidbury's Toll E1 35
Tierfontein A3 55
Tierpoort B4 55
Tina Bridge C1 33
Tip Tree A3 34
Toggekry A1 25
Tombo C2 33
Tompi Seleka A1 22
Tongaat Beach D1 27
Trafalgar A5 27
Trawal B3 45
Trichardtsdal A3 21
Triple Streams C1 33
Trompsburg C5 55
Tshani B2 33
Tsitsa Bridge C1 33
Tsitsikamma Trail **39**
Tsolo C1 33
Tsomo A1 33
Tugela Ferry B3 32
Tugela Mouth A5 25
C3 32
Tulbagh C5 45
Tweeling B1 55
Tweeriviere G2 39
Tweespruit C3 55
Two Oceans
Aquarium 49, 52
Tyata F2 35
Tyira C1 33
Tzaneen 80

Ubombo C1 25
D1 32
Ugie B1 33
Uitenhage B3 34
Uitspankraal C3 45
Ulundi A3 25
C2 32
Umbogintwini C2 27
Umbumbulu C2 27
Umgeni Dam B1 27
Umhlanga Rocks D1 27
Umkomaas C3 27
Umlazi C2 27
Umtentu D2 33
Umtentweni B4 27
uMzinto B3 27
Underberg B5 31
Union Building 16
Uniondale E1 39
Upper Nseleni B3 25
Upper Tuyme E1 35
Utrecht B1 32
Uvongo B5 27
D2 33

Vaal Dam 54
River 72
Vaalhoek B4 21
C1 22

Valley of Desolation 64
Valsrivier C2 55
Van Reenen B1 31
D1 55
Vanderbijlpark A1 55
Vanderkloof B5 55
Vanrhynsdorp B2 45
Vanstadensrus C4 55
Vant's Drift B2 32
Vegkop B2 55
Velddrif B4 45
Ventersburg B3 55
Venterstad C5 55
Vereeniging A1 55
Verkeerdevlei B3 55
Verkykerskop C1 55
Verulam D1 27
Victoria Bay B3 38
Viedgesville B2 33
Vierfontein A2 55
Viljoensdrif B1 55
Viljoenskroon A2 55
Villiers B1 55
Vineyard D5 55
Virginia B3 55
Volksrust A1 32
Voortrekker
Monument (Paarl) 16
Vrede C1 55
Vredefort A2 55
Vredenburg A4 45
Vredendal B2 45
Vryheid B1 32

Wakkerstroom B1 32
Wanda B5 55
Warden C1 55
Warm Baths **78**
Warrenton A4 55
Wasbank D1 31
A2 32
waterfalls 23, 74
Waterford A2 34
Waterfront
Cape Town **52**
Randburg **10**, 12
Waterkloof C5 55
Waterval-Boven B2 22
Wavecrest A2 33
Weenen D3 31
A3 32
Welgeleë B3 55
Welkom B3 55
Wellington C5 45
Welverdiend A1 55
Wepener C4 55
Wesley F2 35
Wesselsbron A3 55
Westleigh B2 55
Westminster C3 55
Westonaria A1 55
Westville C1 27
Weza D1 33
whale route 42
White River B5 21
White River D2 22
Whites B3 55
Whitmore B1 33
Wild Coast **33**
Wilderness C3 38
wildflowers **45**
wildlife **20**, **74**
Willow Grange C3 31
Willowvale A2 33
Winburg B3 55
Windmeul C5 45
Windsorton Road A4 55
winelands **42**, **59**
Winkelpos A2 55
Winsorton A4 55
Winterton B2 31
A3 32
Witbank A2 22
Witkop D5 55
Witpoort A3 55
Witput A5 55
Wittedrif E3 39
Witteklip B4 34
Wolmaransstad A3 55
Wolseley C5 45
Wolvepoort C4 55
Wolwefontein A2 34
Wolwehoek B1 55
Wolwespruit B4 55
Wonderfontein B2 22
Wonderkop B2 55
Wooldridge F2 35
Worcester C5 45
Wuppertal C3 45
Wyford D1 55

Xolobe A1 33

Yellowwood Park C2 27
Yzerfontein B5 45

Zaaimansdal E1 39
Zastron D4 55
Zebediela 80
zoological gardens
Bloemfontein 56
Pretoria 16
Zunckels B2 31
Zwelitsha F1 35

MAIN MAP INDEX

	Grid Ref.	Page No.
Aalwynsfontein	C2	62
Aansluit	H2	69
Abbotsdale	B2	60
Aberdeen	C5	65
Aberdeen Road	C5	65
Aberfeldy	C4	73
Acornhoek	C4	81
Adams Mission	F2	67
Addo	E5	61
Adelaide	F5	65
Adendorp	D5	65
Afguns	B3	79
Aggeneys	C1	62
Agter Sneeuberg	D4	65
Agtertang	E3	65
Ahrens	F1	67
Albertinia	E2	61
Alberton	B1	73
Alderley	D5	66
Aldinville	G1	67
Alettasrus	C1	71
Alexander Bay	A4	68
Alexandria	F5	61
Alheit	F4	69
Alice	F4	61
Alicedale	E4	61
Aliwal North	F3	65
Allandale	F5	71
Allanridge	F3	71
Alldays	D1	79
Alma	B4	79
Amabele	B5	66
Amalia	D2	71
Amanzimtoti	F2	67
Amatikulu	G1	67
Amersfoort	D2	73
Amsterdam	A2	75
Andrieskraal	D5	60
Andriesvale	F2	69
Anysberg	D1	60
Anysspruit	A2	75
Ariamsvlei	E3	69
Arlington	B3	73
Aroab	E2	69
Ashton	C2	60
Askeaton	B4	66
Askham	F2	69
Askraal	D2	60
Assegaaibos	C5	60
Assen	B4	79
Aston Bay	D5	60
Atlanta	B5	79
Atlantis	B2	60
Aurora	C5	62
Austin's Post	E1	65
Avoca	B1	75
Avondrust	D1	60
Avondster	D2	71
Avontuur	B5	60
Babanango	B4	75
Babelegi	C5	79
Badplaas	A1	75
Bailey	F4	65
Baines Drift	C1	79
Bakerville	E1	71
Balfour	C2	73
Balfour	F5	65
Ballito	G1	67
Balmoral	C1	73
Baltimore	C2	79
Bandur	D1	79
Bank	A1	73
Banner Rest	F3	67
Bapsfontein	C1	73
Barakke	D5	65
Barberspan	E1	71
Barberton	B1	75
Barkly East	B3	66
Barkly Pass	C3	66
Barkly West	C4	71
Baroda	E4	65
Baroe	C4	60
Barrington	A5	60
Barrydale	D2	60
Bashee Bridge	C4	66
Bathurst	F5	61
Beacon Bay	G4	61
Beaufort West	A5	64
Beauty	B2	79
Bedford	E5	65
Beestekraal	B5	79
Behulpsaam	D5	65
Beitbridge	B1	81
Bekker	B3	70
Bela Vista	D2	75
Belfast	B5	81
Bell	G4	61
Bellevue	E4	61
Bellville	B2	60
Belmont	C1	65
Benoni	B1	73
Berbice	B3	75
Bereaville	C2	60
Bergen	A2	75
Bergrivier	A1	60
Bergville	D4	73
Berlin	G4	61
Bermolli	A4	70
Bethal	D1	73
Bethel	B5	66
Bethelsdorp	D5	60
Bethlehem	B4	73
Bethulie	E2	65
Bettiesdam	D2	73
Betty's Bay	B3	60
Bewley	G5	77
Bhunya	B2	75
Biesiespoort	B4	64
Biesiesvlei	E1	71
Big Bend	C2	75
Bisho	G4	61
Bisi	E2	67
Bitterfontein	C3	62
Bityi	D4	66
Bivane	B3	75
Bizana	E3	67
Bladgrond	E4	69
Blairbeth	H5	77
Blanco	A5	60
Blesmanspos	C3	71
Bletterman	C3	65
Blikfontein	B3	70
Blinkwater	D2	79
Blinkwater	F5	65
Bloedrivier	A3	75
Bloedrivier	A4	75
Bloemfontein	F1	65
Bloemhoek	D1	63
Bloemhof	E3	71
Bloubergstrand	B2	60
Bloudrif	F3	71
Blouhaak	D2	79
Bluecliff	D4	60
Bluegums	B3	66
Blythdale Beach	G1	67
Bo-Wadrif	E5	63
Boane	D1	75
Bochum	D2	79
Bodenstein	F1	71
Boerboonfontein	D2	60
Boesmanskop	B2	66
Boetsap	C3	71
Bokfontein	B1	60
Bokhara	F3	69
Boknesstrand	F5	61
Bokong	D1	66
Boksburg	B1	73
Bolo Reserve	B5	66
Bolotwa	B4	66
Bonekraal	F4	63
Bonnievale	C2	60
Bonny Ridge	E3	67
Bontrand	E3	67
Boons	A1	73
Borchers	B2	81
Bosbokrand	C4	81
Boshoek	A5	79
Boshof	D4	71
Boskuil	E3	71
Bospoort	E1	71
Bossiekom	E1	63
Bothaville	F3	71
Botlhapatlou	G3	77
Botlokwa	A2	81
Botrivier	B2	60
Botshabelo	F1	65
Bowker's Park	F4	65
Boyne	B3	81
Braemar	F2	67
Brakpan	C1	73
Brakpoort	B3	64
Brakspruit	F2	71
Branddraai	C4	81
Brandfort	F4	71
Brandkop	D3	63
Brandrivier	E2	61
Brandvlei	E2	63
Brandwag	F2	61
Braunschweig	G4	61
Braunville	B4	66
Bray	E5	77
Breakfast Vlei	F4	61
Bredasdorp	C3	60
Breidbach	G4	61
Breipaal	F2	65
Breyten	A1	75
Bridgewater	D1	79
Brits	B5	79
Britstown	B2	64
Broedersput	D2	71
Brombeek	D1	79
Brondal	C5	81
Bronkhorstspruit	C1	73
Brooks Nek	E3	67
Bruintjieshoogte	D5	65
Bucklands	B5	70
Buffelsdrif	A5	60
Buffelsvlei	B4	81
Bulembu	B1	75
Bulletrap	B1	62
Bultfontein	E4	71
Bulwer	E2	67
Buntingville	D4	66
Burgersdorp	F3	65
Burgersfort	B4	81
Burgervilleweg	C3	65
Butha-Buthe	B4	73
Butterworth	C5	66
Buysdorp	D2	79
Bylsteel	D2	79

Name	Grid	Page
Cala	C4	66
Cala Road	C4	66
Caledon	C2	60
Calitzdorp	E2	61
Calvert	B4	75
Calvinia	E4	63
Cambria	C5	60
Cameron's Glen	E5	65
Campbell	B4	70
Camperdown	F2	67
Candover	C3	75
Cape St Francis	D5	60
Cape Town	A2	60
Carletonville	A1	73
Carlisle Bridge	E4	61
Carlow	D1	79
Carlton	D3	65
Carnarvon	G3	63
Carolina	A1	75
Carsonia	E1	71
Catembe	D1	75
Cathcart	B5	66
Catuane	D2	75
Cedarville	D2	66
Cederberg	D5	63
Centurion	B1	73
Ceres	C1	60
Chalumna	G4	61
Changalane	C1	75
Charl Cilliers	D2	73
Charlestown	D3	73
Chicabela	D1	75
Chicualacuala	D1	81
Chieveley	D5	73
Chipise	C1	81
Chrissiesmeer	A1	75
Christiana	D3	71
Chuniespoort	A3	81
Churchhaven	A1	60
Ciko	D5	66
Cintsa	H4	61
Citrusdal	D5	63
Clansthal	F2	67
Clanville	B3	66
Clanwilliam	D5	63
Clarens	C4	73
Clarkebury	C4	66
Clarkson	C5	60
Clermont	G2	67
Clewer	D1	73
Clifford	B3	66
Clocolan	A5	73
Coalville	D1	73
Coega	E5	61
Coerney	E4	61
Coetzersdam	C2	71
Coffee Bay	D5	66
Cofimvaba	B4	66
Coghlan	C4	66
Colchester	E5	61
Colekeplaas	C5	60
Colenso	D5	73
Colesberg	D3	65
Coligny	F1	71
Committees	F4	61
Commondale	B3	75
Concordia	B1	62
Content	D4	71
Conway	D4	65
Cookhouse	E5	65
Copperton	A2	64
Corn Exchange	B5	73
Cornelia	C2	73
Cottondale	C4	81
Cradock	E5	65
Cramond	G2	69
Crecy	C4	79
Creighton	E2	67
Crocodile Bridge	D5	81
Croydon	C1	75
Cullinan	C5	79
Dabenoris	D5	68
Dagbreek	G4	69
Daggaboersnek	E5	65
Daleside	B1	73
Dalmanutha	A1	75
Dalton	F1	67
Daniëlskuil	B3	70
Danielsrus	B3	73
Dannhauser	A4	75
Dargle	F1	67
Darling	A1	60
Darnall	G1	67
Daskop	A5	60
Dasville	C2	73
Davel	D1	73
Daveyton	C1	73
Dawn	G4	61
De Aar	C3	65
De Brug	E1	65
De Doorns	C1	60
De Gracht	D1	79
De Hoek	B1	60
De Hoop	F2	61
De Klerk	B3	64
De Rust	A4	60
De Vlug	B5	60
De Wildt	B5	79
Dealesville	E4	71
Deelfontein	C3	65
Deelpan	E1	71
Delareyville	D2	71
Delportshoop	C4	71
Demistkraal	D5	60
Dendron	D2	79
Deneysville	B2	73
Dennilton	D5	79
Derby	F1	71
Derdepoort	H4	77
Despatch	D5	60
Devon	C1	73
Devonlea	D2	71
Dewetsdorp	F1	65
Dibeng	A3	70
Dibete	H3	77
Die Bos	E4	63
Diemansputs	G2	63
Dieput	C3	65
Dikabeya	A1	79
Dingleton	A3	70
Dinokwe	A2	79
Dirkiesdorp	A2	75
Diti	C1	81
Dohne	B5	66
Donkerpoort	E2	65
Donnybrook	E2	67
Dordrecht	B4	66
Doringbaai	C4	62
Doringbos	D4	63
Douglas	B5	70
Dover	B2	73
Dovesdale	F1	71
Drennan	E5	65
Driefontein	D4	73
Droërivier	A5	64
Drummondlea	D3	79
Duiwelskloof	B3	81
Dullstroom	B5	81
Dundee	A4	75
Dupleston	F2	65
Durban	G2	67
Durbanville	B2	60
Dutlwe	E3	77
Dwaal	D3	65
Dwaalboom	A4	79
Dwarskersbos	C5	62
Dwyka	E1	61
Dysselsdorp	A5	60
East London	G4	61
Eastpoort	E5	65
Ebende	C5	66
Edenburg	E1	65
Edendale	F1	67
Edenvale	B1	73
Edenville	B3	73
Eendekuil	D5	63
Egspagsdrif	C3	71
Eksteenfontein	B5	68
Elands Height	C3	66
Elandsbaai	C5	62
Elandsdrif	E5	65
Elandskraal	A4	75
Elandslaagte	D4	73
Elandsputte	E1	71
Elgin	B2	60
Elim	C3	60
Elim Hospital	B2	81
Elliot	C4	66
Elliotdale	D4	66
Ellisras	B2	79
Elmeston	B3	79
Emangusi	D2	75
Embotyi	E4	67
Empangeni	C5	75
Engcobo	C4	66
Entumeni	G1	67
Erasmia	B1	73
Ermelo	A2	75
Escourt	E1	67
Eshowe	G1	67
Evander	C1	73
Evangelina	D1	79
Evaton	B1	73
Ewbank	B1	70
Excelsior	F5	71
eZibeleni	B4	66
Faans Grove	H2	69
Fairfield	C3	60
Faure	B2	60
Fauresmith	E1	65
Felixton	H1	67
Ferreira	F1	65
Ficksburg	B5	73
Firgrove	B2	60
Fish Hoek	B2	60
Flagstaff	E3	67
Florisbad	E4	71
Fochville	A1	73
Forbes Reef	B1	75
Fort Beaufort	F4	61
Fort Brown	F4	61
Fort Donald	E3	67
Fort Hare	F4	61
Fort Mistake	D4	73
Fort Mtombeni	G1	67
Fouriesburg	B4	73
Frankfort	C2	73
Franklin	E2	67
Franschhoek	B2	60
Fransenhof	A1	64
Fraserburg	G4	63
Frere	D5	73
Ga-Modjadji	B3	81
Ga-Mopedi	B2	70
Ga-Mothibi	B2	70
Ga-Rankuwa	B5	79
Gabane	G4	77
Gaborone	H4	77
Gamoep	C2	62
Gansbaai	C3	60
Ganskuil	A4	79
Ganspan	C3	71
Ganyesa	C1	71
Garies	B3	62
Garryowen	B4	66
Gege	B2	75
Geluk	C2	71
Geluksburg	D4	73
Gelukspruit	F3	69
Gemsbokvlakte	C1	71
Gemvale	E4	67
Genadendal	C2	60
Geneva	F3	71
George	A5	60
Gerdau	E1	71
Germiston	B1	73
Geysdorp	D1	71
Giesenskraal	B2	64

Place	Grid	Page
Gilead	D2	79
Gingindlovu	G1	67
Giyani	C2	81
Gladdeklipkop	D3	79
Glencoe	A4	75
Glenconnor	D4	60
Glenmore Beach	F3	67
Glenrock	B1	66
Glenrock	E5	65
Gloria	D1	73
Gluckstadt	B4	75
Goba	C1	75
Goedemoed	F2	65
Goedewil	B5	81
Golela	C3	75
Gompies	D4	79
Gomvlei	F2	65
Gonubie	H4	61
Good Hope	G5	77
Goodhouse	C5	68
Gordon's Bay	B2	60
Gorges	C3	68
Gouda	B1	60
Gouritsmond	F3	61
Graaff-Reinet	D5	65
Graafwater	C5	62
Grabouw	B2	60
Grahamstown	F4	61
Granaatboskolk	E2	63
Grasfontein	E1	71
Graskop	C4	81
Grasmere	B1	73
Graspan	C1	65
Gravelotte	C3	81
Gregory	D1	79
Greylingstad	C2	73
Greystone	D4	60
Greyton	C2	60
Greytown	F1	67
Griekwastad	B4	70
Groblersdal	D5	79
Groblershoop	H4	69
Groenriviersmond	B3	62
Groenvlei	A3	75
Groesbeek	C3	79
Grondneus	F3	69
Groot Brakrivier	A5	60
Groot Spelonke	B2	81
Groot-Marico	H5	77
Grootdrif	D4	63
Grootdrink	G4	69
Grootkraal	A4	60
Grootmis	A1	62
Grootpan	F1	71
Grootspruit	A3	75
Grootvlei	C2	73
Grünau	C3	68
Gt-Jongensfontein	E3	61
Gumtree	A5	73
Ha-Magoro	B2	81
Haakdoring	C3	79
Haarlem	B5	60
Haenertsburg	B3	81
Haga-Haga	H4	61
Halfweg	E2	63
Halycon Drift	D3	66
Hamab	D3	68
Hamburg	G4	61
Hammarsdale	F2	67
Hankey	D5	60
Hanover	C3	65
Hanover Road	D3	65
Hantam	D4	63
Harding	E3	67
Harrisburg	F2	71
Harrisdale	F3	69
Harrismith	C4	73
Hartbeesfontein	F2	71
Hartbeeskop	B1	75
Hartbeespoort	B5	79
Hartswater	D3	71
Hattingspruit	A4	75
Hauptsrus	E1	71
Hawston	B3	60
Hazyview	C5	81
Hectorspruit	D5	81
Heerenlogement	C4	62
Heidelberg	B1	73
Heidelberg	D2	60
Heilbron	B2	73
Hekpoort	B1	73
Heldina	A1	73
Helpmekaar	A4	75
Hemlock	B5	81
Hendrick's Drift	B4	73
Hendriksdal	C5	81
Hendrina	D1	73
Hennenman	F3	71
Herbertsdale	E2	61
Hereford	D4	79
Herefords	C1	75
Hermanus	C3	60
Hermanusdorings	B3	79
Herold	A5	60
Heroldsbaai	A5	60
Herschel	B3	66
Hertzogville	D3	71
Het Kruis	C5	62
Heuningspruit	A3	73
Heydon	D4	65
Hibberdene	F3	67
Higg's Hope	B1	64
Highflats	F2	67
Hildavale	G5	77
Hildreth Ridge	B2	81
Hillandale	D1	60
Hilton	F1	67
Himeville	E2	67
Hlabisa	C4	75
Hlathikhulu	B2	75
Hlobane	B3	75
Hlogotlou	A4	81
Hlotse	B5	73
Hluhluwe	C4	75
Hluthi	C3	75
Hobeni	D5	66
Hobhouse	B1	66
Hoedspruit	C4	81
Hofmeyr	E4	65
Hogsback	F5	65
Holbank	A2	75
Holme Park	C4	79
Holmedene	C2	73
Holoog	C3	68
Holy Cross	E3	67
Hondefontein	G5	63
Hondeklipbaai	A2	62
Hoopstad	E3	71
Hopefield	A1	60
Hopetown	C1	65
Hotagterklip	C3	60
Hotazel	A2	70
Hottentotskloof	C1	60
Hout Bay	A2	60
Houtkraal	C2	65
Howick	F1	67
Hukuntsi	B3	76
Humansdorp	D5	60
Huntleigh	B1	81
Hutchinson	B4	64
Idutywa	C5	66
Ifafa Beach	F3	67
Immerpan	D4	79
Impisi	E3	67
Inanda	G2	67
Indwe	B4	66
Infanta	D3	60
Ingogo	D3	73
Ingwavumba	C3	75
Inhaca	D1	75
Isipingo	G2	67
Iswepe	A2	75
Itsoseng	E1	71
Ixopo	E2	67
Izingolweni	E3	67
Izotsha	F3	67
Jacobsdal	C5	71
Jagersfontein	E1	65
Jaght Drift	F1	63
Jambila	B1	75
Jameson Park	C1	73
Jamestown	F3	65
Jammerdrif	B1	66
Jan Kempdorp	D3	71
Jansenville	D4	60
Janseput	C2	79
Jeffreys Bay	D5	60
Jeppe's Reef	C1	75
Joel's Drift	B4	73
Johannesburg	B1	73
Joubertina	C5	60
Jozini	C3	75
Jwaneng	F4	77
Kaapmuiden	C5	81
Kaapsehoop	C5	81
Kakamas	F4	69
Kalamare	A1	79
Kalbaskraal	B2	60
Kalkbank	D2	79
Kalkwerf	G4	69
Kameel	D1	71
Kamiesberg	C2	62
Kamieskroon	B2	62
Kampersrus	C4	81
Kang	D2	76
Kanoneiland	G4	69
Kanus	D3	68
Kanye	G4	77
Kao	D1	66
Karasburg	D3	68
Karatara	A5	60
Karee	E5	71
Kareeboskolk	E2	63
Kareedouw	C5	60
Karkams	B2	62
Karos	G4	69
Karringmelkspruit	B3	66
Kasouga	F5	61
Kathu	A3	70
Katlehong	B1	73
Kaya se Put	H4	77
Keate's Drift	A5	75
Kei Mouth	C5	66
Kei Road	B5	66
Keimoes	F4	69
Kelso	F2	67
Kempton Park	B1	73
Kendal	C1	73
Kendrew	C5	65
Kenhardt	F1	63
Kenilworth	D4	71
Kennedy's Vale	B4	81
Kentani	C5	66
Kenton on Sea	F5	61
Kestell	C4	73
Kgagodi	B1	79
Khabo	B5	73
Khakhea	D4	76
Khubus	B4	68
Kidds Beach	G4	61
Kimberley	C4	71
King William's Town	G4	61
Kingsburgh	F2	67
Kingscote	E2	67
Kingsley	A3	75
Kingswood	E3	71
Kinirapoort	D2	66
Kinross	C1	73
Kirkwood	D4	60
Klaarstroom	A4	60
Klawer	C4	62
Klein Drakenstein	B2	60
Klein Letaba	B2	81
Klein Tswaing	C2	71
Kleinbegin	G4	69
Kleinmond	B3	60
Kleinpoort	D4	60
Kleinsee	A1	62

Place	Grid	Page
Klerksdorp	F2	71
Klerkskraal	A1	73
Klipdale	C3	60
Klipfontein	D1	73
Klipfontein	D4	60
Klipplaat	C4	60
Kliprand	C3	62
Klipspruit	B5	81
Knapdaar	F3	65
Knysna	B5	60
Koedoeskop	B4	79
Koegas	A1	64
Koegrabie	G5	69
Koenong	C1	66
Koffiefontein	D1	65
Koiingnaas	A2	62
Kokerboom	E4	69
Kokong	D3	76
Kokstad	E3	67
Kolonyama	C1	66
Komaggas	B2	62
Komatipoort	D5	81
Komga	C5	66
Komkans	C3	62
Kommandokraal	A4	60
Kommetjie	A2	60
Kommissiepoort	B1	66
Koopan-Suid	F2	69
Koopmansfontein	C4	71
Koosfontein	D2	71
Kootjieskolk	E3	63
Koperspruit	C1	79
Kopong	H3	77
Koppies	A2	73
Koringberg	B1	60
Koringplaas	F5	63
Kosmos	B5	79
Koster	F1	71
Kotzesrus	B3	62
Koukraal	F2	65
Koup	E1	61
Koutjie	A5	60
Kraaifontein	B2	60
Kraaldorings	E1	61
Kraankuil	C2	65
Kransfontein	C4	73
Kranskop	G1	67
Kriel	D1	73
Kromdraai	D1	73
Kroonstad	A3	73
Krugers	E2	65
Krugersdorp	B1	73
Kruidfontein	F1	61
Kruisfontein	D5	60
Kruisrivier	F1	61
Ku-Mayima	C4	66
Kubung	C2	66
Kubutsa	B2	75
Kuilsriver	B2	60
Kums	E3	69
Kuruman	B3	70
Kwa Dweshula	F3	67
Kwaggaskop	B5	81
KwaMashu	G2	67
KwaMbonambi	C4	75
Kwamhlanga	C5	79
Kylemore	B2	60
L'Agulhas	C3	60
La Cotte	C3	81
Laaiplek	A1	60
Labera	F5	77
Ladismith	E1	61
Lady Frere	B4	66
Lady Grey	B3	66
Ladybrand	B1	66
Ladysmith	D4	73
Lahlangubo	D3	66
Laingsburg	D1	60
Lambert's Bay	C5	62
Lammerkop	D5	79
Landplaas	C4	62
Langberg	E2	61
Langdon	C4	66
Langebaan	A1	60
Langehorn	C1	71
Langholm	F4	61
Langklip	F4	69
Lavumisa	C3	75
Leandra	C1	73
Lebowakgomo	D3	79
Leeu-Gamka	G5	63
Leeudoringstad	E2	71
Leeupoort	B4	79
Legkraal	A2	81
Lehlohonolo	D2	66
Lehututu	B3	76
Leipoldtville	C5	62
Lekfontein	F4	61
Lekkersing	A1	62
Lemoenshoek	D2	60
Lentsweletau	H3	77
Lephepe	H2	77
Letjiesbos	A5	64
Letlhakeng	F3	77
Letseng-La-Terae	D1	66
Letsitele	B3	81
Leydsdorp	B3	81
Libertas	B4	73
Libode	D4	66
Lichtenburg	E1	71
Lidgetton	F1	67
Limburg	D3	79
Lime Acres	B4	70
Linakeng	D1	66
LIndeshof	C2	60
Lindley	B3	73
Lindleyspoort	A5	79
Llandudno	A2	60
Lobamba	B2	75
Lobatse	G4	77
Loch Vaal	B2	73
Lochiel	B1	75
Loerie	D5	60
Loeriesfontein	D3	63
Lofter	E2	65
Logageng	C1	71
Lohatlha	A3	70
Lokgwabe	B3	76
Long Hope	E4	61
Loskop	E1	67
Lothair	A1	75
Louis Trichardt	B2	81
Louisvale	G4	69
Louterwater	B5	60
Louwna	C2	71
Louwsburg	B3	75
Lower Dikgatlhong	A2	70
Lower Pitseng	C3	66
Loxton	A4	64
Loyengo	B2	75
Luckhoff	D1	65
Lufuta	C4	66
Lulekani	C3	81
Lundin's Nek	C3	66
Luneberg	A3	75
Lusikisiki	E4	67
Luttig	G5	63
Lutumba	B1	81
Lutzputs	F4	69
Lutzville	C4	62
Lydenburg	B5	81
Lykso	C2	71
Maartenshoop	B4	81
Maasstroom	C1	79
Mabaalstad	A5	79
Mabeskraal	A4	79
Mabopane	B5	79
Mabula	B4	79
Machadodorp	B5	81
Machava	D1	75
Macleantown	G4	61
Maclear	C3	66
Madadeni	A3	75
Madiakgama	C1	71
Madibogo	D1	71
Madipelesa	C3	71
Mafeteng	B2	66
Mafikeng	E1	71
Mafube	D2	66
Mafutseni	C2	75
Magaliesburg	A1	73
Magudu	C3	75
Magusheni	E3	67
Mahalapye	A2	79
Mahlabatini	B4	75
Mahlangasi	C3	75
Mahwelereng	D3	79
Maizefield	D2	73
Makopong	D4	76
Makwassie	E2	71
Makwate	A2	79
Malaita	A4	81
Malealea	C2	66
Maleoskop	D5	79
Malgas	D3	60
Malmesbury	B1	60
Maloma	C2	75
Malotwana	H3	77
Mamaila	B2	81
Mamates	C1	66
Mamre	B2	60
Mandini	G1	67
Mangeni	A4	75
Manhoca	D2	75
Mankayane	B2	75
Mankweng	A3	81
Manthestad	D3	71
Mantsonyane	C1	66
Manubi	D5	66
Manzini	B2	75
Maope	A1	79
Mapela	C3	79
Mapumulo	G1	67
Maputo	D1	75
Marakabei	C1	66
Marble Hall	D4	79
Marburg	F3	67
Marchand	F4	69
Margate	F3	67
Maricosdraai	H4	77
Marikana	B5	79
Marite	C4	81
Marken	C2	79
Markramsdraai	A3	70
Marnitz	C2	79
Marquard	A4	73
Marracuene	D1	75
Martin's Drift	B2	79
Marydale	G1	63
Maseru	B1	66
Mashai	D1	66
Mashashane	D3	79
Masisi	C1	81
Matatiele	D2	66
Mateka	C1	66
Matjiesfontein	D1	60
Matjiesrivier	F1	61
Matlabas	B3	79
Matlala	D3	79
Matlameng	B5	73
Matola	D1	75
Matroosberg	C1	60
Matsaile	D2	66
Matvhelo	C1	81
Mavamba	C2	81
Mazenod	B1	66
Mazeppa Bay	D5	66
Mbabane	B1	75
Mbazwana	D3	75
McGregor	C2	60
Mdantsane	G4	61
Meadows	F1	65
Mekaling	B2	66
Melkbosstrand	B2	60
Melmoth	B4	75
Meltonwold	A4	64
Memel	D3	73
Merindol	A1	73

Merweville	G5	63
Mesa	F1	71
Mesklip	B2	62
Messina	B1	81
Methalaneng	D1	66
Mevedja	D1	75
Meyerton	B1	73
Mgwali	B5	66
Mhlambanyatsi	B2	75
Mhlosheni	B3	75
Mhlume	C1	75
Mica	C3	81
Middelburg	D1	73
Middelburg	D4	65
Middelfontein	C4	79
Middelpos	E4	63
Middelwit	A4	79
Middleton	E4	61
Midrand	B1	73
Migdol	D2	71
Miller	C4	60
Millvale	A5	79
Milnerton	B2	60
Mirage	F2	71
Misgund	B5	60
Misty Mount	D4	66
Mkambati	E4	67
Mkuze	C3	75
Mmamabula	A2	79
Mmathethe	G5	77
Moamba	D1	75
Mochudi	H3	77
Modderrivier	C5	71
Moeng	B1	79
Moeswal	H3	69
Mogalakwena	C3	79
Mogapi	B1	79
Mogapinyana	B1	79
Mogwase	A5	79
Mohales Hoek	B2	66
Mokamole	C3	79
Mokhotlong	D1	66
Mokopung	C2	66
Molepolole	G3	77
Moletsane	C1	66
Moloporivier	E5	77
Molteno	F4	65
Mont Pelaan	D3	73
Montagu	D2	60
Monte Christo	B2	79
Mooifontein	E1	71
Mooi River	E1	67
Mooketsi	B2	81
Moordkuil	C2	60
Moorreesburg	B1	60
Mopane	B1	81
Morgan's Bay	H4	61
Morgenzon	D2	73
Morija	B1	66
Morokweng	B1	70
Morone	B4	81
Morristown	B4	66
Mortimer	E5	65
Morupule	A1	79
Morwamosu	D3	76
Moshaneng	G4	77
Moshesh's Ford	C3	66
Mosita	D1	71
Mosomane	H3	77
Mosopa	G4	77
Mossel Bay	A5	60
Mossiesdal	D5	79
Motetema	A4	81
Mothae	D1	66
Motokwe	D3	76
Motshikiri	B5	79
Motsitseng	D1	66
Mount Ayliff	E3	67
Mount Fletcher	D3	66
Mount Frere	D3	66
Mount Stewart	C4	60
Moyeni	C2	66
Mpaka Stn	C2	75
Mpemvana	A3	75
Mpendle	E1	67
Mpetu	C5	66
Mphaki	C2	66
Mpharane	B2	66
Mpolweni	F1	67
Mpumalanga	F2	67
Mqanduli	D4	66
Mt Moorosi	C2	66
Mtonjaneni	B4	75
Mtubatuba	C4	75
Mtunzini	H1	67
Mtwalume	F3	67
Muden	F1	67
Muizenberg	B2	60
Munster	F3	67
Munyu	C4	66
Murchison	C3	81
Murraysburg	C4	65
Mynfontein	C3	65
Nababeep	B1	62
Nabies	E4	69
Naboomspruit	C4	79
Nakop	E3	69
Namaacha	C1	75
Namakgale	C3	81
Namies	D1	63
Napier	C3	60
Nariep	B3	62
Nature's Valley	B5	60
Ncanara	E5	61
Ncora	C4	66
Ndumo	C2	75
Ndundulu	B5	75
Ndwedwe	G1	67
Neilersdrif	F4	69
Nelspoort	B4	64
Nelspruit	C5	81
New Amalfi	D2	66
New England	B3	66
New Hanover	F1	67
New Machavie	F2	71
Newcastle	D3	73
Newington	D4	81
Newsel-Umdloti	G2	67
Ngabeni	E3	67
Ngobeni	B3	75
Ngome	B3	75
Ngqeleni	D4	66
Ngqungu	D4	66
Nhlangano	B2	75
Nhlazatshe	B4	75
Niekerkshoop	B1	64
Nietverdiend	H4	77
Nieu-Bethesda	D4	65
Nieuwoudtville	D4	63
Nigel	C1	73
Nigramoep	B1	62
Nkambak	B3	81
Nkandla	B4	75
Nkau	C2	66
Nkomo	C2	81
Nkwalini	B5	75
Nobantu	D4	66
Nobokwe	C4	66
Noenieput	E3	69
Nohana	C2	66
Noll	A5	60
Nondweni	A4	75
Nongoma	C3	75
Noordhoek	A2	60
Noordkaap	B1	75
Noordkuil	C5	62
Noordoewer	B4	68
Normandien	D3	73
Northam	A4	79
Norvalspont	E3	65
Notintsila	D4	66
Nottingham Road	E1	67
Noupoort	D3	65
Nqabara	D5	66
Nqabeni	E3	67
Nqamakwe	C5	66
Nqutu	A4	75
Nsoko	C2	75
Ntibane	D4	66
Ntseshe	C5	66
Ntshilini	E4	67
Ntywenke	D3	66
Numbi Gate	C5	81
Nutfield	C4	79
Nuwefontein	D3	68
Nuwerus	C3	62
Nuy	C2	60
Nylstroom	C4	79
Nyokana	D5	66
Oatlands	C4	60
Obobogorap	E2	69
Odendaalsrus	F3	71
Ofcolaco	B3	81
Ogies	C1	73
Ohrigstad	B4	81
Okiep	B1	62
Old Bunting	D4	66
Old Morley	D4	66
Olifantshoek	A3	70
Olyfberg	B3	81
Omdraaisvlei	B2	64
Onderstedorings	F2	63
Ons Hoop	B2	79
Onseepkans	D4	68
Ontmoeting	G2	69
Oorwinning	B1	81
Oostermoed	A4	79
Orania	C1	65
Oranjefontein	B2	79
Oranjemund	A4	68
Oranjerivier	C1	65
Oranjeville	B2	73
Orkney	F2	71
Osborn	B4	75
Osizweni	A3	75
Otse	G4	77
Ottosdal	E2	71
Oudtshoorn	A5	60
Oukraal	C3	60
Ouplaas	D3	60
Overyssel	C2	79
Oviston	E3	65
Owendale	B4	70
Oxbow	C4	73
Oyster Bay	D5	60
Paarl	B2	60
Pacaltsdorp	A5	60
Paddock	F3	67
Pafuri	D1	81
Pafuri Gate	C1	81
Palala	C3	79
Palapye	A1	79
Paleisheuwel	C5	62
Palm Beach	F3	67
Palmerton	E4	67
Palmietfontein	B2	66
Pampierstad	C3	71
Pampoenpoort	A3	64
Panbult	A2	75
Pansdrif	B5	79
Papendorp	C4	62
Papiesvlei	C3	60
Papkuil	B4	70
Park Rynie	F2	67
Parow	B2	60
Parys	A2	73
Patensie	D5	60
Paternoster	A1	60
Paterson	E4	61
Patlong	C2	66
Paul Kruger Gate	D4	81
Paul Roux	B4	73
Paulpietersburg	B3	75
Pearly Beach	C3	60
Pearston	D5	65
Peddie	F4	61
Peka	B5	73
Pella	D5	68

Place	Grid	Page
Penge	B4	81
Pennington	F3	67
Perdekop	D2	73
Petersburg	D5	65
Petrus Steyn	B3	73
Petrusburg	E1	65
Petrusville	D2	65
Phalaborwa	C3	81
Phamong	C2	66
Philadelphia	B2	60
Philippolis	D2	65
Philippolis Road	E2	65
Philipstown	C2	65
Phitshane Molopo	G5	77
Phokwane	A4	81
Phuthaditjhaba	C4	73
Pienaarsrivier	C5	79
Piet Plessis	C1	71
Piet Retief	B2	75
Pieter Meintjies	D1	60
Pietermaritzburg	F1	67
Pietersburg	D3	79
Piggs Peak	B1	75
Piketberg	B1	60
Pilane	H3	77
Pilgrim's Rest	C4	81
Pinetown	F2	67
Pitsane	G5	77
Pitseng	C1	66
Plaatbakkies	C2	62
Plathuis	D2	60
Platrand	D2	73
Plettenberg Bay	B5	60
Plooysburg	C5	71
Pniel	B2	60
Pofadder	D1	63
Politsi	B3	81
Pomeroy	A4	75
Pongola	C3	75
Ponta do Ouro	D2	75
Pools	B1	60
Port Alfred	F5	61
Port Beaufort	D3	60
Port Edward	F3	67
Port Elizabeth	E5	61
Port Grosvenor	E4	67
Port Nolloth	A1	62
Port Shepstone	F3	67
Port St Johns	E4	67
Porterville	B1	60
Post Chalmers	E4	65
Postmasburg	A4	70
Potchefstroom	F2	71
Potfontein	C2	65
Potgietersrus	D3	79
Potsdam	G4	61
Poupan	C2	65
Pr. Alfred Hamlet	C1	60
Pretoria	C5	79
Prieska	A1	64
Prince Albert	F1	61
Prince Albert Road	E1	61
Pringle Bay	B3	60
Priors	E2	65
Protem	D2	60
Pudimoe	C2	71
Putsonderwater	G1	63
Qabane	D2	66
Qacha's Nek	D2	66
Qamata	B4	66
Qiba	C4	66
Qobong	C2	66
Qoboqobo	C5	66
Qolora Mouth	C5	66
Qoqodala	B4	66
Qora Mouth	D5	66
Qudeni	B4	75
Queensburgh	G2	67
Queenstown	F4	65
Quko	C5	66
Qumbu	D3	66
Radisele	A1	79
Radium	C4	79
Ralebona	C2	66
Raleqheka	C1	66
Ramabanta	C1	66
Ramatlabama	G5	77
Ramotswa	H4	77
Ramsgate	F3	67
Ranaka	G4	77
Randalhurst	B4	75
Randburg	B1	73
Randfontein	B1	73
Rankin's Pass	B4	79
Rashoop	B5	79
Ratelfontein	C5	62
Rawsonville	C2	60
Rayton	C5	79
Redcliffe	E1	67
Reddersburg	F1	65
Redelinghuys	C5	62
Redoubt	E3	67
Reebokrand	D2	65
Reitz	B3	73
Reitzburg	A2	73
Reivilo	C3	71
Renosterkop	B5	64
Renosterspruit	F2	71
Ressano Garcia	D5	81
Restvale	B4	64
Rex	A5	79
Richards Bay	H1	67
Richmond	C4	65
Richmond	F2	67
Riebeeckstad	F3	71
Riebeek Kasteel	B1	60
Riebeek-Oos	E4	61
Riebeek-Wes	B1	60
Rietbron	B4	60
Rietfontein	E2	69
Rietkolk	D3	79
Rietkuil	C3	73
Rietpoel	C2	60
Rietpoort	B3	62
Rietvlei	F1	67
Rita	D3	79
Ritchie	C5	71
Riversdale	E2	61
Riverside	E2	67
Riverview	C4	75
Riviersonderend	C2	60
Roamer's Rest	D2	66
Robert's Drift	C2	73
Robertson	C2	60
Rode	D3	66
Rodenbeck	F1	65
Roedtan	D4	79
Roma	C1	66
Rondevlei	A5	60
Roodebank	C2	73
Roodepoort	B1	73
Rooiberg	B4	79
Rooibokkraal	A3	79
Rooibosbult	B3	79
Rooigrond	E1	71
Rooikraal	D5	79
Rooipan	D1	65
Rooiwal	A2	73
Roosboom	D4	73
Roossenekal	B5	81
Rorke's Drift	A4	75
Rosebank	F2	67
Rosedene	A4	64
Rosendal	B4	73
Rosetta	E1	67
Rosh Pinah	A3	68
Rosmead	D4	65
Rossouw	B3	66
Rostrataville	E2	71
Rothmere	D5	66
Rouxpos	E1	61
Rouxville	F2	65
Ruitersbos	F2	61
Rust	B1	60
Rust de Winter	C5	79
Rustenburg	A5	79
Rustig	A3	73
Rusverby	A5	79
Saaifontein	G4	63
Sabie	C5	81
Sada	F5	65
Sakrivier	E3	63
Salajwe	F2	77
Salamanga	D2	75
Saldanha	A1	60
Salem	F4	61
Salpeterpan	C2	71
Salt Lake	C1	65
Salt Rock	G1	67
Sand River Valley	D4	73
Sandberg	C5	62
Sandton	B1	73
Sandvlakte	C5	60
Sannaspos	F1	65
Sannieshof	E1	71
Sasolburg	B2	73
Satco	D3	68
Sauer	B1	60
Scarborough	A2	60
Scheepersnek	A3	75
Schmidtsdrif	C4	71
Schoombee	E4	65
Schweizer-Reneke	D2	71
Scottburgh	F2	67
Sea Park	F3	67
Seaview	D5	60
Sebapala	C2	66
Sebayeng	A3	81
Secunda	D1	73
Sedgefield	A5	60
Seekoegat	A4	60
Sefako	C4	73
Sefikeng	C1	66
Sehonghong	D1	66
Sekhukhune	B4	81
Sekoma	E3	77
Selonsrivier	D5	79
Sendelingsdrif	A4	68
Sendelingsfontein	E2	71
Sending	D2	79
Senekal	A4	73
Sengwe	C1	81
Senlac	E5	77
Sentrum	A3	79
Seringkop	C5	79
Serowe	A1	79
Seshego	D3	79
Setlagole	D1	71
Settlers	C4	79
Setuat	C2	71
Sevenoaks	F1	67
Severn	A1	70
Seweweekspoort	E1	61
Seymour	F5	65
Sezela	F3	67
Shaka's Rock	G1	67
Shakaskraal	G1	67
Shannon	F1	65
Sheepmoor	A2	75
Sheffield Beach	G1	67
Sheldon	E4	61
Shelley Beach	F3	67
Sherborne	D3	65
Sherwood Ranch	B1	79
Shoshong	H2	77
Sicunusa	B2	75
Sidvokodvo	B2	75
Sidwadweni	D4	66
Signalberg	C3	68
Sigoga	D2	66
Sihoye	C1	75
Sikwane	H4	77
Silent Valley	A4	79
Silkaatskop	H4	77
Silutshana	A4	75
Silver Streams	B4	70
Simon's Town	B2	60
Sinksabrug	A5	60

Siphofaneni	C2	75
Sir Lowry's Pass	B2	60
Sishen	A3	70
Siteki	C2	75
Sithobela	C2	75
Sittingbourne	G4	61
Siyabuswa	D4	79
Skeerpoort	B5	79
Skipskop	D3	60
Skuinsdrif	H5	77
Slurry	H5	77
Smithfield	F2	65
Smitskraal	C5	60
Sneeukraal	A4	64
Sneezewood	E2	67
Sodium	B2	64
Soebatsfontein	B2	62
Soekmekaar	B2	81
Sojwe	G2	77
Somerset East	E5	65
Somerset West	B2	60
Somkele	C4	75
Sonop	B5	79
Sonstraal	H2	69
Southbroom	F3	67
Southeyville	B4	66
Southport	F3	67
Southwell	F5	61
Soutpan	B5	79
Soutpan	E4	71
Soweto	B1	73
Spanwerk	A3	79
Spes Bona	F2	71
Spitskopvlei	D4	65
Spoegrivier	B2	62
Spring Valley	F5	65
Springbok	B1	62
Springfontein	E2	65
Springs	C1	73
Spytfontein	C5	71
St Faith's	F3	67
St Francis Bay	D5	60
St Helena Bay	C5	62
St Lucia	C4	75
St Marks	B4	66
St Martin	D1	66
Staansaam	F2	69
Stafford's Post	E3	67
Standerton	D2	73
Stanford	C3	60
Stanger	G1	67
Steekdorings	C2	71
Steelpoort	B4	81
Steilloopbrug	C2	79
Steilrand	B3	75
Steinkopf	B1	62
Stella	D1	71
Stellenbosch	B2	60
Sterkaar	C3	65
Sterkspruit	B2	66
Sterkstroom	F4	65
Sterling	G3	63
Steynsburg	E3	65
Steynsrus	A3	73
Steytlerville	C4	60
Stilfontein	F2	71
Still Bay East	E3	61
Still Bay West	E3	61
Stockpoort	A2	79
Stoffberg	A5	81
Stofvlei	C2	62
Stompneusbaai	B5	62
Stoneyridge	D4	66
Stormberg	F3	65
Stormsrivier	C5	60
Stormsvlei	D2	60
Straatsdrif	H5	77
Strand	B2	60
Strandfontein	C4	62
Struisbaai	C3	60
Strydenburg	C2	65
Strydpoort	E2	71
Studtis	C4	60
Stutterheim	B5	66
Summerstrand	E5	61
Sun City/Lost City	A5	79
Sunland	E5	61
Sutherland	F5	63
Sutton	A2	70
Suurbraak	D2	60
Swaershoek	E5	65
Swart Umfolozi	B3	75
Swartberg	E2	67
Swartkops	E5	61
Swartmodder	F3	69
Swartplaas	F1	71
Swartputs	B4	70
Swartruggens	A5	79
Swartwater	C1	79
Swellendam	D2	60
Swempoort	B3	66
Swinburne	D4	73
Syfergat	F4	65
Tabankulu	C1	75
Tabankulu	E3	67
Tafelberg	D4	65
Tainton	H4	61
Takatokwane	E3	77
Taleni	C5	66
Tarkastad	F4	65
Taung	D3	71
Temba	C5	79
Tembisa	B1	73
Terra Firma	D5	76
Teviot	E4	65
Tewane	A1	79
Teyateyaneng	C1	66
Teza	C4	75
Thaba Bosiu	C1	66
Thaba Chitja	C2	66
Thaba 'Nchu	F1	65
Thaba Tseka	D1	66
Thabana Morena	B2	66
Thabazimbi	A4	79
Thamaga	G4	77
The Berg	C4	81
The Crags	B5	60
The Downs	B3	81
The Haven	D5	66
The Heads	B5	60
The Ranch	B5	75
Theron	F4	71
Theunissen	F4	71
Thohoyandou	B2	81
Thorndale	A2	81
Thornville	F2	67
Three Sisters	B4	64
Tierfontein	E3	71
Tierpoort	F1	65
Tina Bridge	D3	66
Tinmyne	C3	79
Tlali	C1	66
Tlhakgameng	C1	71
Tlokoeng	D1	66
Tolwe	C2	79
Tom Burke	B2	79
Tombo	E4	67
Tompi Seleka	D4	79
Tonash	C1	79
Tongaat	G1	67
Tontelbos	E3	63
Tosca	C1	71
Tosing	C2	66
Touwsriver	C1	60
Trawal	C4	62
Trichardt	D1	73
Trichardtsdal	B3	81
Triple Streams	D3	66
Trompsburg	E2	65
Tsatsu	F5	77
Tsazo	C4	66
Tsetsebjwe	C1	79
Tsetseng	D2	76
Tshabong	H1	69
Tshakhuma	B2	81
Tshane	B3	76
Tshaneni	C1	75
Tshani	D4	66
Tshidilamolomo	F5	77
Tshipise	B1	81
Tshiturapadsi	C1	81
Tsineng	A2	70
Tsitsa Bridge	D4	66
Tsoelike	D2	66
Tsolo	D4	66
Tsomo	C5	66
Tugela Ferry	A5	75
Tugela Mouth	G1	67
Tuinplaas	C4	79
Tunnel	C1	60
Turton	F3	67
Twee Rivieren	F1	69
Tweefontein	D5	63
Tweeling	C3	73
Tweespruit	B1	66
Tyira	D3	66
Tylden	B5	66
Tzaneen	B3	81
Ubombo	C3	75
Ugie	C3	66
Uitenhage	D5	60
Uitkyk	C1	62
Uitspankraal	D5	63
Ulco	C4	71
Ulundi	B4	75
Umbogintwini	G2	67
Umbumbulu	F2	67
Umgababa	F2	67
Umhlanga Rocks	G2	67
Umkomaas	F2	67
Umlazi	G2	67
Umtata	D4	66
Umtentu	E4	67
Umtentweni	F3	67
uMzimkhulu	E2	67
uMzinto	F2	67
uMzumbe	F3	67
Underberg	E2	67
Uniondale	B5	60
Upington	G4	69
Usutu	C1	79
Utrecht	A3	75
Uvongo	F3	67
Vaalhoek	C4	81
Vaalplaas	C5	79
Vaalwater	B3	79
Val	C2	73
Valsrivier	B4	73
Van Reenen	D4	73
Van Rooyen	A4	75
Van Wyksdorp	E2	61
Van Wyksvlei	G2	63
Van Zylsrus	H2	69
Vanalphensvlei	C3	79
Vanderbijlpark	B2	73
Vanderkloof	D2	65
Vandyksdrif	D1	73
Vanrhynsdorp	C4	62
Vanstadensrus	B2	66
Vant's Drift	A4	75
Vegkop	B3	73
Velddrif	A1	60
Ventersburg	F3	71
Ventersdorp	F1	71
Venterskroon	A2	73
Venterstad	E3	65
Vereeniging	B2	73
Verena	D5	79
Vergeleë	E5	77
Verkeerdevlei	F4	71
Verkykerskop	D3	73
Vermaaklikheid	E3	61
Vermaas	E1	71
Verster	B4	64
Verulam	G2	67
Victoria West	B3	64
Viedgesville	D4	66
Vier-en-Twintig Riv.	C3	79

Vierfontein	F2	71
Viljoensdrif	B2	73
Viljoenshof	C3	60
Viljoenskroon	F2	71
Villa Nora	B2	79
Villiers	C2	73
Villiersdorp	C2	60
Vineyard	F3	65
Vioolsdrif	B4	68
Virginia	F3	71
Visrivier	E4	65
Vivo	D2	79
Vleesbaai	F3	61
Vleifontein	E1	61
Vleiland	E1	61
Volksrust	D3	73
Volop	H4	69
Volstruisleegte	B4	60
Voortrekkerspos	A3	79
Vorstershoop	D5	76
Vosburg	B2	64
Vrede	C3	73
Vredefort	A2	73
Vredenburg	A1	60
Vredendal	C4	62
Vredesdorp	E2	69
Vroeggedeel	H3	69
Vrouenspan	F3	69
Vryburg	C2	71
Vryheid	A3	75
Waenhuiskrans	D3	60
Wakkerstroom	A3	75
Walkerville	B1	73
Wallekraal	B2	62
Wanda	C1	65
Waqu	B5	66
Warburton	A1	75
Warden	C3	73
Warm Baths	C4	79
Warmbad	D4	68
Warmwaterberg	D2	60
Warrenton	D3	71
Wasbank	A4	75
Waterford	D4	60
Waterkloof	E2	65
Waterpoort	A2	81
Waterval-Boven	B5	81
Wavecrest	C5	66
Waverley	B1	75
Wegdraai	H4	69
Welgeleë	F4	71
Welkom	F3	71
Wellington	B2	60
Welverdiend	A1	73
Wepener	B1	66
Werda	D4	76
Wesley	G4	61
Wesselsbron	F3	71
Wesselsvlei	B2	70
Westerberg	A1	64
Westleigh	A3	73
Westminster	B1	66
Westonaria	B1	73
Weza	E3	67
White River	C5	81
Whites	F3	71
Whitmore	C4	66
Whittlesea	F5	65
Wiegenaarspoort	B5	64
Wilderness	A5	60
Williston	F4	63
Willowmore	B4	60
Willowvale	C5	66
Winburg	F4	71
Wincanton	A3	70
Windmeul	B2	60
Windsorton	C4	71
Windsorton Road	D4	71
Winkelpos	F3	71
Winterton	D5	73
Winterveld	B5	79
Witbank	D1	73
Witdraai	F2	69
Witkop	F3	65
Witmos	E5	65
Witnek	D5	79
Witpoort	E2	71
Witput	C1	65
Witpütz	A3	68
Witsand	D3	60
Wittedrif	B5	60
Witteklip	D5	60
Witwater	C2	62
Wolmaransstad	E2	71
Wolplaas	D3	68
Wolseley	B1	60
Wolvepoort	F2	65
Wolwefontein	D4	60
Wolwehoek	B2	73
Wolwespruit	D4	71
Wonderfontein	A5	81
Wonderkop	A3	73
Wondermere	H5	77
Woodlands	C5	60
Wooldridge	G4	61
Worcester	C2	60
Woudkop	C2	79
Wuppertal	D5	63
Wyford	D4	73
Xolobe	C5	66
Yzerfontein	A1	60
Zaaimansdal	B5	60
Zastron	B2	66
Zebediela	D3	79
Zeerust	H5	77
Zitundo	D2	75
Zoar	E1	61
Zunckels	D5	73
Zwartkop	F2	63
Zwarts	E1	61
Zwelitsha	G4	61
Zwingli	H4	77